Stability and Robustness of Multivariable Feedback Systems

The MIT Press Series in Signal Processing, Optimization, and Control
Alan S. Willsky, editor
1. *Location on Networks: Theory and Algorithms,* Gabriel Y. Handler and Pitu B. Mirchandani, 1979
2. *Digital Signal Processing and Control and Estimation Theory: Points of Tangency, Areas of Intersection, and Parallel Directions,* Alan S. Willsky, 1979
3. *Stability and Robustness of Multivariable Feedback Systems,* Michael George Safonov, 1980.

Stability and Robustness of Multivariable Feedback Systems

Michael George Safonov

The MIT Press
Cambridge,
Massachusetts,
and
London, England

This book was set in Monotype Times Roman
by Komiyama Printing Co., Ltd.,
and printed and bound by Halliday Lithograph Corporation
in the United States of America.

Library of Congress Cataloging in Publication Data

Safonov, Michael George.

Stability and robustness of multivariable feedback systems.

(The MIT Press series in signal processing, optimization, and control ; 3)
Based on the author's thesis, Massachusetts Institute of Technology, 1977, presented under title: Robustness and stability aspects of stochastic multivariable feedback system design.
Bibliography: p.
Includes index.
1. Feedback control systems. 2. Stability.
I. Title, II. Series: MIT Press series in signal processing, optimization, and control ; 3.
TJ216.S22 629.8'3 80–13099
ISBN 0–262–19180–6
ISBN 0-262-69304-6

Contents

3

LQG Robustness and Stability: The Continuous-Time Case

4

LQG Robustness and Stability: The Discrete-Time/Sampled-Data Case

5

Conclusion

Series Foreword

The fields of signal processing, optimization, and control stand as well-developed disciplines with solid theoretical and methodological foundations. While the development of each of these fields is of great importance, many future problems will require the combined efforts of researchers in all of the disciplines. Among these challenges are the analysis, design, and optimization of large and complex systems, the effective utilization of the capabilities provided by recent developments in digital technology for the design of high-performance control and signal processing systems, and the application of systems concepts to a variety of applications such as transportation systems, seismic signal processing, and data communication networks.

This series serves several purposes. It not only includes books at the leading edge of research in each field but also emphasizes theoretical research, analytical techniques, and applications that merit the attention of workers in all disciplines. In this way the series should help acquaint researchers in each field with other perspectives and techniques and provide cornerstones for the development of new research areas within each discipline and across the boundaries.

Michael Safonov's book *Stability and Robustness of Multivariable Feedback Systems* represents an important contribution to the field of feedback control system design. The primary motivation for Safonov's work is the question of robustness, the design of feedback systems that yield satisfactory performance in the face of modeling uncertainties or approximations. While many of the original frequency domain design methods successfully address this problem, these techniques are in general limited to single-input/single-output systems. On the other hand, many of the modern approaches to feedback system design do consider the multivariable case, but in the process the issue of robustness has to some extent fallen by the wayside. In part for this reason many modern techniques have fallen short of becoming general, practical multivariable design procedures.

In this book, the author examines this missing piece, the robustness of multivariable feedback systems, and he brings together the concepts of classical frequency domain techniques and the methods of modern multivariable control. In the process of obtaining specific results for several multiloop design techniques, he develops a new abstract framework for analyzing problems of stability and robustness. For this reason as well as for the detailed results it contains, Safonov's book represents an important step toward the development of a practical multivariable control system design methodology.

Alan S. Willsky

Preface and Acknowledgments

This monograph on stability theory presents a novel and conceptually simple view of nonlinear, multiloop feedback system stability theory based on the "topological separation" of function spaces—a view sufficiently general to encompass both Lyapunov and input-output stability concepts. The main objective of the book is to address the issues that arise in designing feedback systems that are robust against the destabilizing effects of unknown-but-bounded uncertainty in component dynamics. I believe this is the first and only book to provide a completely general mathematical formulation of these issues and to methodically develop techniques for the quantitative analysis of multiloop feedback system robustness. The book is also a significant contribution to stability theory per se because the stability definitions and problem formulations in chapter 2 capture for the first time the essential features of stability problems with a sufficient degree of simplicity and abstraction to enable a completely unified treatment of the concepts and results of Lyapunov and input-output stability. I am hopeful that this book will prove to be timely in providing a rigorous methodology for addressing such inherently "feedback" aspects of system design as robustness and sensitivity at a time when researchers are beginning to recognize that such methodology is mandatory if complex systems are to be designed using modern system theory.

Included in chapter 2 are new multiloop generalizations of the circle stability criterion. Potential applications include nonlinear feedback design, the validity of modeling approximations, hierarchical control system design, and stability margin analysis for multiloop feedback systems. The results interface with modern multivariable feedback design techniques to provide a theoretical basis for the computer-aided design of multiloop feedback systems to meet specifications calling for a robust tolerance or bounded uncertainty in plant dynamics. The theory is applied in chapters 3 and 4 to characterize the stability margins of optimal linear-quadratic Gaussian estimators and controllers. Continuous-time linear-quadratic state-feedback regulator designs are found to be inherently robust, having an infinite gain margin and at least $\pm 60^\circ$ phase margin at each control input channel; sampled-data designs are found to approximate this robustness provided certain conditions are satisfied. Analogous results apply to a constant-gain extended Kalman filter (CGEKF) for which no on-line covariance computations are required. A separation-type result is established for nonlinear systems, proving that nondivergent estimates can, unconditionally, be substituted for true values in nonlinear feedback controllers without inducing instability. The results have applications to gain scheduling for adjustable set-point nonlinear output-feedback regulator designs.

This book is aimed at researchers and advanced graduate students in the areas of feedback control engineering circuits and systems. It will also appeal to mathematicians having an interest in applications of functional analysis to engineering problems.

This book is based on my Ph.D. thesis, which I submitted to the Massachusetts Institute of Technology in August 1977 under the title "Robustness and Stability Aspects of Stochastic Multivariable Feedback System Design." I am grateful to Professor Michael Athans for his guidance, encouragement, and support during the course of this research. As my thesis supervisor, his insight, observations, and suggestions helped establish the overall direction of the research effort and contributed immensely to the success of the work reported here. I thank my thesis readers, Professor Alan S. Willsky, Professor Nils R. Sandell, and Dr. David A. Castanon for their encouragement and for their detailed comments and suggestions during the final phases of the preparation of the thesis. For making possible exchanges with several English scholars, I thank Professor Alistair G. J. MacFarlane of Cambridge University who kindly arranged for me to visit England while the thesis research was in progress. Discussions during my visit with Professor MacFarlane, Dr. A. I.

Mees, Professor H. H. Rosenbrock (UMIST), Dr. P. A. Cook (UMIST), Dr. B. Kouvaritakis, Dr. J. Edmunds, and others provided added motivation for the work reported in chapter 2, and unquestionably influenced the interpretation given to the results. This monograph, and my graduate learning experience, benefited from thought-provoking conversations with Professors Sanjoy K. Mitter, Leonard A. Gould, Gunter Stein, Jan C. Willems, Elijah Polak (Berkeley), and Charles A. Desoer (Berkeley) and with Mr. Jarrell Elliott, Mr. Brian Doolin, and Dr. Raymond Montgomery of NASA. For my indoctrination in the "nuts-and-bolts" aspects of modern control theory, I owe much to my summer work experience at the Analytic Sciences Corporation and especially to Dr. Robert Stengel and Mr. John Broussard. I benefited in many ways from hours of active and intellectually stimulating discussion spent with my fellow students H. Chizeck, D. Birdwell, D. Teneketzis, P. -K. Wong, and many others.

The research reported in this monograph was conducted at the MIT Electronic Systems Laboratory with partial support provided by the NASA Ames Research Center under grant NGL-22–009–124 and by the NASA Langley Research Center under grant NSG-1312 and at the University of Southern California.

Stability and Robustness of Multivariable Feedback Systems

1

Introduction

1.1 Overview

1.1.1 Motivation

Historically, feedback has been used in control system engineering as a means for satisfying design constraints requiring
(i) stabilization of insufficiently stable systems;
(ii) reduction of system response to noise;
(iii) realization of specified transient-response and/or frequency-response characteristics (e.g., prescribed poles and zeroes); and
(iv) improvement of a system's robustness against variations in open-loop dynamics (e.g., parameter variations, unmodeled dynamics or non-linearity, singular perturbations, etc.).
Classical feedback synthesis techniques (viz., the graphical techniques involving Nyquist loci, Bode plots, Nichols charts, etc.) include procedures that ensure directly that each of these types of design constraints is satisfied [16, 43]. Unfortunately, the direct methods of classical feedback theory become overwhelmingly complicated for all but the simplest feedback configurations; in particular, the classical theory cannot cope simply and effectively with multiloop feedback.

Modern feedback design techniques—these include, for example, pole-placement [18], linear-quadratic-Gaussian optimal feedback [9, 10], etc.—have made relatively simple the solution of many *multiloop* control synthesis problems. The modern techniques can be readily applied in a computer-aided-design environment to provide an effective method for solving feedback design problems having constraints of the first three of the aforementioned types. However, the modern methods do not lend themselves naturally to problems in which there are design constraints of the fourth type, i.e., specifications calling for a robust tolerance of bounded uncertainty, nonlinearity, or variations in open-loop dynamics.

The inability of modern feedback synthesis techniques to handle such robustness specifications as easily and naturally as classical techniques stems from a fundamental difference between the classical and modern approaches to feedback design. In classical feedback synthesis techniques, the design model of the plant (typically a Nyquist locus) serves to specify directly the set of stabilizing scalar feedback gains for the plant model: a scalar feedback gain k is stabilizing for the plant model if and only if 1/k lies (on the real axis) in the complement of the region of the complex plane enclosed by the Nyquist locus of the plant. If the plant model is known to be accurate only to within certain bounds, then one can model this bounded uncertainty with a "fuzzy" Nyquist locus, for which the set of stabilizing feedback gains is still given by the complement of the region

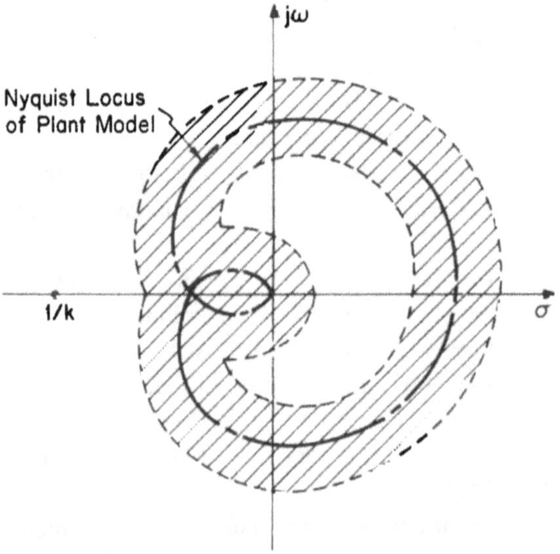

Figure 1.1 The feedback gain k stabilizes every plant whose Nyquist locus lies inside the shaded "fuzzy" band about the plant model.

enclosed by the Nyquist locus (figure 1.1). The property of classical feedback techniques that enables engineers to deal easily with robustness specifications—a property not possessed by modern multivariable feedback synthesis techniques—is this natural characterization of sets of robustly stable feedback laws directly in terms of sets of possible plant dynamics.

In the jargon of classical feedback theory, the maximal variation in plant open-loop dynamics—e.g., the maximum "fuzziness" of the plant Nyquist locus—that can be tolerated before a particular feedback design becomes unstable defines that design's *stability margins: gain margin* and *phase margin* are quantitative measures of stability margin. Engineering experience has shown that the stability margins of a feedback design provide a useful measure of its robustness against the effects of bounded variation in open-loop dynamics; consequently it is common for feedback controller design specifications to include requirements for prescribed minimal gain margin and phase margin.

The fundamental objective of the research reported here has been to develop a means for incorporating robustness specifications—i.e., design specifications calling for prescribed stability margins—into modern multivariable feedback design procedures, including procedures employed in multivariable stochastic model-reference estimator design.[1] One may appropriately view this fundamental objective as being the development of a *theory of approximations* applicable to multivariable dynamical systems, a theory that quantifies the trade-offs between modeling approximations and feedback-law choice by associating with each feedback law stability margins establishing limits to the tolerable imprecision in the system model. Such modeling approximations arise routinely in every engineering problem, not only as a consequence of the unavoidable uncertainly associated with physical processes, but also as a consequence of intentional model simplification. The latter includes such common practices as linearization, neglect of weak coupling between subsystems in decentralized

1 Recall that a *model-reference* estimator is an estimator incorporating an internal model of the process dynamics. In such estimators "residual error" (which is the difference between the model output and the observed process output) is fed back to the internal model so as to control the estimate error [104, p. 403]. Virtually all practical recursive estimator designs (including for example the Kalman filter, the extended Kalman filter, and the Luenberger observer) are model-reference estimators.

designs, and time-scale decomposition into low-, medium-, and high-frequency system models; the latter is a standard engineering strategy employed in developing simplified hierarchical designs.

Accomplishing this fundamental objective has entailed the development of

(i) a means for specifying stability margins for multiloop feedback systems (since classical single-loop characterizations of stability margins, such as gain and phase margin, are in general inadequate for characterizing multiloop stability margins); and

(ii) a new stability theory that provides a direct characterization of sets of robustly stable multiloop feedback laws in terms of "fuzzy" sets of possible multiloop plant dynamics.

1.1.2 Description of Results

The central result described in this book—a fundamental theoretical result which forms the foundation of the entire work—is an abstract and extremely powerful new stability theorem (theorem 2.1). In essence, the theorem shows that a multiloop feedback system is closed-loop stable if there exists a topological separation (into two disjoint sets) of the function space on which the system's dynamical relations are defined, the relation for the forward loop lying in one part of the separated space and the relation for the feedback loop lying in the other. This theorem has a direct bearing on the robustly stable feedback synthesis problem: if one part of the separation is taken to be a bounded region about the plant model and the other part is taken to be the complement of this region, then the theorem provides a direct characterization of the set of robustly stable feedback laws as the complement of the set of possible plant input-output relations, just as the Nyquist theorem does for single-loop classical feedback designs having a nondynamical scalar feedback gain k. The input-output relations may be specified by, for example, transfer function matrices or, possibly, nonlinear state equations: in the former case the topological separation condition can be verified in the frequency domain, leading directly to powerful multiloop generalizations of the circle and Popov stability criteria (see section 2.5); in the latter case one finds that the classical Lyapunov stability theory emerges as a special case in which a positive-definite Lyapunov function is used to establish the topological separation (corollaries 2.1 a, b). Inasmuch as the new stability theorem includes as special cases some of the most powerful existing stability theorems (e.g., Lyapunov, Popov, or circle stability criteria) and inasmuch as it provides a fundamentally new perspective for stability theory (viz., topological separation of function spaces), it constitutes a new theory of stability—the theorem has been designated the *main stability theorem.*

A methodology based on this main stability theorem has been devised for multiloop feedback system robustness and stability margin analysis (section 2.6). The methodology, which is in much the same spirit as the classical approach to single-loop robustness problems, uses frequency-dependent "sector conditions" to characterize the frequency-dependent "fuzziness" in a *multivariable* design model. A special case of the main stability theorem called the *sector stability theorem* (theorem 2.2) together with various *frequency-domain* tests (section 2.5) of the conditions of the sector stability theorem provide a practicable means for specifying multivariable feedback system stability margins and a theoretical basis for the design of robust multiloop feedback laws to meet such specifications; a conceptual computer-aided design procedure is outlined in section 2.6. Potential applications of the results include simplified hierarchical control for large systems and gain scheduling for adjustable set-point nonlinear regulator systems.

The implications of the new theory with regard to the stability margins of modern multivariable linear-quadratic-Gaussian (LQG) optimal estimators and controllers are examined in detail. The continuous-time case is considered in chapter 3, and the discrete-time/sampled-data case in chapter 4.

The design-specific stability margins of optimal linear-quadratic state-feedback (LQSF) designs are characterized in terms of the system matrices, quadratic-performance-index weighting matrices, and the optimal solution of the Riccati equation: these margins are characterized as a convex set of nonlinear dynamical deviations between the design model and the actual plant that can be tolerated without inducing instability. Additionally, it is shown that the continuous-time LQSF optimal design procedure is inherently robust in that it automatically ensures certain minimal stability margins including an infinite gain margin, at least a $\pm 60°$ phase margin, and at least a 50% gain reduction tolerance at each control input channel; discrete-time/sampled-data designs are found to approximate this inherent robustness, but the robustness is degraded as the sampling interval increases.

Viewing the Kalman filter as a feedback system in which residual error is fed back to control the estimation error, the duality between Kalman filters and LQSF controllers is expoloited to provide a characterization of the nonlinearity tolerance of a constant-gain extended Kalman filter (CGEKF); the CGEKF is a nonlinear extended Kalman filter employing a precomputed constant residual-gain matrix and having drastically reduced on-line computational requirements relative to extended Kalman filters employing a time-varying residual-gain matrix that is adaptively updated on-line. The results include analytically verifiable conditions that can be used to confirm the (global!) stability of CGEKF designs and, provided that the CGEKF incorporates an accurate internal model of the nonlinear process dynamics, ensure the nondivergence of CGEKF estimates. The CGEKF design procedure is found to have an inherent robustness which can be interpreted as including an infinite gain margin, at least $\pm 60\%$ phase margin, and at least 50% gain reduction tolerance at each sensor output channel; though it should be noted that, because an accurate internal system model is required for CGEKF nondivergence, the CGEKF robustness results do not have the same interpretation as the dual LQSF robustness results.

The CGEKF and LQSF robustness results are shown to combine in a fashion reminiscent of the separation theorem of estimation and control to suggest a powerful technique, based on linear-quadratic-Gaussian optimal feedback theory, for the synthesis of simplified dynamical output-feedback compensators for nonlinear regulator systems. The technique leads to a feedback compensator design consisting of a cascade of a CGEKF and an optimal constant LQSF gain matrix. It is proved that the inherent robustness of optimal linear-quadratic state feedback against unmodeled nonlinearity combines with the intrinsic robustness of the CGEKF to assure that such feedback designs will be closed-loop stable even in systems with substantial nonlinearity, assuming that the CGEKF incorporates an accurate internal model of the nonlinear plant dynamics.

The aforementioned LQSF regulator stability results and CGEKF stability and nondivergence results are derived in the general context of the class of constant-gain controllers and nonlinear estimators whose design is not necessarily based on statistical considerations; for example, nonlinear estimator designs intended to optimize structural simplicity or error-transient response, i.e., nonlinear observers [107]. This general class of constant-gain controllers and nonlinear estimators includes as special cases LQSF and CGEKF designs. In the context of this broader class of suboptimal nonlinear controllers and estimators, the results provide analytically verifiable conditions which can be used to test for nondivergence and stability and to evaluate robustness against the effects of design approximations; though one cannot in general expect such designs to be as robust as LQSF and CGEKF designs. The output-feedback separation-type property applies to this broader class of controllers and estimators, showing that nondivergent estimates can, unconditionally, be substituted for true values in otherwise-stable feedback systems without ever causing instability.

It is demonstrated that all the CGEKF/LQSF nondivergence and stability results extend to state-augmented designs (section 3.8 and 4.8). Such state-augmented designs include, for example, proportional-integral controller designs which track with zero steady-state error and compensated CGEKF nonlinear estimator designs that have zero steady-state bias error.

1.1.3 Structure of Monograph

This monograph consists of five chapters:

1 Introduction

2 Stability and Robustness: A Geometric Perspective and Frequency-

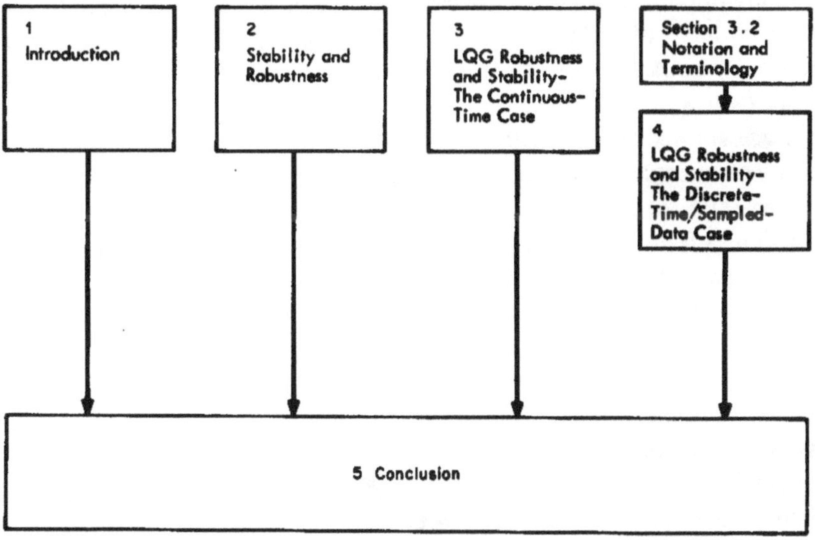

Figure 1.2 Logical relationship of chapters.

Domain Criteria
3, 4 LQG Robustness and Stability
5 Conclusion.
The logical interdependence of the various chapters is illustrated in figure 1.2. The monograph has been arranged so that the first four chapters are logically independent and may be read in any order, though it is recommended that the sections within each chapter be read in sequence. The proofs of the results in chapters 3 and 4, all of which are based on the results developed in chapter 2, are contained in the appendix, a few exceptions being made for proofs that are especially simple or illuminating. The developments in chapters 3 and 4, which concern respectively the continuous- and discrete-time LQG problem, are completely parallel, even to the numbering of sections and theorems; readers wishing to compare the results developed for the two cases will find this parallelism helpful.

1.2 Previous Work and Related Literature

1.2.1 Robustness and Sensitivity of General Feedback Systems

The fundamental work on the robustness of feedback systems is due to Bode [16, pp. 451–488]. Bode's work concerned both the robustness of feedback systems and the closely related issue of differential sensitivity, although Bode did not use these terms. The term *robustness* refers to tolerance of large disturbances (lying within specified bounds) whereas the term *differential sensitivity* concerns the effects of vanishingly small disturbances.

Bode showed that the effects of vanishingly small perturbations in the gains of a single-loop linear feedback system are directly related to the return ratio (or loop gain) and return difference (one minus the return ratio) of a feedback system. Bode's results on differential sensitivity have since been extensively studied [43] and extended [24, 53] to multiloop, nonlinear, time-varying feedback systems. A discrete-time notion of differential sensitivity has also been formulated by Kwakernaak and Sivan [55, p. 427]. It appears that the analysis of differential sensitivity is now well understood; though the development of methods for synthesizing feedback systems with reduced differential sensitivity continues to be an area of active research [37]. Reference [26] is an anthology of many of the key journal articles which have appeared on the subject of differential sensitivity. Reference [25] also contains several relevant articles.

In the area of robustness, Bode's principal contribution was the observation that the amount of tolerable uncertainty in the open-loop dynamics of a single-loop linear feedback system can be expressed in terms of a region in a space whose "points" are open-loop system transfer functions, each such "point" being described by the Nyquist locus of its associated transfer function. Specifically, Bode showed how the notions of gain and phase margin can be exploited to arrive at a simple and useful means for characterizing these regions of tolerable uncertainty. The engineering implications are developed in detail by, e.g., Horowitz [43]. It is shown in [44] that classical Nyquist-Bode theory can be iteratively applied in order to design robustly stable multiloop feedback having the special structure of "cascaded multiloop feedback." Rosenbrock [88; 89, pp. 198–208; 90], McMorran [66], and Belletrutti and MacFarlane [15, 64, 65] have developed and examined the design implications of a multiloop generalization of the Nyquist stability criterion. However, except for the narrow class of "diagonally dominant" (i.e., "weakly-coupled") systems [20, 90, 92], the quantitative robustness implications of the multiloop Nyquist results remain unclear.

Results having a close relation to the issue of feedback system robustness have been developed by Zames [118, 119]. Viewing feedback systems in terms of the dynamical input-output relations of their components, Zames showed that "conic sectors" in an appropriate space of input-output relations can be used to aggregately characterize complex nonlinear dynamical input-output relations in a simple, useful fashion. While the primary emphasis in Zames's work was the use of conic sectors to provide a simple characterization of complex nonlinear relations, he made the following brief observation in his conclusions [118]:

> One of the broader implications of the theory here concerns the use of functional analysis for the study of poorly defined systems. It seems possible, from only coarse information about a system, and perhaps even without knowing details of internal structure, to make useful assessments of qualitative behavior.

Despite the appearance of myriads[2] of publications expanding upon and refining the results in Zames's paper [118], the idea of using functional analysis for poorly defined systems has not previously been fully developed. Nevertheless, this idea is implicit in the classical frequency-domain ap-

2 Among these myriads are, to name a few, [6], [22], [23], [27], [32], [42], [56], [67], [86], [106], [110], and [119]; a complete listing would probably include at least several hundreds of references.

proaches to robust feedback design[3] and this idea forms the thesis upon which the multiloop feedback and stability margin results of this book are built. In particular, it is Zames's work [118, 119] which laid the foundation and provided much of the inspiration for the theory of stability developed in chapter 2.

It should be noted that some authors (e.g., Davison [29]) have used the term "robustness" in connection with linear feedback systems that track with zero steady-state error in the presence of additive disturbance inputs satisfying specified dynamical equations. It is demonstrated in [29] and [30] that if an appropriate servo-compensator is employed then such zero steady-state error tracking occurs and is robust against plant modeling errors, provided that the overall system remains closed-loop stable. In the present monograph, we dwell principally on a different, but related, aspect of robustness: we are concerned primarily with the amount of plant modeling error that can be tolerated before a feedback system becomes unstable.

1.2.2 Linear-Quadratic-Gaussian (LQG) Estimators and Feedback Controllers—General

One of the more powerful approaches to multivariable feedback system design, an approach whose robustness implications are examined in detail in this monograph, is the linear-quadratic-Gaussian (LQG) procedure. The technical and philosophical issues relating to the application of the LQG procedure are discussed by, for example, Athans [9, 10]; the textbooks by Anderson and Moore [5] and Kwakernaak and Sivan [55] are excellent sources of detailed information about the LQG procedure.

Briefly, the LQG method is an algorithm for synthesizing output-feedback compensators which minimizes a designer-selected quadratic performance index for a linear plant subjected to Gaussian white noise of known mean and covariance. Based on the *separation theorem* of estimation and control, an LQG compensator can be split into two parts: a Kalman filter, which estimates the state of the plant, and a memoryless state-feedback gain, which acts on the state estimate generated by the Kalman filter to generate compensating inputs to the plant. In the special case in which the plant output includes noise-free measurements of the

3 Frequency-domain methods and transfer function methods are in fact function space methods. For example, a transfer function may be viewed naturally as a functional operator mapping complex input functions (defined over the complex plane) into complex output functions (likewise defined over the complex plane).

plant state, the Kalman filter is eliminated and the compensator is called a *linear-quadratic state-feedback* (LQSF) regulator.

The LQG technique provides a straightforward means for synthesizing stable multiloop linear feedback systems which are insensitive to Gaussian white noise. Variations of the LQG technique have been devised for the synthesis of feedback systems with specified poles and eigenvectors [5, pp. 77–78; 45; 72; 115; 126] and for systems with constraints on controller structure [19, 59, 60, 101]. By state-augmentation methods the LQG technique can be applied to the design of feedback compensators for systems subject to persistent disturbance inputs and to other types of nonwhite noise [17, 47–49, 57, 101, 102, 117]. It is well known [8, 9] that by substituting a nonlinear extended Kalman filter for the optimal linear estimator (i.e., the Kalman filter) in the LQG controller, one may adapt the LQG procedure to suboptimal nonlinear control problems.[4] Thus, LQG theory has come to play a central role in much of modern multiloop feedback theory.

1.2.3 Stability Margins, Sensitivity, and Robustness of LQG Estimators and Controllers

The fundamental work on the differential sensitivity properties associated with LQG systems is due to Kalman [52]. Kalman showed that (under mild assumptions) a linear single-input state-feedback system is optimal with respect to some quadratic performance index if, and only if, the system is stable and has a return difference of magnitude greater than unity at all frequences. Kalman noted that classical control theory requires this condition on the return difference for reduced sensitivity to component variations. Kalman's sensitivity results have since been more precisely interpreted by Perkins and Cruz [82] and generalized to multi-input LQSF regulators by Anderson [1] and MacFarlane [63]. Perkins and Cruz [83] summarize these results, and Wonham [120, ch. 13] contains a brief critical discussion. The differential sensitivity of the optimal cost to parameter variations is addressed by Barnett [11, 13, 14]. The effects on the optimal quadratic cost of variations in sampling interval is addressed by Levis et al. [61]. Techniques for synthesizing LQSF designs with reduced sensi-

4 While this nonlinear extension of LQG feedback theory is well known, its rigorous justification rests on the nonlinear separation theorems developed in chapters 3 and 4 of this monograph, viz., theorems 3.3 and 4.3.

tivity are proposed in [51, 103].

Relatively little has been produced regarding the differential sensitivity properties associated with Kalman filters and with general LQG regulators incorporating Kalman filters in their feedback loops. With only limited success, Anderson [2] attempted to determine under what circumstances a general LQG regulator is equivalent to an LQSF regulator. Kwakernaak [54] showed (under the assumption that the controlled plant is minimum phase) that in the limit as the control cost-weighting matrix goes to zero (i.e., as the loop gain increases so that the poles of the Kalman filter dominate the system response), general LQG regulators do exhibit reduced differential sensitivity; however, it is not clear that an LQG design dominated by the poles of its filter would be satisfactory in other respects.

Regarding the robustness properties of LQSF systems, perhaps the most significant result is due to Anderson and Moore [5, pp. 70–76]. Employing the Nyquist and the circle stability theorems, Anderson and Moore showed that Kalman's result [52] concerning the return difference of LQSF systems can be used to conclude that single-input LQSF regulators have $\pm 60°$ phase margin, infinite gain margin, and 50% gain reduction tolerance. Moreover, they showed that the gain properties apply to nonlinear time-varying gains. Related results by Moylan [74, 75] generalize results of Barnett and Storey [12] and of Moore [73] to parameterize classes of memoryless, nondynamical feedback perturbations which will not destabilize a multi-input optimal state-feedback regulator with quadratic performance index. Less general multiloop results have been derived independently by Wong [113, 114]. Gilman and Rhodes [36] have developed an upper bound on the quadratic performance index of suboptimal nonlinear LQSF designs; provided the system is cost-observable and provided the bound does not "blow up," their results can be used to evaluate the gain margins and nonlinearity tolerances of LQSF designs. Recent papers dealing with LQSF robustness include [80], [81], and [108], which are in part based on some of the ideas that have been developed in the course of the research reported here. The papers [95]–[97] contain preliminary reports of the result (section 3.4) that all continuous-time LQSF designs have infinite gain margin, at least $\pm 60°$ phase margin, and at least 50% gain reduction tolerance at each control input channel; though it should be noted that the methods of proof employed in [95]–[97] are different.

As an indication of at least one of the limitations of the robustness properties universal to LQSF regulators, Rosenbrock and McMorran

[91] show by means of an example that LQSF regulator designs may be conditionally stable. That is, the failure of a single loop in a multiloop LQSF regulator may destabilize a system which is open-loop stable. Wong [113] examines this problem in greater depth.

The literature on the subject of robustness and computational considerations in nonlinear estimation is sparse and largely inconclusive. The discussion of nonlinear estimation in Schweppe [104, ch. 13] provides a good intuitive understanding of the trade-offs between computational requirements and residual-gain choice; though the possibility of a constant residual gain is not explicitly considered. The idea of using a constant residual gain for linear filtering is well known [34, pp. 238–242], but the connection with nonlinear filtering has not been established. Of the existing literature on nonlinear estimation, [35] and [107] appear to be the most closely related to the present work.

Gilman and Rhodes [35] suggest a procedure for synthesising nonlinear estimators with a pre-computable but time-varying residual gain. Their estimator, like the extended Kalman filter, has the intuitively appealing structure of a *model-reference* estimator [105, p. 403]; i.e., it consists of an internal model of the system dynamics with observations entering via a gain acting on the residual error between the system and model outputs. The distinguishing feature of the estimator suggested in [35] is that the residual gain is chosen so as to minimize a certain upper bound on the mean-square error. This procedure tends to ensure a robust design since, assuming the minimal value of the error bound does not "blow up," the estimator cannot diverge. A limitation of this design procedure is that the error bound may be very loose for systems with substantial nonlinearity; so there is no assurance that the bound-minimizing residual gain is a good choice. Also, there is no a priori guarantee that the resultant estimator will even be stable since the minimal error bound may become arbitrarily large as time elapses. Similar results are developed for discrete-time systems by Gusak and Simkin [38].

Tarn and Rasis [107] have proposed a constant-gain model-reference nonlinear estimator which is a natural extension of Luenberger's observer for linear systems, having a design based solely on stability considerations. The results of [107] show that, given such a nonlinear observer design, if certain Lyapunov functions can be found, then one can conclude that

(i) The estimator is nondivergent; and

(ii) The estimator can be used for state reconstruction in a full-state-feedback system without causing instability.

However, from an engineering standpoint the results of [107] are deficient in that they are nonconstructive: no design synthesis procedure is suggested; no method is proposed for construction the Lyapunov functions required to test the stability of a design; no procedure is suggested for minimizing the estimator's error. The CGEKF results presented in this monograph (sections 3.5–3.7 and 4.5–4.7) address all these deficiencies by providing a constructive procedure for synthesizing stable constant-gain model-reference estimator designs which are to a first approximation optimally accurate. Moreover, these results prove that, provided the estimator is nondivergent, it can be used for state reconstruction without ever causing instability, irrespective of the availability of Lyapunov functions.

The papers of Patel and Toda [121, 122], in contrast to the aforementioned papers on nonlinear estimation and in contrast to the present work, do not require an exact internal model of the process dynamics in their results regarding the robustness of optimal estimators. These authors have developed an upper bound on the mean-square error of mismatched optimal linear estimators, i.e., mismatched Kalman filters. However, their results have the important limitation that they apply only when the control input to the process is identically zero.

Results concerning the robustness of general LQG feedback controllers have been reported by Gilman and Rhodes [35]. These authors have developed an upper bound on the expected value of the quadratic performance index for white-noise-driven, continuous-time, output-feedback systems employing a state-feedback gain matrix acting on a state estimate generated by a nonlinear model-reference estimator which, like the extended Kalman filter, incorporates a nonlinear internal model of the plant dynamics. Provided the system is "cost-observable," provided the upper bound on the cost does not grow unboundedly as time elapses, and provided the nonlinear model incorporated in the estimator exactly models the plant dynamics, then this result can be used to assure the closed-loop stability of the overall system. Since in practical applications the actual value assumed by the performance index is often not of particular engineering interest and since the upper bound on the cost in [35] may be quite loose for systems with substantial nonlinearity, the principal engineering interest in these results appears to be with regard to their stability implication. On the other hand, the separation theorem for nonlinear systems developed in this monograph (theorem 3.3) allows one to ascertain the stability of such systems much more simply and directly.

Underlying the various conclusions about the minimal *inherent* robustness[5] and *inherent* insensitivity of LQG estimator and controller designs are certain more basic properties associated with optimality. The problem of characterizing the various properties associated with optimality is intimately related with the so-called "inverse problem" of optimal control, which concerns the characterization of the set of performance indices for which a given control law is optimal. Related papers are [1], [52], [71], [75], and [116].

5 For example, the inherent infinite gain margin and $\pm 60°$ phase margin robustness properties of single-input LQSF systems proved by Anderson and Moore [5, pp. 70–76].

2

Stability and Robustness: A Geometric Perspective, and Frequency-Domain Criteria

2.1 Introduction

A key step in the synthesis of robustly stable feedback systems is the characterization of a *set* of feedback laws that are stabilizing for *every* element of the set of possible plant dynamics. This type of information is precisely what is provided for single-loop feedback systems by such input-output stability criteria as the Nyquist, Popov, and circle theorems. Indeed, the practical merit of classical feedback design procedures involving Nyquist loci, Bode plots, and Nichols charts is in a large measure directly attributable to the fact that these design procedures provide the designer with an easily interpretable characterization of such sets of robustly stable feedback laws. Available multivariable input-output stability criteria such as Rosenbrock's multivariable Nyquist theorem [88] and Zames's conic-relation and positivity stability theorems [118] have led to useful characterizations of sets of robustly stable feedback laws for only a limited class of problems, viz., interconnections of dissipative systems [106], weakly coupled interconnections of systems [6] (including so-called "diagonally dominant" systems [20, 90, 92]), and "nearly normal" systems [67] (which can be viewed as vector-space isomorphisms of weakly coupled systems).

With a view toward the development of stability criteria suitable for use in the synthesis of robust *multivariable* feedback systems, a new conceptual framework for stability theory is developed in this chapter. The results show that existing stability criteria have a simple geometric interpretation in terms of a sort of topological separation of the function spaces on which the system's dynamical relations are defined. The fundamental result (theorem 2.1) provides an abstract generalization of existing input-output *and* state-space stability criteria in terms of such a topological separation. Motivated by the observation that the conic sectors of Zames's powerful conic relation stability theorem [118] are interpretable as devices to achieve the required topological separation, a generalization of Zames's conic sector, called simply a *sector*, is considered. This generalization of Zames's conic sector is shown to have a number of properties which make it ideally suited to the task of characterizing sets of stabilizing feedback laws in terms of sets of possible plant dynamics for *multivariable* systems. The sector conditions are amenable to verification in the frequency domain, leading to a multivariable generalization of the circle theorem.

2.1.1 Problem Formulation

Our results concern the stability of the following canonical two-subsystem multivariable feedback system (figure 2.1a)

$$\begin{aligned}(y, x) &\in \overline{\mathbf{G}}(u)\\ (x, y) &\in \overline{\mathbf{H}}(v)\end{aligned} \qquad (2.1.1)$$

where

$u \in \mathscr{U}_e$ and $v \in \mathscr{V}_e$ are disturbance inputs to the system;
$x \in \mathscr{X}_e$ and $y \in \mathscr{Y}_e$ are the outputs of the system;
$\overline{\mathbf{G}}(u) \subset \mathscr{Y}_e \times \mathscr{X}_e$ and $\overline{\mathbf{H}}(v) \subset \mathscr{X}_e \times \mathscr{Y}_e$ are nonlinear relations which are dependent of the disturbance inputs $u \in \mathscr{U}_e$ and $v \in \mathscr{V}_e$ respectively;
$\mathscr{U}_e$, $\mathscr{V}_e$, $\mathscr{X}_e$, and $\mathscr{Y}_e$ are vector spaces.[1]

1 A set X is described as a vector space [40, p. 171] (or, equivalently, as a *linear set* [125, pp. 43–44]) if for any two of its elements x_1 and x_2, the sum $x_1 + x_2$ is defined and is an element of X, and similarly the product ax is defined, 'a' being a scalar; additionally, the following axioms must hold:
(1) $(x_1 + x_2) + x_3 = x_1 + (x_2 + x_3)$ (associative addition);
(2) $x_1 + x_2 = x_2 + x_1$ (commutative addition);
(3) an element 0 exists in X such that $0x = 0$ for all x in X;
(4) $(a_1 + a_2)x = a_1x + a_2x$ (distributive laws);
(5) $a(x_1 + x_2) = ax_1 + ax_2$ (distributive laws);
(6) $(ab)x = a(bx)$ (associative multiplication);
(7) $1x = x$.

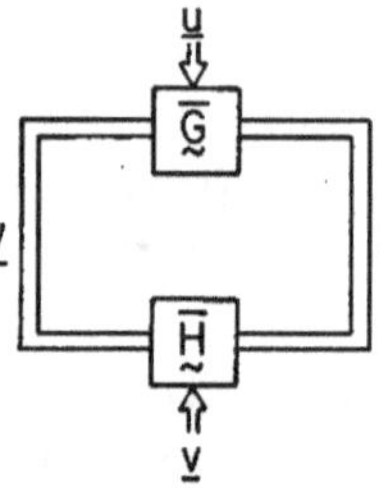

(a) Canonical two-subsystem multivariable feedback system

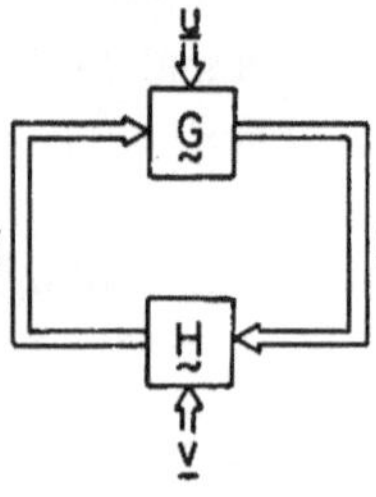

(b) Special case: $\underset{\sim}{G}(\underline{u})$ and $\underset{\sim}{H}(\underline{v})$ operators

Figure **2.1** Canonical two-subsystem multivariable feedback system, and a special case.

It is assumed that $(0, 0) \in \overline{\mathbf{G}}(0)$ and that $(0, 0) \in \overline{\mathbf{H}}(0)$ so that the pair $(x, y) = (0, 0)$ is an equilibrium solution of the undisturbed system. The system (2.1.1) defines a relation between input pairs $(u, v) \in \mathscr{U}_e \times \mathscr{V}_e$ and output pairs $(x, y) \in \mathscr{X}_e \times \mathscr{Y}_e$; equivalently (2.1.1) defines a subset of the space $(\mathscr{U}_e \times \mathscr{V}_e) \times (\mathscr{X}_e \times \mathscr{Y}_e)$.

The vector spaces $\mathscr{U}_e$, $\mathscr{V}_e$, $\mathscr{X}_e$, and $\mathscr{Y}_e$ are *extended normed spaces*, defined in terms of collections of normed spaces $\mathscr{U}_\tau$, $\mathscr{V}_\tau$, $\mathscr{X}_\tau$, and $\mathscr{Y}_\tau$ and a collection of linear projection operators $\mathbf{P}_\tau$ as follows.

Definition Let $\mathscr{X}_e$ be a vector space. If there is associated with $\mathscr{X}_e$ an interval T and a collection of *linear* operators $\mathbf{P}_\tau$ $(\tau \in \mathrm{T})$ mapping $\mathscr{X}_e$ into the collection of *normed* spaces $\mathscr{X}_\tau$ $(\tau \in \mathrm{T})$ then $\mathscr{X}_e$ is the *extended normed space* induced by the collection of operators $\mathbf{P}_\tau$ $(\tau \in \mathrm{T})$. If, additionally, each of the spaces $\mathscr{X}_\tau$ is an inner-product space then we say that $\mathscr{X}_e$ is the *extended inner product space* induced by the collection of operators $\mathbf{P}_\tau$.[2] A vector space $\mathscr{X}_e$ which is itself a normed space is presumed to be the extended normed space for which $\mathscr{X}_\tau = \mathscr{X}_e$ for all τ, and $\mathscr{X}_\tau$ is the identity operator, unless $\mathscr{X}_\tau$ and/or $\mathbf{P}_\tau$ are specifically stated to be otherwise. For brevity we may use the equivalent notation

$$\|z\|_\tau \triangleq \|\mathbf{P}_\tau z\| \tag{2.1.2}$$

$$\langle z_1, z_2\rangle_\tau \triangleq \langle \mathbf{P}_\tau z_1, \mathbf{P}_\tau z_2\rangle. \tag{2.1.3}$$

Comments The foregoing problem formulation is considerably more general than is usual in stability theory. Typically, the interval T represents time and the spaces $\mathscr{X}_e$ and $\mathscr{Y}_e$ consist of functions mapping T into R^n; the operator $\mathbf{P}_\tau$ is typically taken to be the *linear truncation operator* [1]

$$(\mathbf{P}_\tau \cdot \xi)(t) = \begin{cases} \xi(t), & \text{if } t \leq \tau \\ 0, & \text{if } t > \tau \end{cases}. \tag{2.1.4}$$

The interval T might typically be taken to be either the non-negative real numbers R_+ (in the cast of continuous-time systems) or the set of non-negative integers Z_+ (in the case of discrete-time systems). The disturbance vector spaces $\mathscr{U}_e$ and $\mathscr{V}_e$ are typically both either R^n (in the case of Lyapunov state-space results [39]) or spaces of functions mapping T into R^n (in the case of "input-output" stability results [27]).[3]

In the special case in which the relations $\overline{\mathbf{G}}(u)$ and $\overline{\mathbf{H}}(v)$ are induced by operators $\mathbf{G}(u)$: $\mathscr{Y}_e \to \mathscr{X}_e$, and $\mathbf{H}(v)$: $\mathscr{X}_e \to \mathscr{Y}_e$, then one may represent the system (2.1.1) by the equivalent set of feedback equations

2 One can define a variety of "extended norm" functionals $\|\cdot\|_e: \mathscr{Z}_e \to R_+ \cup \{\infty\}$ on the space $\mathscr{Z}_e$, e.g., [118]

$$\|z\|_e = \sup_{\tau \in T} \|z\|_\tau$$

or [5]

$$\|z\|_e = \limsup_{\tau \to (\sup T)} \|z\|_\tau.$$

Since $\|z\|_e$ may in general be infinite, the functional $\|\cdot\|_e$ is not necessarily a norm in the usual sense. However, $\|\cdot\|_e$ does define a norm on the subspace

$$\mathscr{Z} \triangleq \{z \in \mathscr{Z}_e \mid \|z\|_e < \infty\}.$$

For purposes of stability analysis, we have found that it is not necessary to introduce the extended norm $\|\cdot\|_e$ or the normed subspace $\mathscr{Z}$ since the stability properties of each $z \in \mathscr{Z}_e$ can be determined from the τ-dependence of $\|z\|_\tau$.

3 Readers unfamiliar with the notion of a relation, the concept of an extended normed space, the linear truncation operator $\mathbf{P}_\tau$, or other concepts and definitions standard in input-output stability, may find it helpful to refer to one of the authoritative references (e.g., [42], [110], [27]) or to the concise and lucid original exposition of Zames [118].

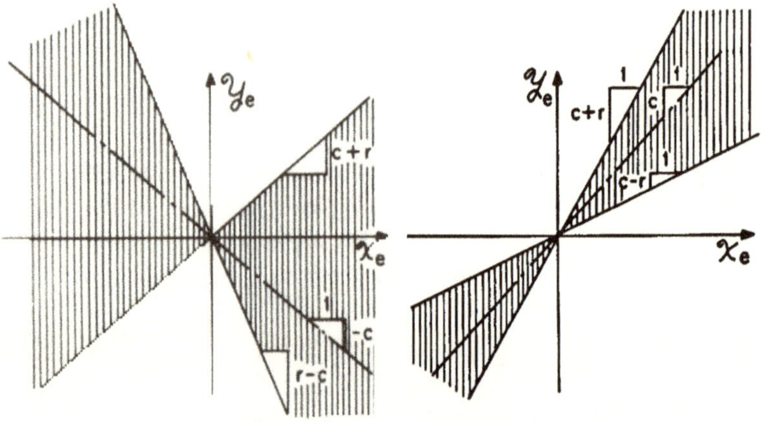

(a) Conic regions in $\mathcal{X}_e \times \mathcal{Y}_e$

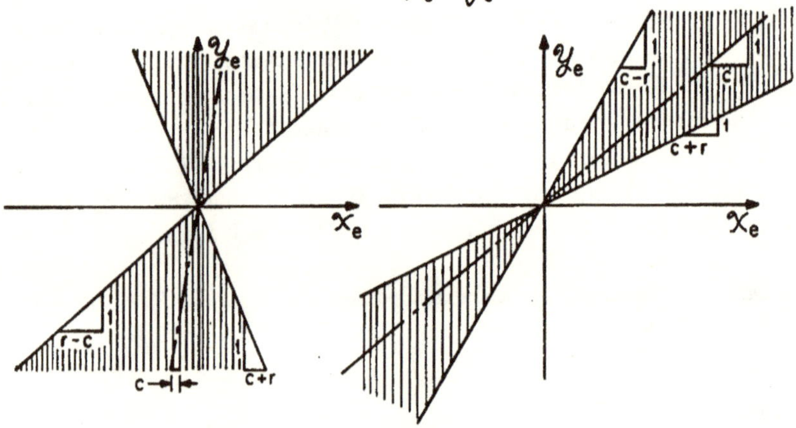

(b) Conic regions in $\mathcal{Y}_e \times \mathcal{X}_e$

Figure 2.2 Conic regions with center c and radius r.

$$x = \mathbf{G}(u)y \qquad (2.1.1')$$
$$y = \mathbf{H}(v)x$$

(see figure 2.1b).

2.1.2 Geometric Interpretation of Zames's Conic Relation Stability Criterion

To provide motivation and a conceptual framework for the development that follows, it is instructive to explain at this point how to give a simple geometric interpretation to the conic-relation stability theorem (Zames [118], thm. 2a), which is among the most powerful results in input-output stability theory.[4] The conditions of the conic relation stability theorem involve "conic" regions of the type

$$\text{Cone}(c, r) \triangleq \{(x, y) \in \mathscr{X}_e \times \mathscr{Y}_e \mid \|\mathbf{P}_\tau(y - cx)\| \leq r\|\mathbf{P}_\tau x\| \text{ for all } \tau \in T\} \subset \mathscr{X}_e \times \mathscr{Y}_e \tag{2.1.5}$$

(figure 2.2) where c and r are scalars called the cone *center* and cone *radius*, respectively.[5] It is said that a relation $\overline{\mathbf{H}} \subset \mathscr{X}_e \times \mathscr{Y}_e$ is *inside* Cone (c, r) if

$$\overline{\mathbf{H}} \subset \text{Cone}(c, r); \tag{2.1.6}$$

$\overline{\mathbf{H}}$ is *strictly inside* Cone (c, r) if for some $r' < r$,

$$\overline{\mathbf{H}} \subset \text{Cone}(c, r') \subset \text{cone}(c, r). \tag{2.1.7}$$

The notions of outside and strictly outside are defined analogously using in place of Cone (c, r) its complement. A property of conic regions such as (2.1.5) that is central to the geometric interpretation of Zames's conic-relation stability theorem is that the complement of such a conic region in $\mathscr{X}_e \times \mathscr{Y}_e$ corresponds to either a conic region or the complement of a conic region in $\mathscr{Y}_e \times \mathscr{X}_e$, as may be seen by comparison of figure 1.2a with figure 1.2b. For technical reasons, apparently having to do with the method of proof used by Zames, the conditions of Zames's conic-relation theorem also require that $\mathscr{U}_e$, $\mathscr{V}_e$, $\mathscr{X}_e$, $\mathscr{Y}_e$ be identical extended inner-product spaces and that the disturbances $u \in \mathscr{U}_e$ and $v \in \mathscr{V}_e$ enter additively, i.e., if $(x_1, y_1) \in \overline{\mathbf{H}}(v)$ and $(y_2, x_2) \in \overline{\mathbf{G}}(u)$, then, respectively,

$$(x_1 + v, y_1) \in \overline{\mathbf{H}}(0), \tag{2.1.8}$$

$$(y_2 + u, x_2) \in \overline{\mathbf{G}}(0) \tag{2.1.9}$$

(figure 2.3). Subject to these restrictions on the class of systems considered, the conditions of Zames's conic relation theorem state quite simply that a sufficient condition for the feedback system (2.1.1) to be stable is that (for appropriately chosen center and radius parameters c and r), the relation

4 The Nyquist, circle, Popov, passivity, and small-gain stability theorems all follow as corollaries to Zames's conic-relation theorem; this is demonstrated in [118] and [119].

5 The notation Cone (c, r) is nonstandard; Zames [118] uses the notation $\{c - r, c + r\}$.

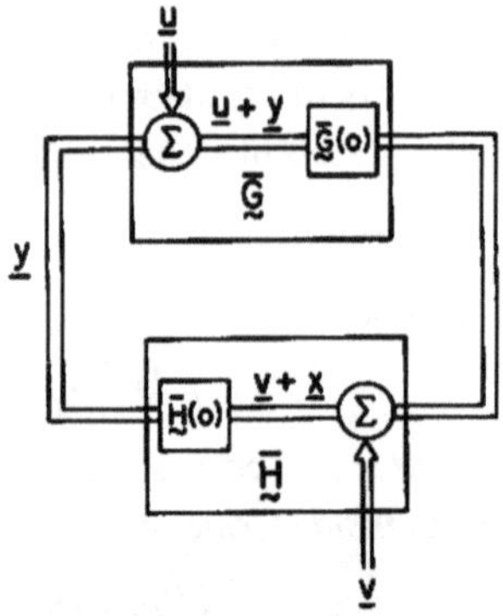

Figure 2.3 Feedback system with disturbances entering additively.

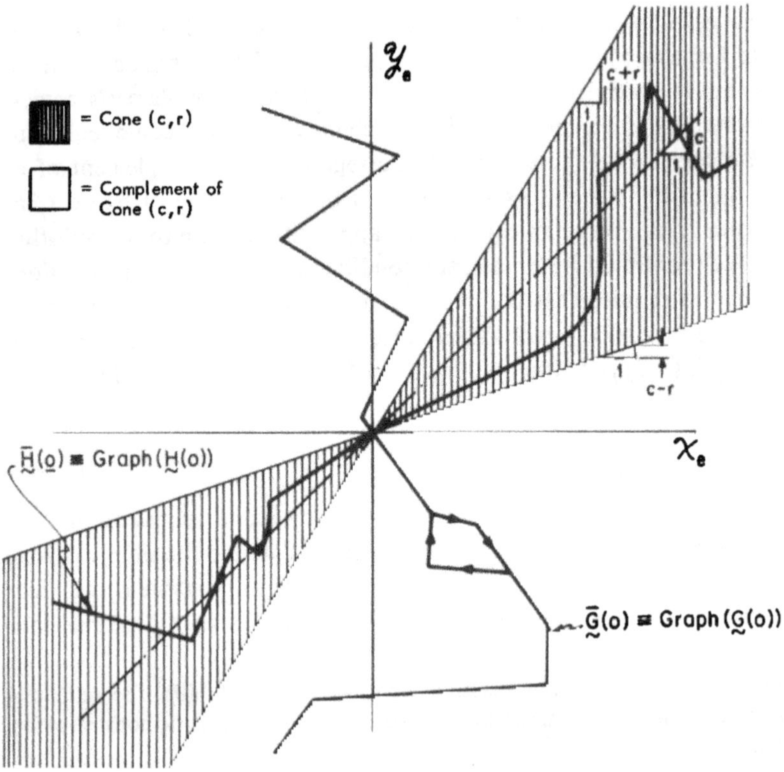

Figure 2.4 Two-dimensional geometric interpretation of Zames's conic-relation theorem.

$\overline{\mathbf{G}}(0)$ be strictly inside Cone $(c, r) \subset \mathscr{Y}_e \times \mathscr{X}_e$ and the relation $\overline{\mathbf{H}}(0)$ be inside the region of $\mathscr{X}_e \times \mathscr{Y}_e$ corresponding to the complement of Cone (c, r) (figure 2.4). The interpretation of the conic relation stability theorem in terms of a *topological separation* is immediately evident: the interior of Cone (c, r) and the interior of the complement of Cone (c, r) form a *topological separation* [76] of the space $\mathscr{X}_e \times \mathscr{Y}_e$ [less the equilibrium point $(x, y) = (0, 0)$ and other points on the boundary of Cone (c, r)] into two disjoint regions, the closure of one region containing all nonzero pairs $(x, y) \in \overline{\mathbf{H}}(0)$ and the interior of the other region containing all nonzero pairs (x, y) such that $(y, x) \in \overline{\mathbf{G}}(0)$.

The results which follow show that it is more than just a coincidence that the conditions of the conic relation stability theorem correspond to a topological separation. The results show in essence that one can use any such partitioning of $\mathscr{X}_e \times \mathscr{Y}_e$ into two disjoint regions, provided the "distance" between the two regions increases unboundedly as the "distance" from the equilibrium increases. What constitutes a suitable measure of "distance" is the subject of section 2.3.

2.2 Notation and Terminology

In this section some of the standard terminology from the stability literature (e.g., [118] and [39]) is reviewed and, where necessary, generalized; frequently used symbols are listed.

2.2.1 Relations (see [118])

A *relation* $\overline{\mathbf{R}}$ is any set of the form $\overline{\mathbf{R}} \subset \mathscr{X} \times \mathscr{Y}$; i.e., a relation is *any* subset of the Cartesian product of *any* two sets. A relation $\overline{\mathbf{R}} \subset \mathscr{X} \times \mathscr{Y}$ can be viewed as a mapping of subsets of $\mathscr{X}$ into subsets of $\mathscr{Y}$ and in this regard, is merely a generalization of the notion of a function mapping $\mathscr{X}$ into $\mathscr{Y}$. Some operations involving relations are defined below.

IMAGE The image $\overline{\mathbf{R}}[\mathscr{A}]$ of a set $\mathscr{A} \subset \mathscr{X}$ under a relation $\overline{\mathbf{R}} \subset \mathscr{X} \times \mathscr{Y}$ is the subset of $\mathscr{Y}$

$$\overline{\mathbf{R}}[\mathscr{A}] \triangleq \{y \mid (x, y) \in \overline{\mathbf{R}} \text{ for some } x \in \mathscr{A}\}. \tag{2.2.1}$$

INVERSE The *inverse* of a relation $\overline{\mathbf{R}} \subset \mathscr{X} \times \mathscr{Y}$ is the relation $\overline{\mathbf{R}}^{\mathbf{I}} \subset \mathscr{Y} \times \mathscr{X}$

$$\overline{\mathbf{R}}^{\mathbf{I}} \triangleq \{(y, x) \in \mathscr{Y} \times \mathscr{X} \mid (x, y) \in \overline{\mathbf{R}}\}; \tag{2.2.2}$$

clearly, the inverse *always* exists.

COMPOSITION PRODUCT The *composition product* of the relations $\overline{\mathbf{R}}_1 \subset \mathscr{X} \times \mathscr{Y}$ followed by $\overline{\mathbf{R}}_2 \subset \mathscr{Y} \times \mathscr{Z}$ is the relation $\overline{\mathbf{R}}_2 \circ \overline{\mathbf{R}}_1 \subset \mathscr{X} \times \mathscr{Z}$, where

$$\overline{\mathbf{R}}_2 \circ \overline{\mathbf{R}}_1 \triangleq \{(x, z) \in \mathscr{X} \times \mathscr{Z} \mid \text{there exists } y \in \mathscr{Y} \text{ such that } (x, y) \in \overline{\mathbf{R}}_1 \text{ and } (y, z) \in \overline{\mathbf{R}}_2\}. \tag{2.2.3}$$

SUM If $\overline{\mathbf{R}}_1, \overline{\mathbf{R}}_2 \subset \mathscr{X} \times \mathscr{Y}$ and if addition is defined on $\mathscr{Y}$, then the *sum* of the relations $\overline{\mathbf{R}}_1$ and $\overline{\mathbf{R}}_2$ is the relation

$$\overline{\mathbf{R}}_1 + \overline{\mathbf{R}}_2 \triangleq \{(x, y) \in \mathscr{X} \times \mathscr{Y} \mid x \in \mathscr{X} \text{ and } y = y_1 + y_2 \text{ for some } y_1 \in \overline{\mathbf{R}}_1[\{x\}] \text{ and } y_2 \in \overline{\mathbf{R}}_2[\{x\}]\}. \tag{2.2.4}$$

GRAPH If $\mathbf{G}$ is a mapping of points $x \in \mathscr{X}$ into points $\mathbf{G}x \in \mathscr{Y}$, then the *graph* of $\mathbf{G}$ is the relation

$$\overline{\mathbf{G}} \equiv \text{Graph}(\mathbf{G}) \triangleq \{(x, y) \in \mathscr{X} \times \mathscr{Y} \mid x \in \mathscr{X} \text{ and } y = \mathbf{G}x\}. \tag{2.2.5}$$

2.2.2 Stability Terminology

CLASS K [39, p. 7] A function ϕ mapping non-negative real numbers into non-negative real numbers is defined to be in *class* K, denoted $\phi \in \mathrm{K}$, if ϕ is continuous and strictly increasing, with $\phi(0) = 0$.

POSITIVE DEFINITE; DECRESCENT; RADIALLY UNBOUNDED [39, pp. 98–99, 195] Let $\mathrm{V}(\cdot)$ be a function mapping a normed space $\mathscr{X}$ into the non-negative real numbers. The function $\mathrm{V}(\cdot)$ is said to be *positive definite* if, for some $\phi \in \mathrm{K}$,

$$\begin{aligned} &\text{(i)} \quad \phi(\|x\|) \le \mathrm{V}(x) \text{ and} \\ &\text{(ii)} \quad \mathrm{V}(0) = 0. \end{aligned} \tag{2.2.6}$$

The function $\mathrm{V}(\cdot)$ is *decrescent* if for some $\phi \in \mathrm{K}$

$$\mathrm{V}(x) \le \phi(\|x\|). \tag{2.2.7}$$

The function V is said to be *radially unbounded* if for some $\phi \in \mathrm{K}$

$$\begin{aligned} &\text{(i)} \quad \phi(\|x\|) \le \mathrm{V}(x) \text{ and} \\ &\text{(ii)} \quad \lim_{\alpha \to \infty} \phi(\alpha) = \infty. \end{aligned} \tag{2.2.8}$$

NEIGHBORHOOD For any extended normed space $\mathscr{X}_e$ [i.e., a space $\mathscr{X}_e$ defined as in (2.1.2) and (2.1.3)], any set $\mathscr{A} \subset \mathscr{X}_e$, and any non-negative number α, the *neighborhood* $N(\mathscr{A}; \alpha)$ is the set

$$N(\mathscr{A}; \alpha) \triangleq \{x \in \mathscr{X}_e \mid \text{for some } x_0 \in \mathscr{A}, \|\mathbf{P}_\tau(x - x_0)\| \leq \alpha \text{ for all } \tau \in T\}. \tag{2.2.9}$$

$\|(x, y)\|$ For any normed spaces $\mathscr{X}$, $\mathscr{Y}$ and any $(x, y) \in \mathscr{X} \times \mathscr{Y}$, the notation $\|(x, y)\|$ is in this book defined to mean

$$\|(x, y)\| \triangleq (\|x\|^2 + \|y\|^2)^{1/2}; \tag{2.2.10}$$

clearly, (2.2.10) defines a norm on $\mathscr{X} \times \mathscr{Y}$.

GAIN; INCREMENTAL GAIN $\mathscr{X}_e$ and $\mathscr{Y}_e$ are extended normed spaces; let $\mathbf{F}$ be a map of points $x \in \mathscr{X}_e$ into sets $\mathbf{F}x \subset \mathscr{Y}_e$. If for some scalar $k < \infty$, for all $x \in \mathscr{X}_e$ and all $\tau \in T$

$$\mathbf{F}x \subset N(\{0\}; k\|x\|_\tau), \tag{2.2.11}$$

then $\mathbf{F}$ has *finite gain*; the smallest k for which (2.2.11) is satisfied is called the *gain* of $\mathbf{F}$. It for some $k < \infty$, all $x_1, x_2 \in \mathscr{X}_e$, and all $\tau \in T$

$$\mathbf{F}x_2 \subset N(\mathbf{F}x_1; k\|x_1 - x_2\|_\tau), \tag{2.2.12}$$

then $\mathbf{F}$ has *finite incremental gain*; the smallest such k is called the *incremental gain* of $\mathbf{F}$.

BOUNDED; STABLE; FINITE-GAIN STABLE Let $\mathscr{X}_e$ and $\mathscr{Y}_e$ be extended normed spaces; let $\mathbf{F}$ be a map of points $x \in \mathscr{X}_e$ into sets $\mathbf{F}x \subset \mathscr{Y}_e$; let $\mathscr{A} \subset \mathscr{Y}_e$. If there exists a continuous increasing function ϕ mapping the non-negative real numbers into itself such that for all $x \in \mathscr{X}_e$ and all $\tau \in T$

$$\mathbf{F}x \subset N[\mathscr{A}; \phi(\|x\|_\tau)], \tag{2.2.13}$$

then $\mathbf{F}$ is *bounded about the set* $\mathscr{A}$; if $\phi \in K$, then we say $\mathbf{F}$ is *stable about the set* $\mathscr{A}$; if ϕ is linear (i.e., if ϕ is of the form $\phi(\|x\|_\tau) = k\|x\|_\tau$), then we say that $\mathbf{F}$ is finite-gain stable about the set $\mathscr{A}$. When $\mathscr{A} = \{0\}$, then we say simply that $\mathbf{F}$ is *bounded*, or *stable*, or *finite-gain stable*, respectively (i.e., we omit the phrase "about the set $\mathscr{A}$"). Evidently, finite-gain stability implies stability which in turn implies boundedness.

OPEN-LOOP BOUNDED, STABLE, FINITE-GAIN STABLE A mapping of points

$u \in \mathscr{U}_e$ into relations $\bar{\mathbf{G}} \subset \mathscr{X}_e \times \mathscr{Y}_e$ is said to be, respectively, *open-loop bounded*, or *open-loop stable*, or *open-loop finite-gain stable* if the induced map of points $(u, x) \in \mathscr{U}_e \times \mathscr{X}_e$ into sets $\bar{\mathbf{G}}(u)[x] \subset \mathscr{Y}_e$ is respectively bounded, or stable, or finite-gain stable.

CLOSED-LOOP BOUNDED, STABLE, FINITE-GAIN STABLE The feedback system (2.1.1) is said to be respectively *closed-loop bounded*, or *closed-loop stable*, or *closed-loop finite-gain stable* if the map of points $(u, v) \in \mathscr{U}_e \times \mathscr{V}_e$ into relations in $\mathscr{X}_e \times \mathscr{Y}_e$ induced by (2.1.1) is respectively bounded, or stable, or finite-gain stable.

NONANTICIPATIVE Let T be an interval, let $\mathscr{X}$ and $\mathscr{Y}$ be sets of functions defined on *T*, and let **F** be a mapping of $\mathscr{X}$ into $\mathscr{Y}$. Suppose that for every $\tau \in \mathrm{T}$ and every pair $x_1, x_2 \in \mathscr{X}$ with $x_1(\mathrm{t}) = x_2(\mathrm{t})$ for all $\mathrm{t} \leq \tau$, that

$(\mathbf{F}x_1)(\mathrm{t}) = (\mathbf{F}x_2)(\mathrm{t})$ for all $\mathrm{t} \leq \tau$;

then the mapping **F** is said to be *nonanticipative.*

Comment 1 It is *necessary* that stability be defined here, because there is no standard definition in the literature. The present definition is most closely related to the definition employed in [32], including that definition as a special case pertaining to a subclass of systems of the form (2.1.1).

The motivation for the present choice of definition is two-fold. First, the definition is more flexible than previous definitions of input-output stability in that:

(i) inputs need not enter additively, and

(ii) by allowing discussion of stability about an arbitrary set, the definition permits one, in principle, to address certain special issues in stability theory, e.g., the stability of time-varying functions or sets of time-varying functions such as the limit cycles of autonomous systems.

Second, the definition meshes well with the classical notion of stability in the sense of Lyapunov [112], as is demonstrated in chapter 3.

Comment 2 It is noteworthy that in the case of linear systems, the definitions of bounded, stable, and finite-gain stable coincide: for such systems ϕ can always be taken to be linear, e.g., in (2.2.13), pick any x_0 with $\|x_0\| \neq 0$ and replace $\phi(\|x\|)$ by $\phi'(\|x\|) \equiv \|x\|/\phi(\|x_0\|)$ [94, thm. 5.4]. Consequently, when speaking of *linear* systems, the terms *bounded, stable,* and *finite-gain stable* may be used interchangeably.

2.2.2 List of Symbols

I The identity matrix, operator, or relation

0 The zero matrix, operator, or relation

∇ The Gateaux derivative of a function or operator (e.g., if $f: R^n \to R^m$, then $\nabla f(x)$ is the Jacobian matrix of f at the point $x \in R^n$) [42, p. 17]

R The real numbers

R_+ The non-negative real numbers

C The complex numbers

Z The integers

Z_+ The non-negative integers

A^T, x^T The transpose of the matrix A or vector x

A^*, x^* The complex conjugate of A^T or x^T

K See sec. 2.2.2

$\mathbf{P}_\tau$ See sec. 2.1.1

$[x(t)]_{t \in T}$ The function x, defined on the set T

Sector (**F**) Defined in sec. 2.4

Comp.-Sector (**F**) Defined in sec. 2.4

inside " "

strictly inside " "

outside " "

strictly outside " "

Cone (**C**, **R**) Defined in sec. 2.5

+-Cone (**K**) " "

$\mathcal{M}_2, \mathcal{M}_{2e}$ Defined in sec. 2.5.1

$\mathcal{L}_2, \mathcal{L}_{2e}$ " "

m_2, m_{2e} " sec 2.5.2

ℓ_2, ℓ_{2e} " "

d_τ Defined in sec. 2.3

$A > 0$ ($A \geq 0$) The matrix A is positive-definite (positive semidefinite)

R^n Euclidian space of dimension n

C^n Complex Euclidian space of dimension n

$R^{n \times m}$ The set of $n \times m$ matrices with real elements

$C^{n \times m}$ The set of $n \times m$ matrices with complex elements

det[A] The determinant of the matrix A

$\overline{\mathbf{G}}^I$ The inverse of the relation $\overline{\mathbf{G}}$, defined in sec. 2.2.1

Graph($\overline{\mathbf{G}}$) The graph of the operator **G**, defined in sec. 2.2.1

$\Rightarrow$ "Implies"

$\Leftrightarrow$ "Implies and is implied by"

2.3 Main Stability Theorem

An abstract stability criterion, based on the topological partitioning of the product space $\mathscr{X}_e \times \mathscr{Y}_e$, will now be stated. Insofar as it has been possible to determine, virtually all existing stability criteria, including the Lyapunov-type state-space criteria, can be viewed as either special cases or corollaries of the result.

THEOREM 2.1 (Main Stability Theorem) **Suppose that one can find for each $\tau \in T$ a functional $d_\tau: \mathscr{X}_e \times \mathscr{Y}_e \to \mathbf{R}$, such that**

$$\bar{\mathbf{G}}^{I}(u) \subset \{(x, y) \mid d_\tau(x, y) \geq \phi_1(\|(x, y)\|_\tau) - \phi_2(\|u\|_\tau) \text{ for all } \tau \in T\} \quad \textbf{(2.3.1)}$$

$$\bar{\mathbf{H}}(v) \subset \{(x, y) \mid d_\tau(x, y) \leq \phi_3(\|v\|_\tau) \text{ for all } \tau \in T\} \quad \textbf{(2.3.2)}$$

where $\phi_i: \mathrm{R}_+ \to \mathrm{R}_+$ (i = **1, 2, 3) are continuous increasing functions and** where ϕ_1 is a radially unbounded function in class K. Then, the system (2.1.1) is closed-loop bounded. If, additionally, the ϕ_i (i = 1, 2, 3) are all in class K, then the system (2.1.1) is closed-loop stable. If, furthermore, the ϕ_i (i = 1, 2, 3) are all linear, then (2.1.1) is closed-loop finite-gain stable.

PROOF Let $(x, y) \in \mathscr{X}_e \times \mathscr{Y}_e$ be a solution of (2.1.1). Then

$$(x, y) \in \bar{\mathbf{G}}^{I}(u) \cap \bar{\mathbf{H}}(v).$$

It follows from statements (2.3.1) and (2.3.2) that for all $\tau \in \mathrm{T}$

$$\phi_1(\|\mathrm{P}_\tau(x, y)\|) - \phi_2(\|u\|_\tau) \leq d_\tau(x, y) \leq \phi_3(\|v\|_\tau).$$

Thus, using the fact that ϕ_1 is strictly increasing and radially unbounded, it follows that for all $\tau \in \mathrm{T}$

$$\|(x, y)\|_\tau \leq \phi_1^{-1}(\phi_2(\|u\|_\tau) + \phi_3(\|v\|_\tau))$$

and

$$\begin{aligned}\|(x, y)\|_\tau &\leq \phi_1^{-1}(\phi_2(\|u\|_\tau) + \phi_3(\|v\|_\tau)) \\ &\leq \phi_1^{-1}(\phi_2(\|(u, v)\|_\tau) + \phi_3(\|(u, v)\|_\tau)) \triangleq \phi_4(\|(u, v)\|_\tau).\end{aligned}$$

Evidently the function $\phi_4: R_+ \to R_+$ is a continuous and increasing function; so the feedback system (2.1.1) is closed-loop bounded. Moreover, if $\phi_i \in K$ (respectively, ϕ_i linear) (i = 1, 2, 3) then $\phi_4 \in \mathrm{K}$ (respectively, ϕ_4 is linear) which implies (2.1.1) is closed-loop stable (respectively, closed-loop finite-gain stable). ▮

Comments The conditions of theorem 2.1 can be motivated and conceptually interpreted as follows. For brevity, we consider only the case $\phi_i \in K$ (i = 1, 2, 3). For each $\tau \in T$, the functional $d_\tau: \mathscr{X}_e \times \mathscr{Y}_e \to R$ partitions the product space $\mathscr{X}_e \times \mathscr{Y}_e$ into two regions, viz., $d_\tau^{-1}((0, \infty))$ and $d_\tau^{-1}((-\infty, 0))$, with the set $d_\tau^{-1}(\{0\})$ forming the boundary between the two regions. The conditions (2.3.1) and (2.3.2) imply that, except for the equilibrium $(x, y) = (0, 0)$, the set $\overline{G}^I(0)$ and the set $\overline{H}(0)$ are disjoint; so $(x, y) = (0, 0)$ is the only solution of the undisturbed system. We can visualize the functional $d_\tau(x, y)$ as defining the "distance" of each point $(x, y) \in \mathscr{X}_e \times \mathscr{Y}_e$ from the boundary $d_\tau^{-1}(\{0\})$ with the sign of $d_\tau(x, y)$ determining on which side of the boundary the point lies. The condition (2.3.1) further says that,

$$d_\tau(x, y) \geq \phi_1(\|(x, y)\|_\tau) \tag{2.3.3}$$

for all $(y, x) \in \overline{G}(0)$: so that the "distance" from the boundary of nonzero points $(x, y) \in \overline{G}^I(0)$ is positive and grows unboundedly as $\|(x, y)\|_\tau$ increases. In this conceptual framework, the quantity $\phi_2(\|u\|_\tau)$ is simply an upper bound on the "distance" that $\overline{G}^I(u)$ shifts toward the boundary as a consequence of the disturbance u. Similarly, the "distance" of $\overline{H}(0)$ from the boundary is nonpositive and $\phi_3(\|v\|_\tau)$ is an upper bound on the distance $\overline{H}(v)$ shifts toward the boundary as a consequence of v. Because solutions of (2.1.1) must lie in the set $\overline{G}^I(u) \cap \overline{H}(v)$, we see that the "distance" of $\phi_1(\|(x, y)\|_\tau)$ must be less than the sum $\phi_2(\|u\|_\tau) + \phi_3(\|v\|_\tau)$, i.e.,

$$\phi_1(\|(x, y)\|_\tau) \leq \phi_2(\|u\|_\tau) + \phi_3(\|v\|_\tau). \tag{2.3.4}$$

Because the "distance" $\phi_1(\|(x, y)\|_\tau)$ increases unboundedly as $\|(x, y)\|_\tau$ increases, it is evident from (2.3.4) that $\|(x, y)\|_\tau$ is bounded; this is illustrated in figure 2.5.

It is noteworthy that theorem 2.1 makes no reference to loop transformations, multipliers, contraction mappings, or any of the other mathematical paraphernalia usually associated with input-output stability results (cf. [27]). This is a consequence of the fact that, in contrast to most previous input-output stability criteria, no fixed-point theorems (e.g., the contraction mapping theorem) are used in the proof of theorem 2.1. This underscores the fact that *existence* of solutions—and existence is always assured

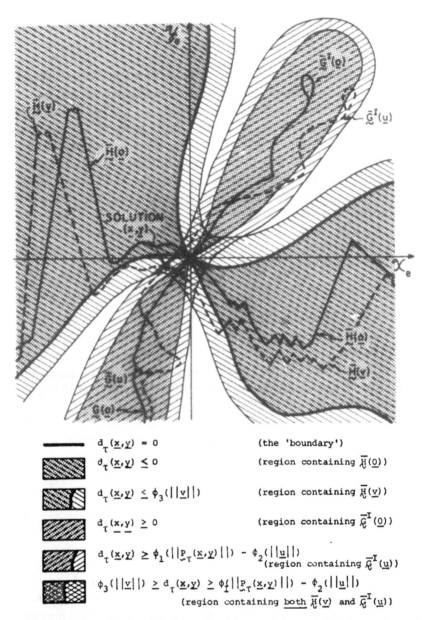

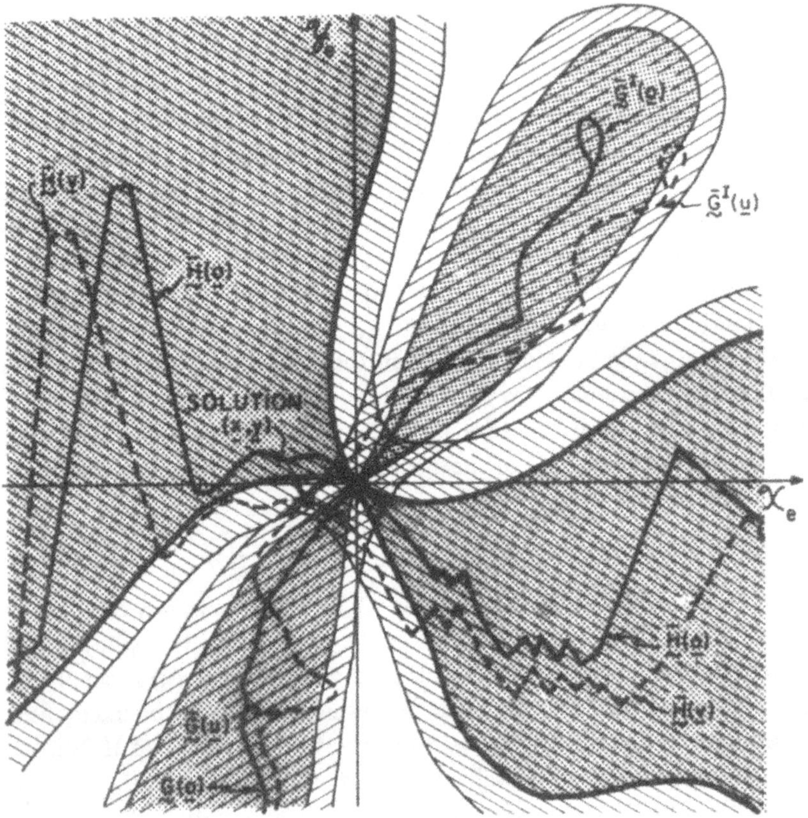

(solid line)	$d_\tau(\underline{x},\underline{y}) = 0$	(the 'boundary')
(shading)	$d_\tau(\underline{x},\underline{y}) \leq 0$	(region containing $\overline{H}(\underline{0})$)
(shading)	$d_\tau(\underline{x},\underline{y}) \leq \phi_3(\|\underline{v}\|)$	(region containing $\overline{H}(\underline{v})$)
(shading)	$d_\tau(\underline{x},\underline{y}) \geq 0$	(region containing $\overline{G}^I(\underline{0})$)
(shading)	$d_\tau(\underline{x},\underline{y}) \geq \phi_1(\|\underline{P}_T(\underline{x},\underline{y})\|) - \phi_2(\|\underline{u}\|)$	(region containing $\overline{G}^I(\underline{u})$)
(shading)	$\phi_3(\|\underline{v}\|) \geq d_\tau(\underline{x},\underline{y}) \geq \phi_1(\|\underline{P}_T(\underline{x},\underline{y})\|) - \phi_2(\|\underline{u}\|)$	(region containing both $\overline{H}(\underline{v})$ and $\overline{G}^I(\underline{u})$)

Figure 2.5 Visualization of the conditions of theorem 2.1 in the "$\mathcal{X}_e \times \mathcal{Y}_e$-plane"—the solution (x, y) must lie in the region containing both $\overline{H}(v)$ and $\overline{G}^1(u)$.

when fixed-point theorems are employed—is not central to the issue of stability. Rather, in stability analysis, we are concerned primarily with ascertaining that all existing solutions are stable. Existence of solutions, which relates to the "well-posedness" of the system equations, can be deduced from entirely separate considerations [110, pp. 93–101].[6]

To demonstrate the powerful generality of theorem 2.1 and to give some insight into the issue of how to select a suitable "distance" functional d_τ, I will now show how classical state-space tests for stability in the sense of Lyapunov [112] emerge as special cases of the theorem.

Example 1. Input-Output Interpretation of Lyapunov Stability (Continuous-Time) In the continuous-time state-space stability problems attacked by Lyapunov methods, the system under consideration is frequently given in the form

$$\dot{x}(t) = f[x(t)] \qquad x(0) = x_0, \tag{2.3.5}$$

where

$t \in R_+$

$x(t) \in X$ for all $t \in R_+$.

X is an inner-product space with inner product $\langle \cdot, \cdot \rangle_X$. This system can be interpreted in terms of the system (2.1.1) as

$$\begin{aligned} x &\equiv [x(t)]_{t \in R_+} = \left(x_0 + \int_0^t y(\tau) d\tau \right)_{t \in R_+} \triangleq \bar{G}(u)y \\ y &\equiv [y(t)]_{t \in R_+} = (f[x(t)])_{t \in R_+} \triangleq H(v)x \\ v &\equiv 0 \in \mathscr{V} \equiv \{0\} \equiv \mathscr{V}_\tau \equiv \mathscr{V}_e \quad \text{for all} \quad \tau \in R_+ \\ u &\equiv x_0 \in \mathscr{U} \equiv \mathscr{X} \equiv \mathscr{U}_\tau \equiv \mathscr{U}_e \quad \text{for all} \quad \tau \in R_+, \end{aligned} \tag{2.3.6}$$

where $x \in \mathscr{X}_e$ and $y \in \mathscr{Y}_e$ and where $\mathscr{X}_e$ and $\mathscr{Y}_e$ are the extended normed spaces induced by the identity operator $P_\tau \xi \equiv \xi$ mapping into the respective spaces

$$\mathscr{X}_\tau \triangleq \{x\colon R_+ \to X \mid x \text{ is once differentiable}\} \tag{2.3.7}$$

6 Well-posedness tests, based on considerations other than stability, are provided in [110]. However, it should be noted that (in contrast to the view taken here and elsewhere in the literature, e.g., in [27], [32], and [118]), [110] *defines* well-posedness to be prerequisite to any discussion of stability or instability.

with norm

$$\|x\|_\tau \triangleq \sup_{t \le \tau} \|x(t)\|_X; \tag{2.3.8}$$

$$\mathscr{Y}_\tau \triangleq \{y : R_+ \to X\} \tag{2.3.9}$$

with (degenerate) norm $\|y\|_\tau \equiv 0$. This is illustrated in figure 2.6.

If we define the inner product on $P_\tau \mathscr{Y}_e$ by

$$\langle x_1, x_2 \rangle_\tau \triangleq \int_0^\tau \langle x_1(t), x_2(t) \rangle_X dt, \tag{2.3.10}$$

let $V: X \to R_+$ be differentiable, and take the "distance" functional

$d_\tau: \mathscr{X}_e \times \mathscr{Y}_e \to R$ to be

$$d_\tau(x, y) \triangleq \sup_{\tau' \in [0,\tau]} \langle [\nabla V(x)]^*, y \rangle_{\tau'}, \tag{2.3.11}$$

where $\nabla V(x) \equiv [\nabla V(x(t))]_{t \in T}$, then we are led directly to the following corollary to theorem 2.1.

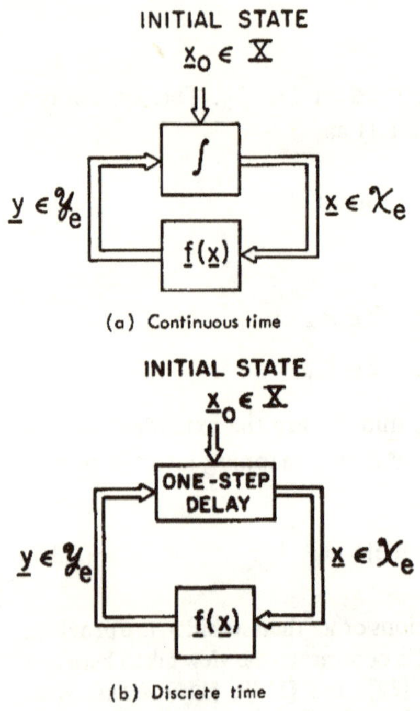

Figure 2.6 Feedback representation of systems amenable to Lyapunov methods.

COROLLARY 2.1a (Stability in the Sense of Lyapunov—Continuous-Time Case) If there exists a differentiable, positive-definite, decrescent, radially unbounded function $V: X \to R_+$, such that

$$[\nabla V(x)]f(x) \leq 0 \tag{2.3.12}$$

for all $x \in X$, then the system (2.3.5) is closed-loop stable.

PROOF For all (x, y) satisfying $x = G(u)y$,

$$\begin{aligned} d_\tau(x, y) &= \sup_{\tau' \in [0,\tau]} \langle [\nabla V(x)]^*, \dot{x} \rangle_{\tau'} \\ &= \sup_{\tau' \in [0,\tau]} \int_0^{\tau'} \left([\nabla V(x(t))] \frac{dx}{dt}(t) \right) dt \\ &= \sup_{\tau' \in [0,\tau]} \int_{x_0}^{x(\tau')} \nabla V(x)\, dx \\ &= \sup_{\tau' \in [0,\tau]} V(x(\tau')) - V(x_0) \\ &\geq \phi_1(\|P_\tau x\|) - \phi_2(\|x_0\|) = \phi_1(\|P_\tau(x, y)\|) - \phi_2(\|x_0\|), \end{aligned}$$

where $\phi_1, \phi_2 \in K$ with ϕ_1 radially unbounded are chosen (using that fact that $V(\cdot)$ is positive-definite, decrescent, radially unbounded) such that

$$\phi_1(\|\xi\|) \leq V(\xi) \leq \phi_2(\|\xi\|)$$

for all $\xi \in X$. For all (x, y) satisfying $y = f(x)$, it follows from (2.3.12) that

$$\begin{aligned} d_\tau(x, y) &= \sup_{\tau \in [0,\tau]} \langle [\nabla V(x)]^*, (f(x(t)))_{t \in T} \rangle_{\tau'} \\ &= \sup_{\tau' \in [0,\tau]} \int_0^{\tau'} \nabla V(x(t)) f(x(t))\, dt \\ &\leq 0 \leq \phi_3(v\|_\tau) \end{aligned}$$

where $\phi_3 \in K$ may be chosen arbitrarily. Corollary 2.1a thus follows from theorem 2.1. ∎

Comparison of this result with classical Lyapunov stability results (see, for example, [112, sec. 2.3], clearly establishes that continuous-time classical results concerning global stability in the sense of Lyapunov can be interpreted as special cases of theorem 2.1 obtainable by restricting the class of systems considered. The same holds true for discrete-time systems, as is shown next. (end of example 1)

Example 2. Input-Output Interpretation of Lyapunov Stability (Discrete Time) In discrete-time state-space stability problems, the system under consideration typically is given in the form

$$x(t+1) = f[x(t)];\; x(0) = x_0, \tag{2.3.13}$$

where

$t \in Z_+$

$x(t) \in X$ for all $t \in Z$

$F: X \to X.$

X is an inner-product space with inner product $\langle \cdot, \cdot \rangle_X$. In analogy to the continuous-time case, this system can be interpreted in terms of (2.1.1′) as

$$\begin{aligned} x &\equiv [x(t)]_{t\in Z_+} = (x_0, \text{ if } t = 0;\; y(t-1) \text{ if } t \geq 1)_{t\in Z_+} \equiv \mathbf{G}(u)y \\ y &\equiv [y(t)]_{t\in Z_+} = (f[x(t)])_{t\in Z_+} \equiv \mathbf{H}(v)x \\ v &= 0 \in \mathscr{V} \equiv \{0\} \\ u &= x_0 \in \mathscr{U} \equiv X, \end{aligned} \tag{2.3.14}$$

where $x \in \mathscr{X}_e$ and $y \in \mathscr{Y}_e$ are the extended normed spaces induced by the identity operator $\mathbf{P}_\tau \xi \equiv \xi$ mapping into the respective spaces

$$\mathscr{X}_\tau \equiv \{x(t): Z_+ \to X\} \tag{2.3.15}$$

with norm

$$\|x\|_\tau \triangleq \sup_{t<\tau} \|x(t)\|_X; \tag{2.3.16}$$

$$\mathscr{Y}_\tau \equiv \{y(t): Z_+ \to X\} \tag{2.3.17}$$

with degenerate norm $\|y\|_\tau \equiv 0$.
Taking the inner product on $\mathbf{P}_\tau\{\xi: Z_+ \to R\}$ to be

$$\langle \xi_1, \xi_2 \rangle_\tau = \sum_{i=0}^{\tau-1} \xi_1(i)\xi_2(i), \tag{2.3.18}$$

letting $V: X \to R$, taking $V: \mathscr{X}_e \to R_+ \times T$ to be $V(x) = [V(x(t)]_{t\in T}$, and taking the "distance" functional $d_\tau: \mathscr{X}_e \times \mathscr{Y}_e \to R$ to be

$$d_\tau(x, y) = \sup_{\tau' \leq \tau} \langle V^{1/2}(y) + V^{1/2}(x), V^{1/2}(y) - V^{1/2}(x) \rangle_{\tau'}, \tag{2.3.19}$$

one is led directly to a corollary to theorem 2.1 establishing that classical results concerning discrete-time global stability in the sense of Lyapunov (see [112; secs. 2.3 and 7.2]) can be interpreted as special cases of theorem 2.1.

COROLLARY 2.1b (Stability in the Sense of Lyapunov—Discrete-Time Case) If there exists a positive-definite, decrescent, radially unbounded function $V: X \to R_+$ such that

$$V[f(x)] - V(x) \leq 0 \tag{2.3.20}$$

for all $x \in X$, then the system (2.3.13) is closed-loop stable.

PROOF For all (x, y) satisfying $x = G(u)y$,

$$\begin{aligned} d_\tau(x, y) &= \sup_{\tau' \leq \tau} \langle V^{1/2}(y) + V^{1/2}(x), V^{1/2}(y) - V^{1/2}(x) \rangle_{\tau'} \\ &= \sup_{t=1,\ldots,\tau} \sum_{i=0}^{t-1} V(y(i)) - V(x(i)) \\ &= \sup_{t=1,\ldots,\tau} \sum_{i=0}^{t-1} V(x(i+1)) - V(x(i)) \\ &= \sup_{t=1,\ldots,\tau} V(x(t)) - V(x_0) \\ &\leq \phi_1(\|P_\tau x\|) - \phi_2(\|x_0\|) = \phi_1(P_\tau(x, y)\|) - \phi_2(\|x_0\|), \end{aligned}$$

where $\phi_1, \phi_2 \in K$ with ϕ_1 radially unbounded are chosen (using the fact that $V(\cdot)$ is positive-definite, decrescent, radially unbounded) such that

$$\phi_1(\|\xi\|) \leq V(\xi) \leq \phi_2(\|\xi\|)$$

for all $\xi \in X$. For all (x, y) satisfying $y(t) = f(x(t))$, it follows from (2.3.20) that

$$\begin{aligned} d_\tau(x, y) &= \sup_{\tau' \leq \tau} \langle V^{1/2}(y) + V^{1/2}(x), V^{1/2}(y) - V^{1/2}(x) \rangle_{\tau'} \\ &= \sup_{t=1,\ldots,\tau} \sum_{i=1}^{t-1} V(f(x(i))) - V(x(i)) \leq 0 \leq \phi_3(\|v\|_\tau), \end{aligned}$$

where $\phi_3 \in K$ may be chosen arbitrarily. Corollary 2.1b thus follows from theorem 2.1. ▮ (end of example 2)

Comment The "distance" functionals d_τ (2.3.11) and (2.3.19) employed in corollaries 2.1a and 2.1b both involve inner products. Likewise, the conic sector (2.1.5) employed by Zames is representable in terms of a distance functional involving an inner product:

$$\text{Cone}(c, r) = \{(x, y) \mid d_\tau(x, y) \leq 0\},$$

where

$$d_\tau(x, y) = \langle P_\tau[y - (c + r)x], P_\tau[y - (c - r)x]\rangle.$$

In the next section, a powerful stability test is developed using general inner product "distance" functionals to accomplish the topological partitioning required by theorem 2.1.

2.4 Sector Stability Criterion

As noted earlier, previous efforts to find useful multivariable extensions of the conic relation stability theorem and its corollaries (e.g., the Nyquist, Popov, circle, small-gain, and positivity theorems) have met with only limited success. Applying theorem 2.1, however, we develop in this section a new generalization of the conic relation stability theorem from which practical frequency-domain stability tests for multivariable systems are obtained directly via Parseval's theorem.

We begin by defining a generalization of the conic sector that plays the key role in Zames's conic-relation stability theorem.

DEFINITION (Sector) Let $\mathscr{X}_e$ and $\mathscr{Y}_e$ be extended normed spaces and let $\mathscr{Z}_e$ be an extended inner product space. Let

$$F(x, y, \tau) \triangleq \langle F_{11}y + F_{12}x, F_{21}y + F_{22}x\rangle_\tau \tag{2.4.1}$$

for each $\tau \in T$, where $F_{ij}0 = 0$ (i, j = 1, 2) and $F_{11}, F_{21}: \mathscr{Y}_e \to \mathscr{Z}_e$ and $F_{12}, F_{22}: \mathscr{X}_e \to \mathscr{Y}_e$. Then the *sector* of F is defined to be

$$\text{Sector}(F) \triangleq \{(x, y) \in \mathscr{X}_e \times \mathscr{Y}_e \mid F(x, y, \tau) \leq 0 \text{ for all } \tau \in T\}. \tag{2.4.2}$$

For notational convenience, the functional F will be denoted by the 2 × 2 array

$$F \triangleq \begin{bmatrix} F_{11} & F_{12} \\ F_{21} & F_{22} \end{bmatrix}. \tag{2.4.3}$$

DEFINITION (inside, outside, strictly inside, strictly outside) A subset $\bar{A}$ of

$\mathscr{X}_e \times \mathscr{Y}_e$ is said to be *inside* Sector (F) if $\tilde{A} \subset$ Sector (F) $\triangleq \{(x, y) \in \mathscr{X}_e \times \mathscr{Y}_e \mid F(x, y, \tau) \leq 0$ for all $\tau \in T\}$; $\tilde{A}$ is said to be *strictly inside* Sector (F) if for some $\varepsilon > 0$, $\tilde{A} \subset \{(x, y) \in \mathscr{X}_e \times \mathscr{Y}_e \mid F(x, y, \tau) \leq -\varepsilon\|(x, y)\|_\tau^2$ for all $\tau \in T\}$; $\tilde{A}$ is said to be *outside* Sector ($\mathscr{F}$) if $\tilde{A} \subset \{(x, y) \in \mathscr{X}_e \times \mathscr{Y}_e \mid F(x, y, \tau) \geq 0$ for all $\tau \in T\}$; and, $\tilde{A}$ is said to be *strictly outside* Sector (F) if for some $\varepsilon > 0$, $\tilde{A} \subset \{(x, y) \in \mathscr{X}_e \times \mathscr{Y}_e \mid F(x, y, \tau) \geq \varepsilon\|(x, y)_\tau^2$ for all $\tau \in T\}$.

We now state a stability result based on theorem 2.1 that employs sectors to accomplish the requisite topological partitioning of the space $\mathscr{X}_e \times \mathscr{Y}_e$. The proof involves a straightforward but tedious verification of the conditions of theorem 2.1.

THEOREM 2.2 (Sector Stability Criterion) Let F be a 2×2 array of operators as in (2.4.3); let the F_{ij} (i, j = 1, 2) have finite incremental gain; let the mappings of $u \in \mathscr{U}$ into $\bar{G}(u)$ and $v \in \mathscr{V}$ into $\bar{H}(v)$ be bounded (respectively, stable; respectively finite-gain stable) about the respective sets $\bar{G}(0)$ and $\bar{H}(0)$. If $\bar{G}^I(0)$ is *strictly inside* Sector (F) and if $\bar{H}(0)$ is *outside* Sector (F), then the system (2.1.1) is closed-loop bounded (respectively, closed-loop stable; respectively, closed-loop finite-gain stable).

PROOF We apply theorem 2.3, taking $d_\tau : \mathscr{X}_e \times \mathscr{Y}_e \to R$ to be the map

$$d_\tau(x, y) = \begin{cases} 0, & \text{if } \|P_\tau(x, y)\| = 0. \\ \dfrac{-1}{\|P_\tau(x, y)\|} F(x, y, \tau), & \text{if } \|P_\tau(x, y)\| \neq 0. \end{cases}$$

We begin by establishing (2.3.1). Let $u \in \mathscr{U}$ be fixed and take $(x, y) \in \bar{G}^I(u)$. Applying the Schwartz inequality, we have that for some $\varepsilon > 0$, for every $(x_0, y_0) \in \bar{G}^I(0)$ and every $\tau \in T$,

$$\begin{aligned} &\|P_\tau(x, y)\| d_\tau(x, y) = -\langle P_\tau(F_{11}y + F_{12}x), P_\tau(F_{21}y + F_{22}x)\rangle \\ &= \|P_\tau(x_0, y_0)\|\, d_\tau(x_0, y_0) \\ &\quad - \langle P_\tau(F_{11}y_0 + F_{12}x_0), P_\tau[(F_{21}y - F_{21}y_0) + (F_{22}x - F_{22}x_0)]\rangle \\ &\quad - \langle P_\tau[(F_{11}y - F_{11}y_0) + (F_{12}x - F_{12}x_0)], P_\tau(F_{21}y + F_{22}x)\rangle \\ &\geq \varepsilon\|P_\tau(x_0, y_0)\|^2 \\ &\quad - \|P_\tau(F_{11}y_0 + F_{12}x_0)\| \cdot \|P_\tau[(F_{21}y - F_{21}y_0) + (F_{22}x - F_{22}x_0)]\| \\ &\quad - \|P_\tau[(F_{11}y - F_{11}y_0) + (F_{12}x - F_{12}x_0)]\| \cdot \|P_\tau(F_{21}y + F_{22}x)\| \\ &\geq \varepsilon\|P_\tau(x_0, y_0)\|^2 \\ &\quad - (k\|P_\tau(x_0, y_0)\|) \cdot (k\|P_\tau[(x, y) - (x_0, y_0)]\|) \\ &\quad - (k\|P_\tau[(x, y) - (x_0, y_0)\|) \cdot (k\|P_\tau(x, y)\|), \end{aligned}$$

where the latter inequality follows with $k < \infty$ an upper bound on the gain and incremental gain of $\mathbf{F}_{ij}$ (i, j = 1, 2). Since by hypothesis the map of $u \in \mathscr{U}$ into $\overline{\mathbf{G}}(u)$ is bounded, there exists a continuous increasing function $\rho_1 : R_+ \to R_+$ and a point $(x_0^{(1)}, y_0^{(1)}) \in \overline{\mathbf{G}}^I(0)$ such that for every $\tau \in T$

$$\|\mathbf{P}_\tau[(x, y) - (x_0^{(1)}, y_0^{(1)})]\| \leq \rho_1(\|\mathbf{P}_\tau u\|).$$

Also, for all $\tau \in T$, there exists a point $(x_0^{(2)}, y_0^{(2)}) \in \overline{\mathbf{G}}^I(0)$ such that

$$\|\mathbf{P}_\tau[(x, y) - (x_0^{(2)}, y_0^{(2)})]\| \leq \|\mathbf{P}_\tau(x, y)\|,$$

namely, the point $(x_0^{(2)}, y_0^{(2)}) = (0, 0)$. It follows that there exists an $(x_0, y_0) \in \overline{\mathbf{G}}^I(0)$ such that for all $\tau \in T$

$$\|\mathbf{P}_\tau[(x, y) - (x_0, y_0)]\| \leq \min\{\|\mathbf{P}_\tau(x, y)\|, \rho_1(\|\mathbf{P}_\tau u\|)\}$$

$$\|\mathbf{P}_\tau(x, y)\| - \rho_1(\|\mathbf{P}_\tau u\|) \leq \|\mathbf{P}_\tau(x_0, y_0)\| \leq 2 \cdot \|\mathbf{P}_\tau(x, y)\|$$

and, from the former inequality, it follows that for all $\tau \in T$

$$\|\mathbf{P}_\tau(x_0, y_0)\|^2 \geq \|\mathbf{P}_\tau(x, y)\|(-2\rho_1(\|\mathbf{P}_\tau u\|) + \|\mathbf{P}_\tau(x, y)\|).$$

It follows that for all $(x, y) \in \overline{\mathbf{G}}^I(u)$ and all $\tau \in T$ sufficiently large,

$$d_\tau(x, y) \geq \varepsilon(\|\mathbf{P}_\tau(x, y)\| - 2\rho_1(\|\mathbf{P}_\tau u\|)) - 2k^2\rho_1(\|\mathbf{P}_\tau u\|) - k^2\rho_1(\|\mathbf{P}_\tau u).$$

Taking $\phi_1, \phi_2 : R_+ \to R_+$ to be

$$\phi_1(\alpha) \triangleq \varepsilon \cdot \alpha$$

$$\phi_2(\alpha) \triangleq (2\varepsilon + 3k^2)\rho_1(\alpha),$$

we see that $\phi_1 \in K$ is linear and radially unbounded and that

$$d_\tau(x, y) \geq [\phi_1(\|\mathbf{P}_\tau(x, y)\|) - \phi_2(\|\mathbf{P}_\tau u\|)]$$

for all $(x, y) \in \overline{\mathbf{G}}^I(u)$ and all $\tau \in T$, which establishes (2.3.1).

Proceeding in an analogous fashion to establish (2.3.2), we have that

$$d_\tau(x, y) \leq 3k^2\rho_2(\|\mathbf{P}_\tau v\|) \triangleq \phi_3(\|\mathbf{P}_\tau v\|)$$

for some $\rho_2 : R_+ \to R_+$, every $(x, y) \in \overline{\mathbf{H}}(z)$, and every $\tau \in T$, where, as before, $k < \infty$ is an upper bound on the gain and incremental gain of $\mathbf{F}_{ij}$ (i, j = 1, 2) and ρ_2, like ρ_1, is continuous and increasing.

The closed-loop boundedness claim of theorem 2.2 follows from theorem 2.1. Moreover, if the maps taking u into $\overline{\mathbf{G}}(u)$ and v into $\overline{\mathbf{H}}(v)$ are stable (respectively, finite-gain stable) about the respective sets $\overline{\mathbf{G}}(0)$ and $\overline{\mathbf{H}}(0)$, then ρ_1 and ρ_2 may be taken to be in class K (respectively, may be taken to be linear) from which it follows as a consequence of theorem 2.1 that (2.1.1) is closed-loop stable (respectively, closed-loop finite-gain stable). ∎

Comment The requirement that the mappings of $u \in \mathscr{U}_e$ into $\overline{\mathbf{G}}(u)$ and $v \in \mathscr{U}_e$ into $\overline{\mathbf{H}}(v)$ be stable about the sets $\overline{\mathbf{G}}(0)$ and $\overline{\mathbf{H}}(0)$ should not be confused with the more restrictive requirement that the subsystems $\overline{\mathbf{G}}$ and $\overline{\mathbf{H}}$ be open-loop stable; open-loop stability demands that the mappings of (u, y) into $\overline{\mathbf{G}}(u)[y]$ and (v, x) into $\overline{\mathbf{H}}(v)[x]$ be stable about $\{(0, 0)\}$. For example, if the disturbances u and v enter additively as in figure 2.3—and this is the only case considered in the majority of the input-output literature—then the stability requirement placed on the mappings $\overline{\mathbf{G}}(\cdot)$ and $\overline{\mathbf{H}}(\cdot)$ in theorem 2.2 is automatically satisfied (with finite gain!). Thus, the stability restriction on the mappings $\overline{\mathbf{G}}(\cdot)$ and $\overline{\mathbf{H}}(\cdot)$ is actually very mild; it can be viewed as a sort of well-posedness condition on the feedback equations, ensuring that small disturbances do not produce unboundedly large dislocations of the dynamical relations in the $\mathscr{X}_e \times \mathscr{Y}_e$-"plane"—cf. [110, p. 90, condition WP. 4].

2.4.1 Properties of Sectors

Zames [118, app. A] demonstrates that his conic sectors have several properties which make them especially well suited to feedback-system stability analysis. Our more general sectors have similar properties, some of which are enumerated in the following lemma.

LEMMA 2.1 (Sector Properties) Let $\mathbf{F}_{ij}$ and $\mathbf{F}_{ij}^{(k)}$ be operators mapping into extended inner-product spaces $\mathscr{Z}_e$ and $\mathscr{Z}_e^{(k)}$ respectively; let $\mathbf{F}_{ij}(0) = 0$ and $\mathbf{F}_{ij}^{(k)}(0) = 0$; let $\overline{\mathbf{A}}$, $\overline{\mathbf{B}}$, and $\overline{\mathbf{A}}^{(k)}$ be relations on extended normed spaces; let $(0, 0) \in \overline{\mathbf{A}}, \overline{\mathbf{B}}, \overline{\mathbf{A}}^{(k)}$; let a and b be scalars with $ab > 0$; let $\mathbf{M}$ and $\mathbf{M}^*$ be operators with the property that $\langle \mathbf{M}z_1, z_2\rangle = \langle z_1, \mathbf{M}^* z_2\rangle_\tau$ for all $z_1, z_2 \in \mathscr{Z}_e$ and all $\tau \in \mathrm{T}$. Then the following properties hold:

(i) Complimentary Sector:

$$\overline{\mathbf{A}} \text{ inside Sector}\left(\begin{bmatrix} \mathbf{F}_{11} & \mathbf{F}_{12} \\ \mathbf{F}_{21} & \mathbf{F}_{22} \end{bmatrix}\right)$$

$\Leftrightarrow$

$$\overline{\mathbf{A}} \text{ outside Sector}\left(\begin{bmatrix} \mathbf{F}_{11} & \mathbf{F}_{12} \\ -\mathbf{F}_{21} & -\mathbf{F}_{22} \end{bmatrix}\right) \triangleq \text{Sector}\left(\begin{bmatrix} I & 0 \\ 0 & -I \end{bmatrix}\right)\cdot \mathbf{F}. \qquad (2.4.4)$$

Furthermore, (2.4.4) holds with *inside* and *outside* replaced respectively by *strictly inside* and *strictly outside*.

(ii) **Multiplier:**

$$\text{Sector}\left(\begin{bmatrix} \mathbf{F}_{11} & \mathbf{F}_{12} \\ \mathbf{M}\cdot\mathbf{F}_{21} & \mathbf{M}\cdot\mathbf{F}_{22} \end{bmatrix}\right) = \text{Sector}\left(\begin{bmatrix} \mathbf{aM}^*\cdot\mathbf{F}_{11} & \mathbf{aM}^*\cdot\mathbf{F}_{12} \\ \mathbf{bF}_{21} & \mathbf{bF}_{22} \end{bmatrix}\right). \quad (2.4.5)$$

(iii) **Inverse relation:**

$$\bar{\mathbf{A}} \text{ inside Sector}\left(\begin{bmatrix} \mathbf{F}_{11} & \mathbf{F}_{12} \\ \mathbf{F}_{21} & \mathbf{F}_{22} \end{bmatrix}\right)$$

$$\Leftrightarrow$$

$$\bar{\mathbf{A}}^{\mathrm{I}} \text{ inside Sector}\left(\begin{bmatrix} \mathbf{F}_{12} & \mathbf{F}_{11} \\ \mathbf{F}_{22} & \mathbf{F}_{21} \end{bmatrix}\right) = \text{Sector}\left(\mathbf{F}\cdot\begin{bmatrix} 0 & I \\ I & 0 \end{bmatrix}\right). \quad (2.4.6)$$

Furthermore, (2.4.6) holds with *inside* replaced by *strictly inside* throughout.

(iv) Sums of relations: If $\bar{\mathbf{B}} = \text{Graph}(\mathbf{B})$ and if $\mathbf{F}_{11}$ and $\mathbf{F}_{21}$ are linear, then

$$\bar{\mathbf{A}} \text{ inside Sector}\left(\begin{bmatrix} \mathbf{F}_{11} & \mathbf{F}_{12} \\ \mathbf{F}_{21} & \mathbf{F}_{22} \end{bmatrix}\right)$$

$$\Leftrightarrow$$

$$\bar{\mathbf{A}} - \bar{\mathbf{B}} \text{ inside Sector}\left(\begin{bmatrix} \mathbf{F}_{11} & (\mathbf{F}_{11}\cdot\mathbf{B} + \mathbf{F}_{12}) \\ \mathbf{F}_{21} & (\mathbf{F}_{21}\cdot\mathbf{B} + \mathbf{F}_{22}) \end{bmatrix}\right)$$

$$\triangleq \text{Sector}\left(\mathbf{F}\cdot\begin{bmatrix} I & \mathbf{B} \\ 0 & I \end{bmatrix}\right). \quad (2.4.7)$$

If $(\bar{\mathbf{A}} - \bar{\mathbf{B}})$ has finite gain, then (2.4.7) holds with *inside* replaced by *strictly inside* throughout.

(v) Composition products of relations:

(a) If $\bar{\mathbf{B}} = \text{Graph}(\mathbf{B})$, then

$$\bar{\mathbf{B}}\cdot\bar{\mathbf{A}} \text{ inside Sector}\left(\begin{bmatrix} \mathbf{F}_{11} & \mathbf{F}_{12} \\ \mathbf{F}_{21} & \mathbf{F}_{22} \end{bmatrix}\right)$$

$$\Rightarrow$$

$$\bar{\mathbf{A}} \text{ inside Sector}\left(\begin{bmatrix} \mathbf{F}_{21}\cdot\mathbf{B} & \mathbf{F}_{12} \\ \mathbf{F}_{21}\cdot\mathbf{B} & \mathbf{F}_{22} \end{bmatrix}\right) \triangleq \text{Sector}\left(\mathbf{F}\cdot\begin{bmatrix} \mathbf{B} & 0 \\ 0 & I \end{bmatrix}\right). \quad (2.4.8)$$

(b) If $\bar{\mathbf{A}}$ = Graph (A) and if $\mathbf{A}^{-1}$ exists, then

$$\bar{\mathbf{B}}\cdot\bar{\mathbf{A}} \text{ inside Sector}\left(\begin{bmatrix}\mathbf{F}_{11} & \mathbf{F}_{12}\\ \mathbf{F}_{21} & \mathbf{F}_{22}\end{bmatrix}\right)$$

$\Rightarrow$

$$\bar{\mathbf{B}} \text{ inside Sector}\left(\begin{bmatrix}\mathbf{F}_{11} & \mathbf{F}_{12}\cdot\mathbf{A}^{-1}\\ \mathbf{F}_{21} & \mathbf{F}_{22}\cdot\mathbf{A}^{-1}\end{bmatrix}\right) \triangleq \text{Sector}\left(\mathbf{F}\cdot\begin{bmatrix}I & 0\\ 0 & \mathbf{A}^{-1}\end{bmatrix}\right). \tag{2.4.9}$$

(c) If $\bar{\mathbf{A}}$ = Graph (A), then

$$\bar{\mathbf{B}} \text{ inside Sector}\left(\begin{bmatrix}\mathbf{F}_{11}\cdot\mathbf{A} & \mathbf{F}_{12}\\ \mathbf{F}_{21}\cdot\mathbf{A} & \mathbf{F}_{22}\end{bmatrix}\right)$$

$\Rightarrow$

$$\bar{\mathbf{A}}\cdot\bar{\mathbf{B}} \text{ inside Sector}\left(\begin{bmatrix}\mathbf{F}_{11} & \mathbf{F}_{12}\\ \mathbf{F}_{21} & \mathbf{F}_{22}\end{bmatrix}\right). \tag{2.4.10}$$

Furthermore, if **A** has finite gain, then (2.4.8)–(2.4.10) hold with *inside* replaced by *strictly inside* throughout.

(vi) Composites of relations: Suppose $\bar{\mathbf{A}} = \{(x^{(1)}, \ldots, x^{(n)}), (y^{(1)}, \ldots, y^{(n)}) \mid (x^{(k)}, y^{(k)}) \in \bar{\mathbf{A}}^{(k)} \text{ for all k} = 1, \ldots, n\}$; suppose $\mathbf{F}_{ij}(\xi^{(1)}, \ldots, \xi^{n}) = (\mathbf{F}_{ij}^{(1)}\xi^{(1)}, \ldots, \mathbf{F}_{ij}^{(n)}\xi^{(n)})$ for (i, j = 1, 2); and suppose that $\mathscr{X}_e = \mathscr{X}_e^{(1)} \times \ldots \times \mathscr{X}_e^{(n)}$ and that the associated inner products satisfy

$$\langle(z_1^{(1)}, \ldots, z_1^{(n)}), (z_2^{(1)}, \ldots, z_2^{(n)})\rangle_\tau = \sum_{k=1}^{n} \langle z_1^{(k)}, z_2^{(k)}\rangle_\tau.$$

Then

$$\bar{\mathbf{A}} \text{ inside Sector}\left(\begin{bmatrix}\mathbf{F}_{11} & \mathbf{F}_{12}\\ \mathbf{F}_{21} & \mathbf{F}_{22}\end{bmatrix}\right)$$

$\Leftrightarrow$

$$\bar{\mathbf{A}}^{(k)} \text{ inside Sector}\left(\begin{bmatrix}\mathbf{F}_{11}^{(k)} & \mathbf{F}_{12}^{(k)}\\ \mathbf{F}_{21}^{(k)} & \mathbf{F}_{22}^{(k)}\end{bmatrix}\right) \text{ for all k} = 1, \ldots, n. \tag{2.4.11}$$

Furthermore, (2.4.11) holds if *inside* is replaced by *strictly inside* throughout.

(vii) Properties (i)–(iv) hold if throughout *inside* is replaced by *outside* and *strictly inside* is replaced by *strictly outside*.

PROOF We prove properties (i)–(vii) in sequence.

Proof of Property (i):

$$\bar{\mathbf{A}} \text{ inside (strictly inside) Sector}\left(\begin{bmatrix} \mathbf{F}_{11} & \mathbf{F}_{12} \\ \mathbf{F}_{21} & \mathbf{F}_{22} \end{bmatrix}\right) \tag{2.4.12}$$

$\Leftrightarrow$

$$\langle \mathbf{F}_{11}y + \mathbf{F}_{12}x, \mathbf{F}_{21}y + \mathbf{F}_{22}x\rangle_\tau \leq -\varepsilon\|(x, y)\|_\tau^2 \tag{2.4.13}$$

for some $\varepsilon \geq 0$ ($\varepsilon > 0$), all $\tau \in \mathrm{T}$, and all $(x, y) \in \bar{\mathbf{A}}$

$\Leftrightarrow$

$$\langle \mathbf{F}_{11}y + \mathbf{F}_{12}x, \mathbf{F}_{21}y - \mathbf{F}_{22}x\rangle_\tau \geq \varepsilon\|(x, y)\|_\tau^2 \tag{2.4.14}$$

for some $\varepsilon \geq 0$ ($\varepsilon > 0$), all $\tau \in \mathrm{T}$ and all $(x, y) \in \bar{\mathbf{A}}$

$\Leftrightarrow$

$$\bar{\mathbf{A}} \text{ outside (strictly outside) Sector}\left(\begin{bmatrix} \mathbf{F}_{11} & \mathbf{F}_{12} \\ -\mathbf{F}_{21} & -\mathbf{F}_{22} \end{bmatrix}\right). \tag{2.4.15}$$

This proves property (i).

Proof of Property (ii):

$$(x, y) \in \text{Sector}\left(\begin{bmatrix} \mathbf{F}_{11} & \mathbf{F}_{12} \\ \mathbf{M}\cdot\mathbf{F}_{21} & \mathbf{M}\cdot\mathbf{F}_{22} \end{bmatrix}\right) \tag{2.4.16}$$

$\Leftrightarrow$

$$\langle \mathbf{F}_{11}y + \mathbf{F}_{12}x, \mathbf{M}\cdot\mathbf{F}_{21}y + \mathbf{M}\cdot\mathbf{F}_{22}x\rangle_\tau \leq 0 \tag{2.4.17}$$

for all $\tau \in \mathrm{T}$

$\Leftrightarrow$

$$\begin{aligned}&\langle \mathbf{F}_{11}y, \mathbf{M}\cdot\mathbf{F}_{21}y\rangle_\tau + \langle \mathbf{F}_{11}y, \mathbf{M}\cdot\mathbf{F}_{22}x\rangle_\tau + \langle \mathbf{F}_{12}x, \mathbf{M}\cdot\mathbf{F}_{21}y\rangle_\tau \\ &\quad + \langle \mathbf{F}_{12}x, \mathbf{F}\cdot\mathbf{F}_{22}x\rangle_\tau \leq 0\end{aligned} \tag{2.4.18}$$

for all $\tau \in \mathrm{T}$

$\Leftrightarrow$

$$\begin{aligned}&\{1/\mathrm{ab}\langle \mathrm{a}\mathbf{M}^*\cdot\mathbf{F}_{11}y, \mathrm{b}\mathbf{F}_{21}y\rangle_\tau + 1/\mathrm{ab}\langle \mathrm{a}\mathbf{M}^*\cdot\mathbf{F}_{11}y, \mathrm{b}\mathbf{F}_{22}x\rangle_\tau \\ &\quad + 1/\mathrm{ab}\langle \mathrm{a}\mathbf{M}^*\cdot\mathbf{F}_{12}x, \mathrm{b}\mathbf{F}_{21}y\rangle_\tau + 1/\mathrm{ab}\langle \mathrm{a}\mathbf{M}^*\cdot\mathbf{F}_{12}x, \mathrm{b}\mathbf{F}_{22}x\rangle_\tau\} \leq 0\end{aligned} \tag{2.4.19}$$

for all $\tau \in \mathrm{T}$

$\Leftrightarrow$

$$\langle aM^*\cdot F_{11}y + aM^*\cdot F_{12}x, bF_{21}y + bF_{22}x\rangle_\tau \le 0 \tag{2.4.20}$$

for all $\tau \in T$

$\Leftrightarrow$

$$(x, y) \in \text{Sector}\left(\begin{bmatrix} aM^*\cdot F_{11} + aM^*\cdot F_{12} \\ bF_{21} \quad\quad bF_{22} \end{bmatrix}\right). \tag{2.4.21}$$

From (2.4.16)–(2.4.21), property (ii) follows.

Proof of Property (iii):

$$\bar{A} \text{ inside (strictly inside) Sector}\left(\begin{bmatrix} F_{11} & F_{12} \\ F_{21} & F_{22} \end{bmatrix}\right) \tag{2.4.22}$$

$\Leftrightarrow$

$$\langle F_{11}y + F_{12}x, F_{21}y + F_{22}x\rangle_\tau \le -\varepsilon\|(x, y)\|_\tau^2 \tag{2.4.23}$$

for some $\varepsilon \ge 0$ ($\varepsilon > 0$), all $\tau \in T$, and all $(x, y) \in \bar{A}$

$\Leftrightarrow$

$$\langle F_{12}x + F_{11}y, F_{22}x + F_{21}y\rangle_\tau \le -\varepsilon\|(y, x)\|_\tau^2 \tag{2.4.24}$$

for some $\varepsilon \le 0$ ($\varepsilon > 0$), all $\tau \in T$, and all $(y, x) \in \bar{A}^I$

$\Leftrightarrow$

$$\bar{A}^I \text{ inside (strictly inside) Sector}\left(\begin{bmatrix} F_{12} & F_{11} \\ F_{22} & F_{21} \end{bmatrix}\right). \tag{2.4.25}$$

This proves property (iii).

Proof of Property (iv): Let $k = \text{Gain}(\bar{A} - \bar{B})$. Then

$$\bar{A} \text{ inside (strictly inside) Sector}\left(\begin{bmatrix} F_{11} & F_{12} \\ F_{21} & F_{22} \end{bmatrix}\right) \tag{2.4.26}$$

$\Leftrightarrow$

$$\langle F_{11}y + F_{12}x, F_{21}y + F_{22}x\rangle_\tau \le -\varepsilon\|(x, y)\|_\tau^2 \tag{2.4.27}$$

for all $(x, y) \in \bar{A}$, some $\varepsilon \ge 0$ ($\varepsilon > 0$) and all $\tau \in T$

$\Leftrightarrow$

$$\langle F_{11}y - F_{11}\cdot Bx + F_{11}\cdot Bx + F_{12}x,$$
$$F_{21}y - F_{21}{}^*Bx + F_{21}\cdot Bx + F_{22}x\rangle_\tau \le -\varepsilon\|(x, y)\|_\tau^2 \tag{2.4.28}$$

for all $(x, y) \in \overline{\mathbf{A}}$, some $\varepsilon \geq 0$ ($\varepsilon > 0$) and all $\tau \in \mathrm{T}$

$\Leftrightarrow$

$$\langle \mathbf{F}_{11}(y - \mathbf{B}x) + (\mathbf{F}_{11}\cdot\mathbf{B} + \mathbf{F}_{11})x,\\ \mathbf{F}_{21}(y - \mathbf{B}x) + (\mathbf{F}_{21}\cdot\mathbf{B} + \mathbf{F}_{22})x\rangle_\tau \leq -\varepsilon\|(x, y)\|_\tau^2 \tag{2.4.29}$$

for all $(x, y) \in \overline{\mathbf{A}}$, some $\varepsilon \geq 0$ ($\varepsilon > 0$), and all $\tau \in \mathrm{T}$

$\Leftrightarrow$

$$\langle \mathbf{F}_{11}\tilde{y} + (\mathbf{F}_{11}\cdot\mathbf{B} + \mathbf{F}_{12})x, \mathbf{F}_{21}\tilde{y} + (\mathbf{F}_{21}\cdot\mathbf{B} + \mathbf{F}_{22})x\rangle_\tau\\ \leq -\varepsilon\|(x, \tilde{y} + \mathbf{B}x\|_\tau^2 \leq -\varepsilon\|x\|_\tau^2 \leq -\varepsilon/1 + \mathrm{k}^2\|(x, \tilde{y})\|_\tau^2 \tag{2.4.30}$$

for all $(x, \tilde{y}) \in (\overline{\mathbf{A}} - \overline{\mathbf{B}})$, some $\varepsilon \geq 0$ ($\varepsilon > 0$), and all $\tau \in \mathrm{T}$

$\Leftrightarrow$

$$(\overline{\mathbf{A}} - \overline{\mathbf{B}}) \text{ inside Sector}\left(\begin{bmatrix} \mathbf{F}_{11} & (\mathbf{F}_{11}\cdot\mathbf{B} + \mathbf{F}_{12}) \\ \mathbf{F}_{21} & (\mathbf{F}_{21}\cdot\mathbf{B} + \mathbf{F}_{22}) \end{bmatrix}\right);$$

and, provided $\mathrm{k} < \infty$ and (2.4.26) holds with the parenthetical *strictly inside*,

$$(\overline{\mathbf{A}} - \overline{\mathbf{B}}) \text{ strictly inside Sector}\left(\begin{bmatrix} \mathbf{F}_{11} & (\mathbf{F}_{11}\cdot\mathbf{B} + \mathbf{F}_{12}) \\ \mathbf{F}_{21} & (\mathbf{F}_{21}\cdot\mathbf{B} + \mathbf{F}_{22}) \end{bmatrix}\right). \tag{2.4.31}$$

This proves property (iv).

Proof of Property (v): Let $\mathrm{k} = \mathrm{Gain}\,(\overline{\mathbf{A}})$. Then

(a) $$\overline{\mathbf{B}}\cdot\overline{\mathbf{A}} \text{ inside (strictly inside) Sector}\left(\begin{bmatrix} \mathbf{F}_{11} & \mathbf{F}_{12} \\ \mathbf{F}_{21} & \mathbf{F}_{22} \end{bmatrix}\right) \tag{2.4.32}$$

$\Leftrightarrow$

$$\langle \mathbf{F}_{11}y + \mathbf{F}_{12}x, \mathbf{F}_{21}y + \mathbf{F}_{22}x\rangle_\tau \leq -\varepsilon\|(x, y)\|_\tau^2 \tag{2.4.33}$$

for all $(x, y) \in \overline{\mathbf{B}}\cdot\overline{\mathbf{A}}$, some $\varepsilon \geq 0$ ($\varepsilon > 0$), and all $\tau \in \mathrm{T}$

$\Leftrightarrow$

$$\langle \mathbf{F}_{11}\mathbf{B}\tilde{y} + \mathbf{F}_{12}x, \mathbf{F}_{21}\mathbf{B}\tilde{y} + \mathbf{F}_{22}x\rangle_\tau \leq -\varepsilon(x, \mathbf{B}\tilde{y})\|_\tau^2 \leq -\varepsilon\|x\|_\tau^2\\ \leq -\varepsilon/1 + \mathrm{k}^2\|(x, \tilde{y})\|_\tau^2 \tag{2.4.34}$$

for all $(x, \tilde{y}) \in \bar{A}$, some $\varepsilon \geq 0$ $(\varepsilon > 0)$ and all $\tau \in T$

$\Leftrightarrow$

$$\bar{A} \text{ inside Sector}\left(\begin{bmatrix} F_{11}\cdot B & F_{12} \\ F_{21}\cdot B & F_{22} \end{bmatrix}\right);$$

and, provided $k < \infty$ and (2.4.32) holds with the parenthetical *strictly inside*,

$$\bar{A} \text{ strictly inside Sector}\left(\begin{bmatrix} F_{11}\cdot B & F_{12} \\ F_{21}\cdot B & F_{22} \end{bmatrix}\right). \tag{2.4.35}$$

(b) $$\bar{B}\cdot\bar{A} \text{ inside (strictly inside) Sector}\left(\begin{bmatrix} F_{11} & F_{12} \\ F_{21} & F_{22} \end{bmatrix}\right) \tag{2.4.36}$$

$\Leftrightarrow$

$$\langle F_{11}y + F_{12}\cdot A^{-1}\cdot Ax, F_{21}y + F_{22}\cdot A^{-1}\cdot Ax\rangle_\tau \leq -\varepsilon\|(x, y)\|_\tau^2 \tag{2.4.37}$$

for all $(x, y) \in \bar{B}\cdot\bar{A}$, some $\varepsilon \geq 0$ $(\varepsilon > 0)$, and all $\tau \in T$

$\Leftrightarrow$

$$\begin{aligned}\langle F_{11}y + F_{12}A^{-1}\tilde{x}, F_{21}y + F_{22}A^{-1}\tilde{x}\rangle_\tau &\leq -\varepsilon\|(A^{-1}\tilde{x}, y)\|_\tau^2 \\ \leq -\varepsilon(\|y\|_\tau^2 + \|A^{-1}\tilde{x}\|_\tau^2) &\leq -\varepsilon(\|y\|_\tau^2 + 1/k^2\|\tilde{x}\|_\tau^2) \\ &\leq -\varepsilon\cdot\min\{1, 1/k^2\}\cdot\|(\tilde{x}, y)_\tau^2\end{aligned} \tag{2.4.38}$$

for all $(\tilde{x}, y) \in \bar{B}$, some $\varepsilon \geq 0$ $(\varepsilon > 0)$, and all $\tau \in T$

$\Leftrightarrow$

$$\bar{B} \text{ inside Sector}\left(\begin{bmatrix} F_{11} & F_{12}\cdot A^{-1} \\ F_{21} & F_{22}\cdot A^{-1} \end{bmatrix}\right); \tag{2.4.39}$$

and, provided $k < \infty$ and (2.4.36) holds with the parenthetical *strictly inside*,

$$\bar{B} \text{ strictly inside Sector}\left(\begin{bmatrix} F_{11} & F_{12}\cdot A^{-1} \\ F_{21} & F_{22}\cdot A^{-1} \end{bmatrix}\right). \tag{2.4.40}$$

(c) $$\bar{B} \text{ inside (strictly inside) Sector}\left(\begin{bmatrix} F_{11}\cdot A & F_{12} \\ F_{21}\cdot A & F_{22} \end{bmatrix}\right) \tag{2.4.41}$$

$\Leftrightarrow$

$$\langle \mathbf{F}_{11}\cdot \mathbf{A}y + \mathbf{F}_{12}x, \mathbf{F}_{21}\cdot \mathbf{A}y + \mathbf{F}_{22}x\rangle_\tau \leq -\varepsilon\|(x, y)\|_\tau^2 \tag{2.4.42}$$

for all $(x, y) \in \overline{\mathbf{B}}$, some $\varepsilon \geq 0$ $(\varepsilon > 0)$, and all $\tau \in T$

$\Leftrightarrow$

$$\begin{aligned}&\langle \mathbf{F}_{11}\tilde{y} + \mathbf{F}_{12}x, \mathbf{F}_{21}\tilde{y} + \mathbf{F}_{22}x\rangle_\tau \leq -\varepsilon\|x, y\|_\tau^2\\ &= -\varepsilon(\|x\|_\tau^3 + \|y\|_\tau^2) \leq -\varepsilon(\|x\|_\tau^2 + 1/k^2\cdot\|\tilde{y}\|_\tau^2)\\ &\leq -\varepsilon\cdot\min\{1, 1/k^2\}\cdot\|(x, \tilde{y})\|_\tau^2\end{aligned} \tag{2.4.43}$$

for all $(x, \tilde{y}) \in \overline{\mathbf{A}}\cdot\overline{\mathbf{B}}$, some $\varepsilon \geq 0$ $(\varepsilon > 0)$, and all $\tau \in T$

$\Rightarrow$

$$\overline{\mathbf{A}}\cdot\overline{\mathbf{B}} \text{ inside Sector}\left(\begin{bmatrix}\mathbf{F}_{11} & \mathbf{F}_{12}\\ \mathbf{F}_{21} & \mathbf{F}_{22}\end{bmatrix}\right);$$

and, provided $k < \infty$ and (2.4.41) holds with the parenthetical *strictly inside*,

$$\overline{\mathbf{A}}\cdot\overline{\mathbf{B}} \text{ strictly inside Sector}\left(\begin{bmatrix}\mathbf{F}_{11} & \mathbf{F}_{12}\\ \mathbf{F}_{21} & \mathbf{F}_{22}\end{bmatrix}\right). \tag{2.4.44}$$

This proves property (v).

Proof of Property (vi):

$$\overline{\mathbf{A}}^{(k)} \text{ inside (strictly inside) Sector}\left(\begin{bmatrix}\mathbf{F}_{11}^{(k)} & \mathbf{F}_{12}^{(k)}\\ \mathbf{F}_{21}^{(k)} & \mathbf{F}_{22}^{(k)}\end{bmatrix}\right) \tag{2.4.45}$$

for all $k = 1, \ldots, n$

$\Leftrightarrow$

$$\langle \mathbf{F}_{11}^{(k)}y^{(k)} + \mathbf{F}_{12}x^{(k)}, \mathbf{F}_{21}^{(k)}y^{(k)} + \mathbf{F}_{22}^{(k)}x^{(k)}\rangle_\tau \leq -\varepsilon^{(k)}\|(x^{(k)}, y^{(k)})\|_\tau^2 \tag{2.4.46}$$

for all $(x^{(k)}, y^{(k)}) \in \overline{\mathbf{A}}^{(k)}$, some $\varepsilon^{(k)} \geq 0$ $(\varepsilon^{(k)} > 0)$, all $\tau \in T$, and all $k = 1, \ldots, n$

$\Leftrightarrow$

$$\begin{aligned}&\sum_{k=1}^{n} \langle \mathbf{F}_{11}^{(k)}y^{(k)} + \mathbf{F}_{12}^{(k)}x^{(k)}, \mathbf{F}_{21}^{(k)}y^{(k)} + \mathbf{F}_{22}^{(k)}x^{(k)}\rangle_\tau\\ &\leq -\min\{\varepsilon^{(k)} \mid k = 1, \ldots, n\}\cdot\sum_{k=1}^{n}\|(x^{(k)}, y^{(k)}\|_\tau^2\\ &= -\min\{\varepsilon^{(k)} \mid k = 1, \ldots, n\}\cdot\|((x^{(1)}, \ldots, x^{(n)}, (y^{(1)}, \ldots, y^{(n)}))\|_\tau^2\end{aligned}$$

for all $((x^{(1)}, \ldots, x^{(n)}), (y^{(1)}, \ldots, y^{(n)})) \in \bar{\mathbf{A}}$, for some $\varepsilon^{(k)} \geq 0$ ($\varepsilon^{(k)} > 0$) $k = 1, \ldots, n$, and for all $\tau \in T$

$\Leftrightarrow$

$$\bar{\mathbf{A}} \text{ inside (strictly inside) Sector}\left(\begin{bmatrix} \mathbf{F}_{11} & \mathbf{F}_{12} \\ \mathbf{F}_{21} & \mathbf{F}_{22} \end{bmatrix}\right). \tag{2.4.48}$$

This proves property (vi).

Proof of Property (vii): This follows directly from property (i). ∎

2.5 Conic Sectors and Frequency-Domain Criteria

The practical application of theorem 2.2 requires the availability of a verifiable set of conditions that can be used to test the *sectoricity* of a relation, i.e., to determine whether a given relation lies in a given sector. In the case of memoryless relations and sectors defined by memoryless $\mathbf{F}_{ij}$ ($i, j = 1, 2$), this is relatively straightforward: we simply check algebraically that the sector condition holds at each time $t \in T$. For dynamical operators, it is in certain cases possible to check sectoricity with analogous algebraic tests in the frequency domain; several such tests are developed in this section.

The class of sectors considered are those whose defining array $\mathbf{F}$ can be expressed in the special form

$$\mathbf{F} \equiv \begin{bmatrix} \mathbf{F}_{11} & \mathbf{F}_{12} \\ \mathbf{F}_{21} & \mathbf{F}_{22} \end{bmatrix} = \begin{bmatrix} I & (-\mathbf{C} - \mathbf{R}) \\ I & (-\mathbf{C} + \mathbf{R}) \end{bmatrix} \tag{2.5.1}$$

where $\mathbf{C}, \mathbf{R}: \mathscr{X}_e \to \mathscr{Y}_e$. We designate any sector of this type a *conic sector*, denoted Cone $(\mathbf{C}, \mathbf{R})$, because, as may be easily checked,

$$\begin{aligned} \text{Cone}(\mathbf{C}, \mathbf{R}) &\triangleq \text{Sector}\left(\begin{bmatrix} I & (-\mathbf{C} - \mathbf{R}) \\ I & (-\mathbf{C} + \mathbf{R}) \end{bmatrix}\right) \\ &= \{(x, y) \in \mathscr{X}_e \times \mathscr{Y}_e \mid \|\mathbf{P}_\tau(y - \mathbf{C}x)\| \leq \|\mathbf{P}_\tau \mathbf{R}x\| \text{ for all } \tau \in T\}. \end{aligned} \tag{2.5.2}$$

This is simply a generalization of the conic sector employed by Zames, but admitting dynamical operators $\mathbf{C}$ and $\mathbf{R}$ as cone *center* and *radius* parameters in place of the scalars c and r introduced in equation (2.1.5).

Also considered are sectors whose defining array $\mathbf{F}$ is of the form

$$\mathbf{F} = \begin{bmatrix} 0 & -I \\ I & \mathbf{K} \end{bmatrix}. \tag{2.5.3}$$

Such sectors can be viewed as degenerate limiting cases of conic sectors in which $\mathbf{C} + \mathbf{R} = \mathrm{k}I$ and $\mathrm{k} \to \infty$. These types of sectors are closely related to the positive sectors (i.e., the sectors containing all positive relations) considered by Zames [118]—a positive sector corresponding precisely to the case $\mathbf{K} \equiv 0$. Accordingly, such sectors are designated *positive-conic sectors*, denoted

$$+\text{-Cone}\,(\mathbf{K}) \triangleq \text{Sector}\begin{bmatrix} 0 & -I \\ I & \mathbf{K} \end{bmatrix} \tag{2.5.4}$$

Relations that are either inside or outside a conic or positive-conic sector are said to be *conic.*

Besides being amenable to frequency-domain verification of sectoricity, conic sectors have certain convexity properties which make them especially attractive for robustness analysis and may also prove useful in numerical robustness optimization problems; though this latter issue is not addressed here.

LEMMA 2.2 (Convexity of Conic Sectors) Let $\mathbf{G}_1, \mathbf{G}_2 \colon \mathscr{X}_e \to \mathscr{Y}_e$ and let Graph $(\mathbf{G}_1)$ and Graph $(\mathbf{G}_2)$ both be inside Cone $(\mathbf{C}, \mathbf{R})$. Then, for every constant λ with $1 \geq \lambda \geq 0$,

$$\text{Graph}\,[\lambda\mathbf{G}_1 + (1 - \lambda)\mathbf{G}_2] \text{ inside Cone}\,(\mathbf{C}, \mathbf{R}). \tag{2.5.5}$$

The word *inside* may be replaced by *strictly inside* throughout.

PROOF For all $(x, y) \in \text{Graph}\,(\lambda\mathbf{G}_1 + (1 - \lambda)\mathbf{G}_2)$

$$y = \lambda\mathbf{G}_1 x + (1 - \lambda)\mathbf{G}_2 x;$$

and so for all $\tau \in \mathrm{T}$

$$\begin{aligned} \|\mathbf{P}_\tau(y - \mathbf{C}x)\|_\tau &= \|\mathbf{P}_\tau[(\lambda\mathbf{G}_1 x + (1 - \lambda)\mathbf{G}_2 x) - \mathbf{C}x]\|_\tau \\ &= \|\lambda\mathbf{P}_\tau(\mathbf{G}_1 x - \mathbf{C}x) + (1 - \lambda)\mathbf{P}_\tau(\mathbf{G}_2 x - \mathbf{C}x)\|_\tau \\ &\leq \lambda\|\mathbf{P}_\tau(\mathbf{G}_1 x - \mathbf{C}x)\|_\tau + (1 - \lambda)\|\mathbf{P}_\tau(\mathbf{G}_2 x - \mathbf{C}x)\|_\tau \\ &\leq \lambda\|\mathbf{P}_\tau\mathbf{R}x\|_\tau + (1 - \lambda)\|\mathbf{P}_\tau\mathbf{R}x\|_\tau \\ &= \|\mathbf{P}_\tau\mathbf{R}x\|_\tau. \end{aligned}$$

Thus, by (2.5.2),

Graph $(\lambda \mathbf{G}_1 + (1 - \lambda)\mathbf{G}_2)$ inside Cone (C, R).

The strictly inside case follows analogously. ∎

Another important property of conic sectors is embodied in the following result.

LEMMA 2.3 (Conicity by Differentiation) Let $\mathbf{G}: \mathscr{X}_e \to \mathscr{Y}_e$ be a Gateaux-differentiable operator with $\mathbf{G}0 = 0$. Let $\mathbf{C}, \mathbf{K}: \mathscr{X}_e \to \mathscr{Y}_e$ be linear.

(a) If uniformly[7] for all $x \in \mathscr{X}_e$

$$\text{Graph}\,[\nabla\mathbf{G}(x)] \text{ inside (strictly inside) Cone}\,(\mathbf{C}, \mathbf{R}), \tag{2.5.6a}$$

then

$$\text{Graph}(\mathbf{G}) \text{ inside (strictly inside) Cone}\,(\mathbf{C}, \mathbf{R}). \tag{2.5.6b}$$

(b) If uniformly[8] for all $x \in \mathscr{X}_e$

$$\text{Graph}\,(\nabla\mathbf{G}(x)] \text{ inside (strictly inside, outside, strictly outside) } +\text{-Cone}(\mathbf{K}), \tag{2.5.7a}$$

then

$$\text{Graph}(\mathbf{G}) \text{ inside (strictly inside, outside, strictly outside) } +\text{-Cone}\,(\mathbf{K}). \tag{2.5.7b}$$

PROOF **Suppose (2.5.6a) holds. For all $(x, y) \in$ Graph (G) and all $\tau \in T$**

$$\begin{aligned}\|\mathbf{P}_\tau(y - \mathbf{C}x)\| &= \|\mathbf{P}_\tau(\mathbf{G} - \mathbf{C})x\| \\ &= \left\|\mathbf{P}_\tau \int_0^x \nabla(\mathbf{G} - \mathbf{C})(z)\, dz\right\| \\ &= \left\|\mathbf{P}_\tau \int_0^1 \nabla(\mathbf{G} - \mathbf{C})(\rho x)x\, d\rho\right\|\end{aligned}$$

7, 8 The adverb *uniformly* indicates that the constant ε of (2.4.7) may be chosen to be the same for every operator in the collection of linear derivative operators $\{\nabla\mathbf{G}(x) \mid x \in \mathscr{X}_e\}$; evidently this is of significance only in the case when (2.5.6a) and (2.5.7a) hold *strictly*, i.e., when the term *strictly inside* or the term *strictly outside* applies in (2.5.6a), (2.5.7a).

$$= \left\| \int_0^1 \mathbf{P}_\tau(\nabla\mathbf{G}(\rho x) - \mathbf{C})x \, d\rho \right\| \quad \text{(since } \mathbf{P}_\tau \text{ and } \mathbf{C} \text{ are linear)}$$
$$\leq \int_0^1 \|\mathbf{P}_\tau(\nabla\mathbf{G}(\rho x) - \mathbf{C})x\| \, d\rho \quad \text{(by the triangle inequality)}$$
$$\leq \sup_{z \in \mathscr{X}_e} \|\mathbf{P}_\tau(\nabla\mathbf{G}(z) - \mathbf{C})x\|.$$

Equation (2.5.6b) follows.

Suppose (2.5.7a) holds. For all $(x, y) \in$ Graph (G) and all $\tau \in T$

$$\begin{aligned}\langle \mathbf{P}_\tau(y - \mathbf{K}x), \mathbf{P}_\tau(-Ix)\rangle &= -\langle \mathbf{P}_\tau(\mathbf{G} - \mathbf{K})x, \mathbf{P}_\tau x\rangle \\ &= -\left\langle \int_0^1 \mathbf{P}_\tau(\nabla\mathbf{G}(\rho x) - \mathbf{K})x \, d\rho, \mathbf{P}_\tau x \right\rangle \\ &= \int_0^1 \langle \mathbf{P}_\tau(\nabla\mathbf{G}(\rho x) - \mathbf{K})x, \mathbf{P}_\tau(-Ix)\rangle \, d\rho.\end{aligned}$$

Equation (2.5.7b) follows.

Comment Lemma 2.3 makes it possible to verify the conicity of the nonlinear operator **G** by checking the conicity of the collection of *linear* operators $\{\nabla\mathbf{G}(x) \mid x \in \mathscr{X}_e\}$.

2.5.1 Frequency-Domain Tests for Sectoricity—Continuous-Time

We begin by developing frequency-domain tests for conicity of linear time-invariant operators (i.e., transfer-function operators) defined on extended inner-product spaces of either of two types:

(i) $\mathscr{X}_e = \mathscr{Y}_e = \mathscr{L}_{2e}(\mathrm{R}_+, \mathrm{R}^n)$ (2.5.8)

induced (see equations (2.1.2)–(2.1.4)) by the linear truncation operator (2.1.4) mapping the vector space $\{\xi: \mathrm{R}_+ \to \mathrm{R}^n\}$ into the spaces

$$\left.\begin{aligned}&\mathscr{X}_\tau = \mathscr{Y}_\tau = \{\mathbf{P}_\tau\xi: \mathrm{R}_+ \to \mathrm{R}^n \\ &\text{with} \\ &\langle \mathbf{P}_\tau\xi_1, \mathbf{P}_\tau\xi_2\rangle = \int_0^\tau \xi_1^T(t)\xi_2(t) \, dt \\ &\|\mathbf{P}_\tau\xi\| = (\langle \mathbf{P}_\tau\xi, \mathbf{P}_\tau\xi\rangle)^{1/2}\};\end{aligned}\right\} \qquad (2.5.9)$$

(ii) $\mathscr{X}_e = \mathscr{Y}_e = \mathscr{M}_{2e}(\mathrm{R}_+, \mathrm{R}^n)$ (2.5.10)

induced (see equations (2.1.2)–(2.1.4)) by the linear truncation operator

(2.1.4) mapping the vector space $\{\xi: R_+ \to R^n\}$ into the spaces

$$\left.\begin{array}{l} \mathscr{X}_\tau = \mathscr{Y}_\tau = \{P_\tau\xi: R_+ \to R^N \\ \text{with} \\ \langle P_\tau\xi_1 P_\tau\xi_2\rangle = 1/\tau \int_0^\tau \xi_1^T(t)\xi_2(t)\,dt \\ \|P_\tau\xi\| = (\langle P_\tau\xi, P_\tau\xi\rangle)^{1/2}\}. \end{array}\right\} \tag{2.5.11}$$

The difference between the space $\mathscr{L}_{2e}$ and the space $\mathscr{M}_{2e}$ is the factor $1/\tau$ in the inner product of $P_\tau\mathscr{M}_2$, giving the $\mathscr{M}_2$-norm an "average power" interpretation in contrast to the $\mathscr{L}_2$-norm which is more appropriately interpreted in terms of "total energy."

LEMMA 2.4 (Conicity) Let $\mathscr{X}_e$, $\mathscr{Y}_e$ be either as in (2.5.8) or as in (2.5.10); let $\mathbf{G}$, $\mathbf{C}$, $\mathbf{R}: \mathscr{X}_e \to \mathscr{Y}_e$ be nonanticipative linear time-invariant operators with respective transfer functions $G(s)$, $C(s)$, $R(s)$; let $\mathbf{R}$ have a nonanticipative inverse $\mathbf{R}^{-1}$; let $\mathbf{G}$, $\mathbf{C}$, and $\mathbf{R}^{-1}$ be stable. If

$$R^T(-j\omega)R(j\omega) - [G(-j\omega) - C(-j\omega)]^T[G(j\omega) - C(j\omega)] - \varepsilon I \geq 0 \tag{2.5.12}$$

for some $\varepsilon \geq 0$ and all $\omega \in R_+$, then Graph ($\mathbf{G}$) is inside Cone ($\mathbf{C}$, $\mathbf{R}$). If, additionally, (2.5.12) holds for some $\varepsilon > 0$, the Graph ($\mathbf{G}$) is strictly inside Cone ($\mathbf{C}$, $\mathbf{R}$).

PROOF We assume that (2.5.8) applies; so $\mathscr{X}_e = \mathscr{Y}_e = \mathscr{L}_{2e}(R_+, R^n)$. The proofs for the case $\mathscr{X}_e = \mathscr{Y}_e = \mathscr{M}_{2e}(R_+, R^n)$ follow with a normalizing factor $1/\tau$ inserted in appropriate places throughout.

Let $(x, y) \in$ Graph ($\mathbf{G}$) $= \{(x, y) \mid y = \mathbf{G}x; x \in \mathscr{X}_e\}$. Since $\mathbf{R}$ is invertible, there exists $v \in \mathscr{L}_{2e}$ such that $x = \mathbf{R}^{-1}v$. Thus, for each $\tau \in T$

$$\begin{aligned} \|P_\tau(y - \mathbf{C}x)\|^2 &= \|P_\tau(\mathbf{G} - \mathbf{C})\mathbf{R}^{-1}v\|^2 \\ &= \|P_\tau(\mathbf{G} - \mathbf{C})\mathbf{R}^{-1}P_\tau v\|^2 \\ &\qquad \text{(by the nonanticipativeness of } \mathbf{G} - \mathbf{C} \text{ and } \mathbf{R}^{-1}) \\ &\leq \frac{1}{2\pi}\int_{-\infty}^{\infty} \|(G(j\omega) - C(j\omega))R^{-1}(j\omega)V_\tau(j\omega)\|^2\,d\omega \\ &\qquad \text{(by Parseval's theorem and by the stability of } \mathbf{G} - \mathbf{C} \text{ and of } \mathbf{R}^{-1}) \\ &\leq \frac{1}{2\pi}\int_{-\infty}^{\infty} \|V_\tau(j\omega)\|^2 - \varepsilon\|R^{-1}(j\omega)V_\tau(j\omega)\|^2\,d\omega \\ &\qquad \text{(by (2.5.12))} \end{aligned}$$

$$\le \|\mathbf{P}_t v\|^2 - \varepsilon\|\mathbf{R}^{-1}\mathbf{P}_\tau v\|^2 \le \|\mathbf{P}_\tau v\|^2 - \varepsilon\|\mathbf{P}_\tau \mathbf{R}^{-1} v\|^2$$

(by Parseval's theorem and the nonantivipativeness of $\mathbf{R}^{-1}$)

$$= \|\mathbf{P}_\tau \mathbf{R}x\|^2 - \varepsilon\|\mathbf{P}_\tau x\|^2,$$

where $V_\tau(j\omega)$ denotes the Fourier transform of $\mathbf{P}_\tau v$. Hence,

$$\langle \mathbf{P}_\tau[y + (-\mathbf{C} - \mathbf{R})x], \mathbf{P}_\tau[y + (-\mathbf{C} + \mathbf{R})x]\rangle \le \|\mathbf{P}_\tau x\|^2 \le 0,$$

which proves Graph (**G**) is inside Cone (**C**, **R**). If additionally $\varepsilon > 0$, then (taking $k < \infty$ an upper bound on the gain of **G**)

$$\|\mathbf{P}_\tau x\|^2 \le \frac{\varepsilon}{1 + k^2} \|\mathbf{P}_\tau(x, y)\|^2;$$

it follows that Graph (**G**) is strictly inside Cone (**C**, **R**). ▮

Comment A necessary and sufficient condition for **R** to have a nonanticipative inverse with $\mathbf{R}^{-1}$ stable is [27, p. 250]

$$\inf_{\mathrm{Re}(s)\ge 0} |\det[R(s)]| > 0,$$

provided that **R** satisfies certain assumptions which are virtually certain to be satisfied in any conceivable engineering problem [27, p. 246, eq. (5)].

LEMMA 2.5 (Conicity of Inverse Relations) Let $\mathscr{X}_e$, $\mathscr{Y}_e$ be either as in (2.5.8) or as in (2.5.10); let $\mathbf{G}: \mathscr{X}_e \to \mathscr{Y}_e$ and $\mathbf{C}, \mathbf{R}: \mathscr{Y}_e \to \mathscr{X}_e$ be nonanticipative linear time-invariant operators with respective transfer function matrices $G(s)$, $C(s)$, and $R(s)$. Assume that **R** is stable and that $\det[G(j\omega)] \ne 0$ or ∞ for all $\omega \in \mathrm{R}$. Then, $[\mathrm{Graph}(\mathbf{G})]^{\mathrm{I}}$ is outside Cone (**C**, **R**) if the following two conditions are satisfied:

(i) The linear time-invariant feedback system

$$\begin{aligned} x &= \mathbf{G}(y + u) \\ y &= \mathbf{C}(x + v) \\ u &\in \mathscr{Y}_e \\ v &\in \mathscr{X}_e \end{aligned} \tag{2.5.13}$$

is nonanticipative and closed-loop stable.

(ii) For all $\omega \in \mathrm{R}_+$

$$[[I - C(-s)G(-s)]^{\mathrm{T}}[I - C(s)G(s)] - [R(-s)G(-s)]^{\mathrm{T}}[R(s)G(s)]]_{s=j\omega} \ge 0. \tag{2.5.14}$$

PROOF For each $s \in \mathrm{C}$, $G(s)$, $C(s)$, and $R(s)$ are operators mapping C^n into itself. Moreover, since $\det [G(j\omega)] \neq 0$ or ∞, $G^{-1}(j\omega)$ exists and Graph $(G^{-1}(j\omega)) = [\text{Graph}\,(G(j\omega))]^I$. By (2.5.14),

$$\text{Graph}\,(G(j\omega)) \text{ outside Sector}\begin{bmatrix} (-C(j\omega) + R(j\omega)) & I \\ (-C(j\omega) - R(j\omega)) & I \end{bmatrix};$$

and hence, from sector property (iii),

$$\text{Graph}\,(G^{-1}(j\omega)) \text{ outside Sector}\begin{bmatrix} I & (-C(j\omega) + R(j\omega)) \\ I & (-C(j\omega) - R(j\omega)) \end{bmatrix}.$$

So, applying sector properties (iv), (iii), and (v), and using the fact that (2.5.13) is closed-loop stable to assure that $(G^{-1}(j\omega) - C(j\omega))^{-1}$ exists for all ω,

$$\text{Graph}\,[R(j\omega)[G^{-1}(j\omega) - C(j\omega)]^{-1}] \text{ inside Sector}\begin{bmatrix} I & I \\ I & -I \end{bmatrix} = \text{Cone}\,(0, I).$$

Applying Parseval's theorem and using the nonanticipativeness and stability of (2.5.13), we have that for all $\tau \in \mathrm{T}$ and all $v \in \mathscr{L}_{2e}(\mathrm{R}_+, \mathrm{R}^n)$

$$\|\mathbf{P}_\tau \mathbf{R}\mathbf{G}(I - \mathbf{C}\mathbf{G})^{-1} v\|^2 = \|\mathbf{P}_\tau \mathbf{R}\mathbf{G}(I - \mathbf{C}\mathbf{G})^{-1}\mathbf{P}_\tau v\|^2$$

(by nonanticipativeness)

$$\leq \frac{1}{2\pi}\int_{-\infty}^{\infty} \|R(j\omega)G(j\omega)(I - C(j\omega)G(j\omega))^{-1} V_\tau(j\omega)\|^2 \, d\omega$$

(by the stability of (2.5.13) and by Parseval's theorem)

$$= \frac{1}{2\pi}\int_{-\infty}^{\infty} \|R(j\omega)(G^{-1}(j\omega) - C(j\omega))^{-1} V_\tau(j\omega)\|^2 \, d\omega$$

$$\leq \frac{1}{2\pi}\int_{-\infty}^{\infty} \|V_\tau(j\omega)\|^2 \, d\omega$$

$= \|P_\tau v\|^2$ (by Parseval's theorem),

where $V_\tau(j\omega)$ denotes the Fourier transform of $\mathbf{P}_\tau v$. So,

$$\text{Graph}\,(\mathbf{R}\mathbf{G}(I - \mathbf{C}\mathbf{G})^{-1}) \text{ inside Cone}\,(0, I) = \text{Sector}\begin{bmatrix} I & I \\ I & -I \end{bmatrix};$$

and hence, applying sector property (vi),

$$\text{Graph}\,(\mathbf{G}(I - \mathbf{C}\mathbf{G})^{-1}) \text{ inside Sector}\begin{bmatrix} \mathbf{R} & I \\ \mathbf{R} & -I \end{bmatrix}$$

and (denoting $\bar{\mathbf{G}} \equiv$ Graph (G) and $\bar{\mathbf{C}} \equiv$ Graph (C))

$$\bar{\mathbf{G}} \circ (I - \bar{\mathbf{C}} \circ \bar{\mathbf{G}})^{\mathrm{I}} \text{ inside Sector} \begin{bmatrix} \mathbf{R} & I \\ \mathbf{R} & -I \end{bmatrix}$$

Now,

$$[\bar{\mathbf{G}}^{\mathrm{I}} - \bar{\mathbf{C}}]^{\mathrm{I}} \subset [\bar{\mathbf{G}}^{\mathrm{I}} - \bar{\mathbf{C}} \circ \bar{\mathbf{G}} \circ \bar{\mathbf{G}}^{\mathrm{I}}]^{\mathrm{I}} = [(I - \bar{\mathbf{C}} \circ \bar{\mathbf{G}}) \circ \bar{\mathbf{G}}^{\mathrm{I}}]^{\mathrm{I}} = \bar{\mathbf{G}} \circ (I - \bar{\mathbf{C}} \circ \bar{\mathbf{G}})^{\mathrm{I}}.$$

So, applying sector properties (iii), (iv), and (i), we have

$$\bar{\mathbf{G}}^{\mathrm{I}} \text{ outside Sector} \left(\begin{bmatrix} I & 0 \\ 0 & -I \end{bmatrix} \begin{bmatrix} \mathbf{R} & I \\ \mathbf{R} & -I \end{bmatrix} \begin{bmatrix} 0 & I \\ I & 0 \end{bmatrix} \begin{bmatrix} I & -\mathbf{C} \\ 0 & I \end{bmatrix} \right)$$

$$= \text{Sector} \begin{bmatrix} I & -\mathbf{C} + \mathbf{R} \\ I & -\mathbf{C} - \mathbf{R} \end{bmatrix} \triangleq \text{Cone}(\mathbf{C}, \mathbf{R}). \quad \blacksquare$$

LEMMA 2.6 (+-Conicity) Let $\mathscr{X}_e$, $\mathscr{Y}_e$ be as in either (2.5.8) or (2.5.10); let $\mathbf{G}, \mathbf{K}: \mathscr{X}_e \to \mathscr{Y}_e$ be nonanticipative, linear time-invariant operators with respective transfer functions $G(s)$, $K(s)$; let **G** and **K** be stable. If

$$\mathrm{G}(\mathrm{j}\omega) + \mathrm{K}(\mathrm{j}\omega) + [\mathrm{G}(-\mathrm{j}\omega) + \mathrm{K}(-\mathrm{j}\omega)]^{\mathrm{T}} - \varepsilon I \geq 0 \tag{2.5.15}$$

for some $\varepsilon \geq 0$ and all $\omega \in \mathrm{R}_+$, then Graph (G) is *inside* +-Cone (K). Furthermore, if (2.5.15) holds for some $\varepsilon > 0$, then **G** is *strictly inside* +-Cone (K).

PROOF We consider the case $\mathscr{X}_e = \mathscr{Y}_e = \mathscr{L}_{2e}(\mathrm{R}_+, \mathrm{R}^n)$; the proof for the case $\mathscr{X}_e = \mathscr{Y}_e = \mathscr{M}_{2e}(\mathrm{R}_+, \mathrm{R}^n)$ follows with the factor $1/\tau$ inserted in appropriate places throughout.

Let $(x, y) \in$ Graph (G). Then

$$\begin{aligned}
\langle \mathbf{P}_\tau(y + \mathbf{K}x), -\mathbf{P}_\tau x \rangle &= \langle \mathbf{P}_\tau(\mathbf{G} + \mathbf{K})x, -\mathbf{P}_\tau x \rangle \\
&= \int_0^\infty [((\mathbf{G} + \mathbf{K})\mathbf{P}_\tau x)(t)]^{\mathrm{T}} [(\mathbf{P}_\tau x)(t)]\, dt \\
&\quad \text{(by the nonanticipativeness and stability of } \mathbf{G} + \mathbf{K}) \\
&= \frac{1}{2\pi} \int_{-\infty}^{\infty} X_\tau^*(\mathrm{j}\omega)[G(\mathrm{j}\omega) + \mathrm{K}(\mathrm{j}\omega)] X_\tau(\mathrm{j}\omega)\, d\omega \\
&\quad \text{(by Parseval's theorem)} \\
&\leq \frac{-\varepsilon}{2\pi} \int_{-\infty}^{\infty} \|X_\tau(\mathrm{j}\omega)\|^2\, d\omega \quad \text{(by (2.5.15))} \\
&= -\varepsilon \|\mathbf{P}_\tau x\|^2 \leq 0 \quad \text{(by Parseval's theorem),}
\end{aligned}$$

where $X_\tau(j\omega)$ denotes the Fourier transform of $\mathbf{P}_\tau x$. Thus,

$$\text{Graph}(\mathbf{G}) \text{ inside Sector}\begin{bmatrix} I & \mathbf{K} \\ 0 & -I \end{bmatrix} = +\text{-Cone}(\mathbf{K}).$$

To prove that Graph (**G**) is strictly inside +-Cone (**K**), we observe that since Graph (**G**) is open-loop stable and linear, it has finite gain, say $k < \infty$. Hence

$$\|\mathbf{P}_\tau(x, y)\|^2 = \|\mathbf{P}_\tau x\|^2 + \|\mathbf{P}_\tau y\|^2 \leq (1 + k^2)\|\mathbf{P}_\tau x\|^2$$

for all $(x, y) \in$ Graph (**G**) and all $\tau \in$ T. It follows that

$$\langle \mathbf{P}_\tau(y - \mathbf{K}x), \mathbf{P}_\tau x\rangle \leq \frac{-\varepsilon}{1 + k^2}\|\mathbf{P}_\tau(x, y)\|^2$$

for all $(x, y) \in$ Graph (**G**), which proves that, provided (2.5.15) holds with $\varepsilon > 0$, Graph (**G**) is strictly inside +-Cone (**K**). ∎

LEMMA 2.7 (+-Conicity of Inverse Relations) Let $\mathscr{X}_e$ and $\mathscr{Y}_e$ be as in either (2.5.8) or (2.5.10) and let $\mathbf{G}: \mathscr{Y}_e \to \mathscr{X}_e$ and $\mathbf{K}: \mathscr{X}_e \to \mathscr{Y}_e$ be nonanticipative linear time-invariant operators with respective transfer function matrices $G(s)$, $K(s)$. Assume that $\det[G(j\omega)] \neq 0$ or ∞ for all $\omega \in R$. Then $[\text{Graph}(\mathbf{G})]^{\mathrm{I}}$ is outside +-Cone (**K**) if the following two conditions are satisfied:

(i) The linear time-invariant system

$$\begin{aligned} x &= \mathbf{G}(y + u) \\ y &= -\mathbf{K}(x + v) \\ u &\in \mathscr{Y}_e \\ v &\in \mathscr{X}_e \end{aligned} \tag{2.5.16}$$

is nonanticipative and closed-loop stable.

(ii) For all $\omega \in R_+$,

$$-(G^{\mathrm{T}}(-j\omega)[I + K(j\omega)G(j\omega)] + [I + K(-j\omega)G(-j\omega)]^{\mathrm{T}}G(j\omega)) \geq 0. \tag{2.5.17}$$

PROOF For each $s \in C$, $G(s)$ and $K(s)$ are operators mapping C^n into itself. Moreover, since $\det[G(j\omega)] \neq 0$, $\mathbf{G}^{-1}(j\omega)$ exists for all $\omega \in R_+$ and $\text{Graph}(G^{-1}(j\omega)) = [\text{Graph}(G(j\omega))]^{\mathrm{I}}$. By (2.5.17),

$$\text{Graph}(G(j\omega)) \text{ outside Sector}\begin{bmatrix} -I & 0 \\ K(j\omega) & I \end{bmatrix}.$$

So, applying sector properties (iii), (iv), and (iii), and using the fact that (2.5.16) is closed-loop stable to assure that $(G^{-1}(j\omega) + K(j\omega))^{-1}$ exists, we have that, for all $\omega \in R_+$,

$$\begin{aligned}
&\text{Graph}([G^{-1}(j\omega) + K(j\omega)]^{-1}) \\
&\text{outside Sector}\left(\begin{bmatrix} -I & 0 \\ K(j\omega) & I \end{bmatrix}\begin{bmatrix} 0 & I \\ I & 0 \end{bmatrix}\begin{bmatrix} I & -K(j\omega) \\ 0 & I \end{bmatrix}\begin{bmatrix} 0 & I \\ I & 0 \end{bmatrix}\right) \\
&= \text{Sector}\begin{bmatrix} -I & 0 \\ 0 & I \end{bmatrix}.
\end{aligned}$$

Applying Parseval's theorem and using the nonanticipativeness and stability of (2.5.16), we have

$$\begin{aligned}
\langle \mathbf{P}_\tau \mathbf{G}(I + \mathbf{KG})^{-1} v, \mathbf{P}_\tau v \rangle &= \int_0^\infty [(\mathbf{P}_\tau \mathbf{G}(I + \mathbf{KG})^{-1} \mathbf{P}_\tau v)(t)]^T [(\mathbf{P}_\tau v)(t)]\, dt \\
&\qquad \text{(by nonanticipativeness)} \\
&= \frac{1}{2\pi}\int_{-\infty}^{\infty} (G(j\omega)(I + K(j\omega)G(j\omega))^{-1} V_\tau(j\omega))^* V_\tau(j\omega)\, d\omega \\
&\qquad \text{(by stability and Parseval's theorem)} \\
&= \frac{1}{2\pi}\int_{-\infty}^{\infty} ((G^{-1}(j\omega) + K(j\omega))^{-1} V_\tau(j\omega))^* V_\tau(j\omega)\, d\omega, \\
&\geq 0,
\end{aligned}$$

where $V_\tau(j\omega)$ denotes the Fourier transform of $\mathbf{P}_\tau v$. So,

$$\text{Graph}\,(\mathbf{G}(I + \mathbf{KG})^{-1}) \text{ inside Sector}\begin{bmatrix} -I & 0 \\ 0 & I \end{bmatrix};$$

and (denoting $\overline{\mathbf{G}} \equiv \text{Graph}\,(\mathbf{G})$ and $\overline{\mathbf{K}} \equiv \text{Graph}\,(\mathbf{K})$)

$$(\overline{\mathbf{G}} \circ (I + \overline{\mathbf{K}} \circ \overline{\mathbf{G}}) \text{ inside Sector}\begin{bmatrix} -I & 0 \\ 0 & I \end{bmatrix}.$$

Now,

$$\begin{aligned}
(\overline{\mathbf{G}}^{\mathrm{I}} + \overline{\mathbf{K}})^{\mathrm{I}} &\subset (\overline{\mathbf{G}}^{\mathrm{I}} + \overline{\mathbf{K}} \circ \overline{\mathbf{G}} \circ \overline{\mathbf{G}}^{\mathrm{I}})^{\mathrm{I}} \\
&= [(\mathbf{I} + \overline{\mathbf{K}} \circ \overline{\mathbf{G}}) \circ \overline{\mathbf{G}}^{\mathrm{I}}]^{\mathrm{I}} = \overline{\mathbf{G}} \circ (\mathbf{I} + \overline{\mathbf{K}} \circ \overline{\mathbf{G}})^{\mathrm{I}}.
\end{aligned}$$

So,

$$(\bar{\mathbf{G}}^{\mathrm{I}} + \bar{\mathbf{K}})^{\mathrm{I}} \text{ outside Sector}\begin{bmatrix} -I & 0 \\ 0 & I \end{bmatrix};$$

and hence, applying sector properties (iii) and (iv),

$$\bar{\mathbf{G}}^{\mathrm{I}} \text{ outside Sector}\left(\begin{bmatrix} -I & 0 \\ 0 & I \end{bmatrix}\begin{bmatrix} 0 & I \\ I & 0 \end{bmatrix}\begin{bmatrix} I & \mathbf{K} \\ 0 & I \end{bmatrix}\right)$$

$$= \text{Sector}\begin{bmatrix} 0 & -I \\ I & \mathbf{K} \end{bmatrix} = +\text{-Cone}(\mathbf{K}). \quad ∎$$

Example: Multivariable Circle Theorem Lemma 2.5 together with the sector stability criterion and the multivariable Nyquist theorem [123] combine to form a very powerful generalization of the circle stability theorem:

THEOREM 2.3 (Multivariable Circle Theorem) In the feedback system (2.1.1′), let the disturbance inputs u, v be additive (see (2.1.8) and (2.1.9)); let Graph ($\mathbf{H}(0)$) be strictly inside Cone ($\mathbf{C}$, $\mathbf{R}$); let $\mathbf{G}(0)$, $\mathbf{C}$, and $\mathbf{R}$ be linear time-invariant operators with respective transfer function matrices $G(s)$, $C(s)$, and $R(s) \in \mathrm{C}^{n \times n}$; let $\mathbf{R}$ be stable; let $T(s) \in \mathrm{C}^{n \times n}$ denote the "return ratio" matrix $T(s) \equiv C(s)G(s)$; and let $t_i(j\omega)$ ($i = 1, \ldots, n$) denote the characteristic loci of $T(s)$ (i.e., the eigenvalues of $T(j\omega)$). Suppose that the transfer functions det $[C(s)]$ and det $[G(s)]$ have, respectively, n_C and n_G poles (counting multiplicities) in the open right half of the complex plane and no poles or zeroes on the complex axis, and suppose that the characteristic loci $t_i(j\omega)$ encircle the point $+1 + j0$ in C precisely n_i times counterclockwise. Then, the feedback system (2.1.1) is closed-loop finite-gain stable if the following conditions are satisfied:

(i) $$\sum_{i=1}^{n} n_i = n_C + n_G. \tag{2.5.18}$$

(ii) The characteristic loci (i.e., the eigenvalues evaluated at $s = j\omega$) of

$$[I - T(-s)]^{T}[I - T(s)] - [R(-s)G(-s)]^{T}[R(s)G(s)] \tag{2.5.19}$$

lie in the closed right half complex plane.

PROOF The multivariable Nyquist theorem [123] together with the encirclement condition (i) ensure that (2.5.13) holds. Condition (ii) ensures that (2.5.14) holds. So, from Lemma 2.5 [Graph (**G**)]^{I} is outside Cone (**C**, **R**). The result follows from theorem 2.2. ∎

Comment 1 Theorem 2.3 can be readily incorporated into the computer-aided design procedures developed by MacFarlane and his colleagues [65, 124] to permit the evaluation of the robustness of designs against variations of plant transfer function (**H** in this case) within the conic sector Cone (**C**, **R**); the conic sector Cone (**C**, **R**) is characterized in the frequency domain by lemma 2.3.

Theorem 2.3 appears to fill the void in existing stability results pointed out by Rosenbrock and Cook [93].

Because the expression (2.5.19) is a Hermitian matrix (i.e., it is equal to its complex conjugate transposed), its characteristic loci lie on the real axis [40, p. 319].

The well-known circle theorem for single-input single-output feedback systems is a special case of theorem 2.3 in which the cone center and radius parameters are scalars c and r. In the single-input single-output case, we require that the Nyquist locus of $G(s) \in \mathbf{C}^{1\times 1}$ avoid the "critical disc" of radius $\frac{1}{2}\left(\frac{1}{c-r} - \frac{1}{c+r}\right)$ centered at the point $\frac{1}{2}\left(\frac{1}{c-r} + \frac{1}{c+r}\right) + j0 \in \mathbf{C}$, encircling the disc counterclockwise once for each unstable pole of $G(s)$. In theorem 2.3 condition (ii) ensures that the critical disc is avoided and condition (i) ensures that the encirclement condition is satisfied.

Comment 2 It is conjectured that it is possible to relax somewhat condition (i) of lemmas 2.5 and 2.7, possibly even allowing the substitution of *any* $\mathbf{C}' \in$ Cone (**C**, **R**) for **C** in (2.5.13) and *any* $\mathbf{K}' \in +$-Cone (**K**) for **K** in (2.5.16); the latter appears to be consistent with the conditions of the single-input single-output circle theorem. If this conjecture is correct, the testing of conicity would be greatly simplified in some applications. Further research is needed in this area.

2.5.2 Frequency-Domain Tests for Sectoricity—Discrete-Time

Conicity tests analogous to those provided by lemmas 2.4–2.7 are possible for discrete-time systems using z-transforms [50]. In place of $\mathscr{L}_{2e}(\mathrm{R}_+, \mathrm{R}^n)$ and $\mathscr{M}_{2e}(\mathrm{R}_+, \mathrm{R}^n)$, the discrete-time results concern systems defined on extended inner-product spaces of either of the following two types:

$$\text{(i)} \quad \mathscr{X}_e = \mathscr{Y}_e = \ell_{2e}(\mathrm{Z}_+, \mathrm{R}^n) \tag{2.5.20}$$

induced (see equations (2.1.2)–(2.1.4)) by the linear truncation operator (2.1.4) mapping the vector space $\{\xi: Z_+ \to R^n\}$ into

$$\left.\begin{aligned} &\mathscr{X}_\tau = \mathscr{Y}_\tau = \{P_\tau\xi: Z_+ \to R^n \\ &\text{with} \\ &\langle P_\tau\xi_1, P_\tau\xi_2\rangle = \sum_{i=0}^{\tau} \xi_1^T(\tau)\xi_2(\tau) \\ &\|P_\tau\xi\| = (\langle P_\tau\xi, P_\tau\xi\rangle)^{1/2}\}; \end{aligned}\right\} \quad (2.5.21)$$

(ii) $\mathscr{X}_e = \mathscr{Y}_e = {}_{2e}(Z_+, R^n)$ (2.5.22)

induced (see equations (2.1.2)–(2.1.4)] by the linear truncation operator (2.1.4) mapping the vector space $\{\xi: Z_+ \to R^n\}$ into

$$\left.\begin{aligned} &\mathscr{X}_\tau = \mathscr{Y}_\tau = \{P_\tau\xi: Z_+ \to R^n \\ &\text{with} \\ &\langle P_\tau\xi_1, P_\tau\xi_2\rangle = \frac{1}{\tau}\sum_{i=1}^{\tau} \xi_1{}^T(i)\xi_2(i) \\ &\|P_\tau\xi\| = (\langle P_\tau\xi, P_\tau\xi\rangle)^{1/2}\}. \end{aligned}\right\} \quad (2.5.23)$$

The discrete-time analogous lemmas 2.4 and 2.5 are now stated. The only differences between the discrete-time and continuous-time lemmas are the substitution of z-transforms for continuous-time transfer functions and the substitution of complex frequency $e^{j\theta}$ for $j\omega$. The proofs of the following discrete analogues of lemmas 2.6 and 2.7 are not given; they are completely parallel to the continuous-time proofs.

LEMMA 2.8 (Discrete-time Conicity) Let $\mathscr{X}_e$, $\mathscr{Y}_e$ be either as in (2.5.20) or (2.5.22); let $\mathbf{G}$, $\mathbf{C}$, $\mathbf{R}: \mathscr{X}_e \to \mathscr{Y}_e$ be nonanticipative linear time-invariant operators with respective z-transform transfer functions $G(z)$, $C(z)$, $R(z)$; let $\mathbf{R}$ have a nonanticipative inverse $\mathbf{R}^{-1}$; let $\mathbf{G}$, $\mathbf{C}$, and $\mathbf{R}^{-1}$ be stable. If

$$R^T(e^{-j\theta})R(e^{j\theta}) - [G(e^{-j\theta}) - C(e^{-j\theta})]^T[G(e^{j\theta}) - C(e^{j\theta})] - \varepsilon I \geq 0 \quad (2.5.24)$$

for some $\varepsilon \geq 0$ and all $\theta \in [0, \pi]$, then Graph ($\mathbf{G}$) is *inside* Cone ($\mathbf{C}$, $\mathbf{R}$). If (2.5.24) holds with some $\varepsilon > 0$, then Graph ($\mathbf{G}$) is *strictly inside* Cone ($\mathbf{C}$, $\mathbf{R}$).

LEMMA 2.9 (Discrete-time Conicity of Inverse Relations) Let $\mathscr{X}_e$, $\mathscr{Y}_e$ be as in either (2.5.10) or (2.5.22); let $\mathbf{G}: \mathscr{X}_e \to \mathscr{Y}_e$, $\mathbf{C}$, $\mathbf{R}: \mathscr{Y}_e \to \mathscr{X}_e$ be nonanticipative linear time-invariant operators with respective z-transform transfer functions $G(z)$, $C(z)$, $R(z)$. Assume that **R** is stable, and that det $[G(e^{j\theta})] \neq 0$ or ∞ for all $\theta \in [0, \pi]$. Then, [Graph (**G**)]$^{\mathbf{I}}$ is *outside* Cone (**C**, **R**) if the following two conditions are satisfied:

(i) The *linear time-invariant* feedback system

$$\begin{aligned} x &= \mathbf{G}(y + u) \\ y &= \mathbf{C}(x + v) \\ u &\in \mathscr{Y}_e \\ v &\in \mathscr{X}_e \end{aligned} \tag{2.5.25}$$

is nonanticipative and closed-loop stable.

(ii) For all $\theta \in [0, \pi]$,

$$\begin{aligned} &[I - C(e^{-j\theta})G(e^{-j\theta})]^T[I - C(e^{j\theta})G(e^{j\theta})] \\ &\quad - [R(e^{-j\theta})G(e^{-j\theta})]^T[R(e^{j\theta})G(e^{j\theta})] \geq 0. \quad \blacksquare \end{aligned} \tag{2.5.26}$$

2.6 Design of Robustly Stable Feedback

In this section, we discuss the application of theorem 2.2 to the design of robustly stable feedback laws for systems consisting of an arbitrary interconnection of conic elements. It is assumed that there are a finite number of elements, say N, and that the precise dynamical relations associated with the elements, say $\mathbf{H}_i$ (i = 1, . . . , N), are not known; it is known only that the $\mathbf{H}_i$ are *strictly inside* conic sectors Cone $(\mathbf{C}_i, \mathbf{R}_i) \subset \mathscr{X}_e^{(i)} \times \mathscr{Y}_e^{(i)}$ (i = 1, . . . , N). The cone center and radius parameters $\mathbf{C}_i$ and $\mathbf{R}_i$ are presumed to be linear time-invariant operators with respective transfer functions $\mathbf{C}_i(s)$ and $\mathbf{R}_i(s)$. The relations $\overline{\mathbf{H}}_i$ are presumed to be the graphs of either memoryless nonlinear operators or linear time-invariant operators; this ensures that the results of section 2.5 can be used to check conicity.[9]

For simplicity, we assume that the decomposition is such that the $\mathbf{H}_i$ are single-input single-output—in this case, cone parameters for memoryless elements can be obtained by inspection of experimentally acquired ensembles of graphs in the real plane and cone parameters for linear dynamical elements can be obtained from experimentally acquired ensembles of Bode-plot data. The interconnection structure of the system is specified by

9 Some nonlinear dynamical operators can also be admitted by using lemma 2.3.

an N × N matrix $A(s)$ whose elements are single-input single-output transfer functions

$$A_{ij}(s) = \begin{cases}\text{The transfer function of the interconnection between} \\ \text{the output of element i and the input of element j.}\end{cases} \tag{2.6.1}$$

The inputs available for control and outputs available for measurement are likewise specified by matrices $B_1(s)$ and $B_2(s)$ respectively, the elements of which are transfer functions. We define the composite spaces $\mathscr{X}_e$, $\mathscr{Y}_e$ and the operator $\mathbf{H}: \mathscr{X}_e \to \mathscr{Y}_e$ by

$$\mathscr{X}_e = \mathscr{X}_e^{(1)} \times \cdots \times \mathscr{X}_e^{(N)} \tag{2.6.2}$$

$$\mathscr{Y}_e = \mathscr{Y}_e^{(1)} \times \cdots \times \mathscr{Y}_e^{(N)} \tag{2.6.3}$$

$$\mathbf{H}x = \begin{bmatrix} \mathbf{H}_1 x_1 \\ \vdots \\ \mathbf{H}_N x_N \end{bmatrix} \tag{2.6.4}$$

for all $x \equiv (x_1, \ldots, x_N) \in \mathscr{X}_e$. Assuming that the available measurements are fed back to the available inputs through a linear time-invariant feedback operator $\mathbf{F}$ with transfer function $F(s)$, the (undisturbed) composite interconnected system is governed by the feedback equations

$$\begin{aligned} y &= \mathbf{H}x \\ x &= \mathbf{G}y, \end{aligned} \tag{2.6.5}$$

where

$$\mathbf{G} \equiv \mathbf{B}_1 \circ \mathbf{F} \circ \mathbf{B}_2 + \mathbf{A} \tag{2.6.6}$$

(figure 2.7).

To characterize the set of admissible feedbacks $F(s)$, we observe that, by sector property (vi), Graph ($\mathbf{H}$) is inside Cone ($\mathbf{C}, \mathbf{R}$) where $\mathbf{C}, \mathbf{R}: \mathscr{X}_e \to \mathscr{Y}_e$ are the mappings defined by

$$\begin{aligned} \mathbf{C}x &= (\mathbf{C}_1 x_1, \ldots, \mathbf{C}_N x_N) \\ \mathbf{R}x &= (\mathbf{R}_1 x_1, \ldots, \mathbf{R}_N x_N) \end{aligned} \tag{2.6.7}$$

By the theorem 2.2, the system (2.6.5) is closed-loop stable if

$$[\text{Graph}(\mathbf{B}_1 \circ \mathbf{F} \circ \mathbf{B}_2 + \mathbf{A})]^{\mathrm{I}} \text{ outside Cone}(\mathbf{C}, \mathbf{R}), \tag{2.6.8}$$

a condition which may be checked in the frequency domain using lemma

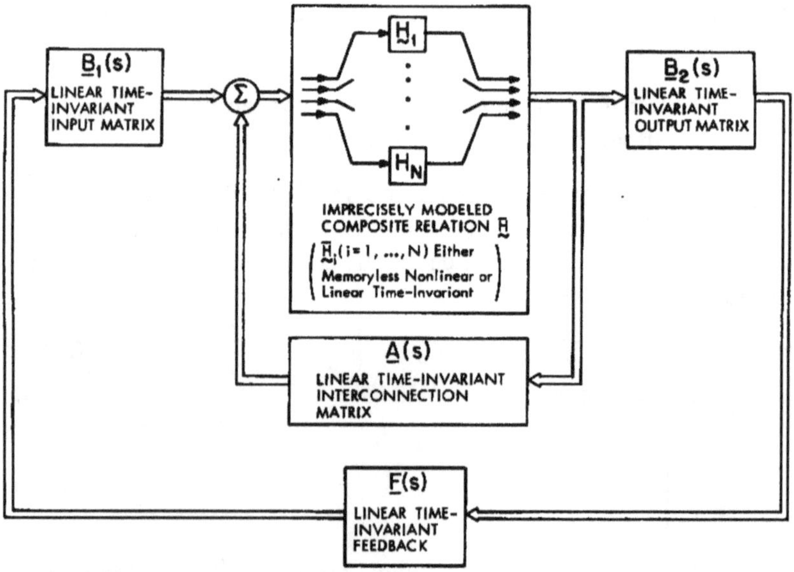

Figure **2.7** Composite interconnected system.

2.5 (and a digital computer to assist with the computations).

This provides the design engineer with a practical test for the robustness of a given feedback design $F(s)$. However, the task of finding a feedback law $F(s)$ satisfying (2.6.8) (and any other design constraints in addition to closed-loop stability) is a problem for which no systematic solution is as yet available. An obvious approach is to design the feedback $\mathbf{F}$ assuming that $\mathbf{H} = \mathbf{C}$ so that the system meets specifications at least when $\mathbf{R} \rightarrow O$—any multivariable linear time-invariant feedback synthesis technique can be used for this (e.g., LQG [9], characteristic locus [65], inverse Nyquist array [90], or pole assignment [18, ch. 7]). The design can then be iteratively adjusted to achieve the required robustness (i.e., to increase the radius of the cone that $\mathbf{B}_1 \circ \mathbf{F} \circ \mathbf{B}_2 + \mathbf{A}$ lies outside).

This procedure for the design of robustly stable feedback laws is summarized in the following four steps:

STEP 1 Decompose the system into an interconnection of imprecisely modeled single-input single output subsystems $\mathbf{H}_i$ which are either linear time-invariant or nondynamical; from experimental data, determine conic sectors including the relations of the subsystems $\mathbf{H}_i$.

STEP 2 Compute the sector of the composite **H** and compute the interconnection matrix $A(s)$, the control input matrix $B_1(s)$ and the measurement output matrix $B(s)$.

STEP 3 Compute the sector of admissible feedbacks (2.6.8).

STEP 4 Design the feedback $F(s)$ for the nominal linear system **C** using standard linear design techniques; iteratively adjust the design to satisfy the robustness constraint (2.6.8).

Comment In practice, step 4 may be the most difficult, as no well-defined algorithm is, as yet, available for iteratively adjusting the design to satisfy (2.6.8)—though the numerical methods such as [84] or [85] may prove to be of value here.

2.7 Critique

From a theoretical viewpoint, the simple geometric interpretation of the stability of feedback systems in terms of a topological separation constitutes a substantial simplification in the conceptual model required to explain stability theory. Besides leading directly to a powerful abstraction of previous input-output stability results (theorem 2.1), it makes clear the general approach that must be taken to generate new results such as theorem 2.2. The conceptual simplicity of the geometric interpretation of stability theory is also of considerable pedagogical value, since it makes it possible to adequately illustrate the fundamental concepts underlying the various stability criteria and their proofs using a single two-dimensional drawing, e.g., figure 2.5.

From an engineering standpoint, the significance of the results appears to be primarily with regard to the design of robustly stable multivariable feedback laws for imprecisely modeled linear or nonlinear multivariable plants. Used in connection with available linear system-feedback design techniques, the results provide a multivariable stability criterion, well suited to a computer-aided design environment, which can be used to verify that a given feedback design meets specifications calling for closed-loop stability in the presence of nonlinearity and parameter variations, singular perturbations, and other sorts of bounded imprecision in the design model.

2.7.1 Relation to Classical Feedback Theory

The results provide a practical multivariable generalization of "classical" single-input single-output (SISO) system-feedback design tools involving Bode plots, Nichols charts, Nyquist loci, etc. In particular, classical frequency-domain concerns having to do with gain margin, phase margin, and bandwidth fit neatly into the multivariable theory developed in sections 2.4–2.6.

For example, consider the cones Cone $(\mathbf{C}_i, \mathbf{R}_i)$ associated with the subsystems $\mathbf{H}_i$ $(i = 1, \ldots, N)$ of the multivariable feedback system considered in section 2.6. The specification of the cone parameters $\mathbf{C}_i$ and $\mathbf{R}_i$ can be viewed as equivalent to a specification of *frequency-dependent* gain and phase margins [43, p. 148] for the composite multivariable feedback system; these conicity conditions give *each subsystem* $\mathbf{H}_i$ a *gain margin* of $20 \log [1 + |R_i(j\omega)|/|C_i(j\omega)|]$ db and a *phase margin* of $2 \arcsin [|R_i(j\omega)|/|2C_i(j\omega)|]$, the margins being relative to the ideal situation $\mathbf{H}_i = \mathbf{C}_i$ $(i = 1, \ldots, N)$. Any variations in the open-loop dynamics of the subsystems producing either gain changes or phase changes within these margins cannot destabilize the closed-loop composite system even when the variations occur simultaneously in several or all of the subsystems. Because the conicity conditions permit frequency-dependent specification of the stability margins, they are in this regard more flexible than the classical notion of gain and phase margin; but it should be noted that the conicity conditions do not permit gain and phase margin to be specified independently.

As a second example of the tie between the present results and the concerns of classical feedback theory, consider the issue of bandwidth. In classical feedback design, a rule of thumb is that the loop gain of a SISO system must be much less than one at frequencies above which the uncertainty in the plant transfer function becomes comparable in magnitude to the plant transfer function itself [43, p. 297]. This qualitative notion is made precise and extended to multivariable systems in condition (ii) of lemma 2.5 and of theorem 2.3.

2.7.2 Relation to Lyapunov Theory and Optimal Control

From corollaries 2.1a and 2.1b, it can be seen that a Lyapunov function for a stable system, either discrete or continuous time, naturally induces a conicity condition on the system which, if satisfied, ensures the stability of the system. Consequently, in situations where there is available a Lyapunov function for a feedback design, the conic sector induced by the Lyapunov function is a logical choice for evaluating the robustness of the feedback design against variations in the system's dynamics.

In the case of feedback laws designed using optimal control methods, the optimal solution of the Hamilton-Jacobi equation [7, p. 357] naturally provides a Lyapunov function for the optimal feedback design. In chapters 3 and 4 of this monograph, there is an in-depth discussion of the robustness of linear-quadratic-Gaussian optimal feedback designs [9, 10] based on the sectors induced by the Lyapunov functions generated by the Hamilton-Jacobi equation; for the linear-quadratic-Gaussian optimal control problem, the optimal solution of the Hamilton-Jacobi equation is a quadratic form involving the solution of the well-known matrix Riccati equation.

2.7.3 Limitations of Stability as a Criterion for Robustness

In practical feedback-system design, we are generally interested in ensuring that the design robustly meets a variety of specifications, in addition to the requirement of closed-loop stability, e.g., specifications involving response time, overshoot, disturbance rejection, etc. These other types of considerations must be accounted for in the feedback design by imposing constraints on the class of admissible feedback laws in addition to the sector conditions imposed to ensure closed-loop stability.

For example, to achieve faster response time or improvements in other properties related to stability, the norms on the spaces $\mathscr{X}_\tau$, $\mathscr{Y}_\tau$ can be chosen such that functions which do not behave as desired are unstable, i.e., have an unbounded norm—e.g., an exponentially weighted norm can be used. It has been shown in [27, pp. 143–146] that in the case of certain frequency-domain stability tests for SISO systems, the use of an exponentially weighted norm leads to the conclusion that exponential stability with exponential rate of decay $\theta^{-\alpha t}$ is assured if $j\omega - \alpha$ is substituted for $j\omega$ in the stability tests; these results extend easily to the multivariable frequency-domain tests of the conditions of the sector stability criterion developed in section 2.5.

With regard to robust disturbance rejection, it is known (see, e.g., [29] or [30]) that for linear systems to reject disturbances with zero steady-state error—and this includes tracking set-point changes in adjustable set-point regulator designs with zero steady-state error—a servo-compensator containing an internal model of the disturbance process should be incorporated in the feedback. For meeting disturbance rejection specifications, this constraint should be imposed on the feedback in addition to the sector constraints imposed to meet stability and response-time specifications.

2.7.4 Potential Applications and Extensions

Gain Scheduling In the design of adjustable set-point regulators for nonlinear systems, it is common engineering practice to "schedule" the feedback gains according to the system's current operating point. Feedback gains are designed for each of several system operating points using a linearized model of the system which approximates the dynamical behavior of the actual nonlinear system at, and near, the corresponding operating point; the actual feedback used with other operating points is usually obtained through some sort of interpolation. Sector conditions can provide a rigorous justification of the approximations used in gain scheduling, and, more important from a practical point of view, they can give an engineer the insight needed to make constructive design modifications when simulation results show that the approximations have failed. The latter can be accomplished by examining where the sector conditions are violated: this provides information helpful in choosing additional feedback design points, in adjusting the interpolation procedure, and in identifying other possible types of corrective action.

Hierarchical Design In the design of feedback laws for large complex systems, it has long been recognized that reasonably simple practical feedback laws can be obtained via decomposition and aggregation methods: the system in question is decomposed hierarchically into groups of subsystems, sub-subsystems, etc.; controls are designed for the elements at the bottom of the hierarchy, say the sub-subsystems, assuming no interaction among sub-subsystems; an aggregated (i.e., simplified) model of each subsystem (each group of sub-subsystems) is then developed retaining only those inputs and outputs deemed necessary and frequently neglecting fast time constants. A control is designed for each aggregated subsystem, and so forth. Justification of the approximations inherent in this procedure has been based largely on its empirically proven success, engineers gaining the insight needed to make the design approximations from physical insight and from classical feedback considerations pertaining to the admissible trade-offs between modeling uncertainty and bandwidth [43, p. 297]. The sector stability criterion appears to be capable of providing a rigorous justification for approximations made in hierarchical feedback design by providing quantitative sector-type bounds on just how crude the approximations may be, but further research is needed to determine to what extent the sector stability criterion can be of use as a hierarchical-system design tool.

Random Sectors A limitation of the sector constraints is that they may tend to be overly restrictive for large systems. This is a consequence of the fact that theorem 2.2 ensures stability even under "worst case" conditions when all of the system relations are at the very boundaries of their respective sectors: a situation which may in fact be improbable. For example, in electrical circuits having components the values of which are imprecisely known (but known to satisfy some probability distribution), it may make sense to specify that the circuit be unstable with at most some finite probability, say 10^{-5}. Circuits which, after assembly, test out unstable, could then be economically repaired or discarded. It may prove to be feasible to use random cone center and radius operators **C** and **R** to characterize the probabilistic nature of the imprecision of the design model; thus, it would be possible to specify a probability that the sector conditions would be violated, giving an upper bound on the likelihood of the system being unstable.

Further research is needed in this area. With appropriate assumptions on the random distributions (e.g., Gaussian), it may actually prove to be computationally simpler to verify conicity by using random cone parameters in some problems—much as the Gaussian assumption in linear estimation results in a simpler estimator than the unknown-but-bounded assumption (see [104]).

3

LQG Robustness and Stability: The Continuous-Time Case

3.1 Introduction

A limitation of the linear-quadratic Gaussian (LQG) procedure for estimator and controller design [9] lies in its failure to explicitly incorporate consideration of the stability margins of the resultant designs. That is, the LQG procedure overlooks the possible destabilizing effects of modeling errors; such errors can arise due to parameter variations, neglect of short time constants, linearization, etc. In the following chapters, results are developed which provide a characterization of the stability margins of LQG designs.

Following a discussion of notation and a formal statement of the problem in sections 3.2 and 3.3, we examine in section 3.4 the stability margins of the optimal linear-quadratic state-feedback (LQSF) regulator, explicitly parameterizing a convex set of nondestabilizing deviations in open-loop dynamics about the linear design model and showing that the LQSF optimal-design procedure has a certain inherent robustness. It is shown that the optimal-design procedure automatically ensures an infinite gain margin, at least a $\pm 60°$ phase margin and at least a 50% gain reduction tolerance in each control input channel, as well as substantial tolerance of nonlinearity.

In section 3.5, a suboptimal estimator for nonlinear stochastic systems is proposed and results are developed that provide a characterization of the stability margins of the estimator and give sufficient conditions for its nondivergence. An important practical implication of the result is that in many suboptimal nonlinear filtering applications, one can obtain satisfactory performance from a constant-gain extended Kalman filter (CGEKF), i.e., an extended Kalman filter employing a precomputed constant residual-gain matrix. Because its residual gain is precomputed, the real-time computational burden of the CGEKF is an order of magnitude smaller than that of the usual extended Kalman filter (which employs a time-varying residual-gain matrix that is adaptively updated on-line). The results prove that the CGEKF is intrinsically robust against the effects of approximations introduced in the design of its residual-gain matrix; i.e., the results prove that the CGEKF design approach yields a *nondivergent* nonlinear estimator, even when a relatively crude stochastic model is used in designing the residual gain. The stability margin results take the form of analytically verifiable conditions on the system nonlinearities which can also be used to test specific CGEKF designs for nondivergence, reducing the engineer's dependence on Monte Carlo simulation for design validation and providing insight useful for constructively making design modifications.

The linear-quadratic state-feedback robustness results combine with the constant-gain extended Kalman filter estimator results in a fashion reminiscent of the separation theorem of estimation and control. It is proven in section 3.6 that a nondivergent CGEKF can be cascaded with an otherwise stable linear-quadratic state-feedback gain matrix to produce a dynamical output-feedback compensator for which closed-loop stability is assured. The inherent robustness of the CGEKF and of linear-quadratic state feedback combine to ensure that such designs will be closed-loop stable, even in systems with substantial nonlinearity.

Moreover, the nondivergence and stability margin results are such as to provide a basis for the constructive modification and improvement of estimator and compensator designs. The design implications are discussed in section 3.7, where it is explained how the results can be especially useful in solving gain-scheduling problems for nonlinear systems.

In section 3.8, we discuss the implications of the results with regard to various modifications of the linear-quadratic Gaussian procedure. It is shown that the results extend directly to modifications involving simple state augmentation, e.g., linear-quadratic proportional integral feedback [47, 49, 99] and to a nonlinear constant-gain extension of the compensated Kalman filter [8].

The proofs, which are based on theorem 2.2, are contained in the appendixes.

3.2 Notation and Terminology

The input-output view of systems is taken, considering a system to be an interconnection of "black boxes" each representable by its input-output characteristics. As will become apparent, the input-output view provides a convenient and natural setting for the discussion and analysis of estimator robustness and divergence, as well as feedback system stability. In this section the pertinent terminology drawn from [27], [42], [110], and [118] is reviewed and the notion of estimator divergence is formalized.

An *operator* is a mapping of functions into functions—such as is defined by a black box which maps input time functions into output time functions. A operator is said to be *nonanticipative* if the value assumed by its output function at any time instant t_0 does not depend on the values assumed by its input function at times $t > t_0$. An operator is said to be *memoryless* or equivalently *nondynamical* if the instantaneous value of its output at time t_0 depends only on the value of its input at time t_0. A *dynamical* operator is an operator which is not necessarily nondynamical.

To facilitate the discussion, the continuous-time input and output functions considered herein are presumed to be imbedded in extended normed spaces of the type

$$\mathscr{M}_{2e}(R_+, R^r) \triangleq \{z: R_+ \to R^r\} \tag{3.2.1}$$

[23, p. 125], with which are associated for each $\tau \in R_+$ the inner product and norm

$$\langle z_1, z_2 \rangle_\tau \triangleq \frac{1}{\tau} \int_0^\tau z_1^T(t) z_2(t)\, dt \tag{3.2.2}$$

$$\|z\|_\tau \triangleq \sqrt{\langle z, z \rangle_\tau}. \tag{3.2.3}$$

The discrete-time input and output functions considered in chapter 4 are presumed to be imbedded in extended normed spaces of the type[1]

1 Z_+ denotes the nonnegative integers.

$$m_{2e}(Z_+, R^r) \triangleq \{x: Z_+ \to R^r\} \tag{3.2.4}$$

with which are associated for each $\tau \in Z_+$ the inner product and norm

$$\langle x_1, x_2 \rangle_\tau = \frac{1}{\tau} \sum_{t=0}^{\tau} x_1^T(t) x_2(t) \tag{3.2.5}$$

$$\|x\|_\tau = (\langle x, x \rangle)^{1/2}. \tag{3.2.6}$$

The quantity $\|z\|_\tau^2$ can be viewed as the "average power" in the function z; in fact, if z is generated by an ergodic random process [78, pg. 327], then $\lim_{\tau\to\infty} \|z\|_\tau^2$ is simply the expected value of $z^T(t)z(t)$.

Because the space $\mathscr{M}_{2e}$ may be unfamiliar to many readers, I briefly discuss its relation to the similar, but distinct, space $\mathscr{L}_{2e}$ which is more widely used in input-output system analysis. The feature that distinguishes $\mathscr{M}_{2e}$ from $\mathscr{L}_{2e}$ is the introduction of the normalizing factor $1/\tau$ into the inner product (3.2.2). Whereas the $\mathscr{L}_{2e}$-norm is appropriately viewed as a measure of the "total energy" of a function, the normalizing factor $1/\tau$ leads to the "average power" interpretation of the norm (3.2.3). The space $\mathscr{M}_{2e}$ is larger than $\mathscr{L}_{2e}$, every function in $\mathscr{L}_{2e}$ being included in the subspace of $\mathscr{M}_{2e}$ comprised of functions of zero norm. The space m_{2e} has an analogous relation to the space l_{2e}.

The *gain* and *norm* of an operator **F**, denoted g(**F**) and $\|\mathbf{F}\|$ respectively, are defined by

$$g(\mathbf{F}) \triangleq \|\mathbf{F}\| \triangleq \sup_{0<\|z\|_\tau<\infty} \frac{\|\mathbf{F}z\|_\tau}{\|z\|_\tau}. \tag{3.2.7}$$

The *incremental gain* of **F** is

$$\tilde{g}(\mathbf{F}) \triangleq \sup_{0<\|z_1-z_2\|_\tau<\infty} \frac{\|\mathbf{F}z_1 - \mathbf{F}z_2\|_\tau}{\|z_1 - z_2\|_\tau}. \tag{3.2.8}$$

If $g(\mathbf{F}) < \infty$, **F** is said to have *finite gain*. Likewise, if $\tilde{g}(\mathbf{F}) < \infty$, then **F** is said to have *finite incremental gain*. The operator **F** is *bounded* if inputs of finite norm produce outputs of finite norm; i.e., there exists a continuous increasing function $\rho: R \to R$ such that for all z $\|\mathbf{F}z\| < \rho(\|z\|)$. A dynamical system is said to be *bounded* if the operator describing its input-output characteristics is bounded; the system is said to be *finite-gain stable* if the operator has finite gain. An operator **F** is said to be *strongly positive*, denoted $\mathbf{F} > 0$, if for some $\varepsilon > 0$ and all z and all τ

$$\langle z, \mathbf{F}z \rangle_\tau \geq \varepsilon \|z\|_\tau^2. \tag{3.2.9}$$

If $\{\mathbf{F}(x) | x \in \mathscr{X}\}$ is a collection of operators whose input-output relations are dependent upon the variable $x \in \mathscr{X}$, and if for some constant $\varepsilon > 0$ (3.2.6) holds for every $\mathbf{F} \in \{\mathscr{F}(x) | x \in \mathscr{X}\}$, then the collection of operators $\{\mathbf{F}(x) | x \in \mathscr{X}\}$ is said to be *uniformly strongly positive*; equivalently, one may write "uniformly $\mathbf{F}(x) > 0$." An operator $\mathbf{F}$ is said to be *positive*, denoted $\mathbf{F} > 0$, if (3.2.6) holds with $\varepsilon = 0$. The *derivative* of the operator $\mathbf{F}$ at the point z_0 is defined to be the linear operator $\nabla\mathbf{F}(z_0)$ having the property that for all z

$$\nabla\mathbf{F}(z_0)z = \lim_{\varepsilon \to 0} \frac{1}{\varepsilon}[\mathbf{F}(z_0 + \varepsilon z) - \mathbf{F}z_0], \tag{3.2.10}$$

provided that the indicated limit exists. When the derivative $\nabla\mathbf{F}(z_0)$ exists, $\mathbf{F}$ is said to be *differentiable* at z_0. For example, if $\mathbf{F}$ is memoryless, i.e., if $(\mathbf{F}z)(t) = f[z(t)]$ for some $f\colon R^r \to R^p$, then $\nabla\mathbf{F}(z)$ is simply the *Jacobian matrix* $\partial f/\partial z$ [42, p. 17]. Alternatively, if $\mathbf{F}$ is a linear operator, then $\nabla\mathbf{F}(z) = \mathbf{F}$ for all z.

If $\mathbf{F}$ is an operator mapping the set $\mathscr{X}$ into the set $\mathscr{Y}$, Graph ($\mathbf{F}$) is the set of all pairs $(x, y) \in \mathscr{X} \times \mathscr{Y}$ such that $y = \mathbf{F}x$ for some $x \in \mathscr{X}$, i.e.,

$$\mathrm{Graph}(\mathbf{F}) \triangleq \{(x, y) \mid y = \mathbf{F}x;\, x \in \mathscr{X}\}. \tag{3.2.11}$$

If $\mathbf{C}$ and $\mathbf{R}$ are finite-gain mappings of an inner-product space $\mathscr{X}$ into itself, then Cone ($\mathbf{C}, \mathbf{R}$) is the set of all pairs $(x, y) \in \mathscr{X} \times \mathscr{X}$ such that $\|y - \mathbf{C}x\|_\tau^2 \le \|\mathbf{R}x\|_\tau^2$; $\mathbf{C}$ and $\mathbf{R}$ are called respectively the cone *center* and *radius*. If

$$\mathrm{Graph}(\mathbf{F}) \subset \mathrm{Cone}(\mathbf{C}, \mathbf{R}), \tag{3.2.12}$$

then we say Graph ($\mathbf{F}$) is *inside* Cone ($\mathbf{C}, \mathbf{R}$), denoted equivalently by

$$\mathrm{Graph}(\mathbf{F}) \text{ inside } \mathrm{Cone}(\mathbf{C}, \mathbf{R}). \tag{3.2.13}$$

If

$$\|y - \mathbf{C}x\|_\tau^2 \le \|\mathbf{R}x\|_\tau^2 - \varepsilon(\|x\|_\tau^2 + \|y\|_\tau^2) \tag{3.2.14}$$

for some $\varepsilon > 0$ and for every $(x, y) \in$ Graph ($\mathbf{F}$), then we may say Graph ($\mathbf{F}$) is *strictly inside* Cone ($\mathbf{C}, \mathbf{R}$), denoted

$$\mathrm{Graph}(\mathbf{F}) \text{ strictly inside } \mathrm{Cone}(\mathbf{C}, \mathbf{R}). \tag{3.2.15}$$

If $\{\mathscr{F}(x) \mid x \in \mathscr{X}\}$ is a collection of operators whose input-output relations are dependent upon the variable $x \in \mathscr{X}$ and if for some constant $\varepsilon > 0$

(3.2.10) holds for every $\mathbf{F} \in \{\mathbf{F}(x) \mid x \in \mathscr{X}\}$, then the collection $\{\mathbf{F}(x) \mid x \in \mathscr{X}\}$ is said to be *uniformly strictly inside* Cone $(\mathbf{C}, \mathbf{R})$; equivalently one may write "uniformly Graph $(\mathbf{F}(x))$ strictly inside Cone $(\mathbf{C}, \mathbf{R})$."

The relevance of the foregoing terminology to estimation stems from the fact that for each control input function u, the error $e \triangleq \hat{x} - x$ of an estimator can be represented as the output of an operator $\mathbf{E}_u$ whose inputs are the system noise, say ξ, and measurement noise, say θ; i.e.,

$$e \triangleq \hat{x} - x = \mathbf{E}_u(\xi, \theta). \tag{3.2.16}$$

To formalize the notion of estimator divergence, the following definitions are introduced: an estimator is *nondivergent* if its error operator is bounded uniformly in u, i.e., if there exists a continuous increasing function $\rho: \mathrm{R} \rightarrow \mathrm{R}$ such that

$$\sup_{u,\tau} \|\mathbf{E}_u(\xi, \theta)\|_\tau \leq \rho(\|(\xi, \theta)\|_\tau). \tag{3.2.17}$$

It is *convergent* if $\rho(\cdot) \equiv 0$; it is *nondivergent with finite gain* if

$$\sup_u g(\mathbf{E}_u) < \infty. \tag{3.2.18}$$

Evidently, convergence implies nondivergence with finite gain, which in turn implies nondivergence. These definitions can be loosely interpreted as follows: an estimator is nondivergent if mean-square-bounded disturbances produce mean-square-bounded error in the estimate; it is nondivergent with finite gain if the mean-square error in the estimate is proportional to the magnitude of the disturbances; it is convergent if the mean-square error always tends to zero. An estimator that is not nondivergent is said to be *divergent.*

3.3 Problem Formulation

The results that follow concern the problems of estimation and control for the nonlinear dynamical system (figure 3.1)

$$\begin{aligned} \frac{\mathrm{d}}{\mathrm{dt}} x &= \mathbf{A}(\mathrm{v}) + \mathbf{B}(\mathrm{v})u + \xi; \qquad x(0^-) = 0, \\ y &= \mathbf{C}(\mathrm{v})x + \theta, \end{aligned} \tag{3.3.1}$$

where

v is a vector of functions including y, u, t as well as all other *known* or *observed* functions (e.g., estimates $\hat{x}$ of x generated from observations and

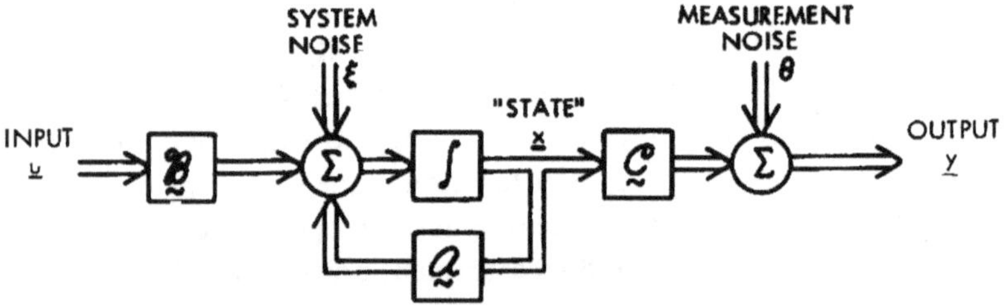

Figure 3.1 The system (A, B, C nonlinear dynamical elements).

known exogenous inputs to the system);
A, **B**, **C** are nonanticipative, differentiable, dynamical nonlinear operators with finite incremental gain and which may in general be nonanticipatively dependent of v;[2]
$\xi \in \mathcal{M}_{2e}(R_+, R^n)$, $\theta \in \mathcal{M}_{2e}(R_+, R^p)$ are disturbance input functions (i.e., noise);
y is an R^p-valued observed output function;
u is an R^m-valued control input function;
x is an R^n-valued function which is to be controlled and/or estimated, depending on the problem specifications.
For simplicity, it is further assumed that the coordinates have been chosen such that $\mathbf{A}0 = 0$, $\mathbf{B}0 = 0$, and $\mathbf{C}0 = 0$. It is conceptually helpful to think of the vector $x(t)$ as the "state" of the system (3.3.1), though this is not rigorously correct except when **A**, **B**, and **C** are nondynamical.

For estimation and control of the system (3.3.1), three structures are considered:

(i) *Nonlinear State-Feedback Controller* (figure 3.2a):

$$u = G(v)x, \tag{3.3.2}$$

where $G(v)$ is an m × n matrix whose elements are dependent on v.

(ii) *Nonlinear Observer Estimator* (figure 3.2b):

$$\frac{d}{dt}\hat{x} = \mathbf{A}\hat{x} + \mathbf{B}u - H(v)(\hat{y} - y); \qquad \hat{x}(0^-) = 0$$
$$\hat{y} = \mathbf{C}\hat{x}, \tag{3.3.3}$$

2 For brevity of notation the dependence of **A**, **B**, **C** on ν is suppressed here and in the sequel, except where clarity mandates its presence.

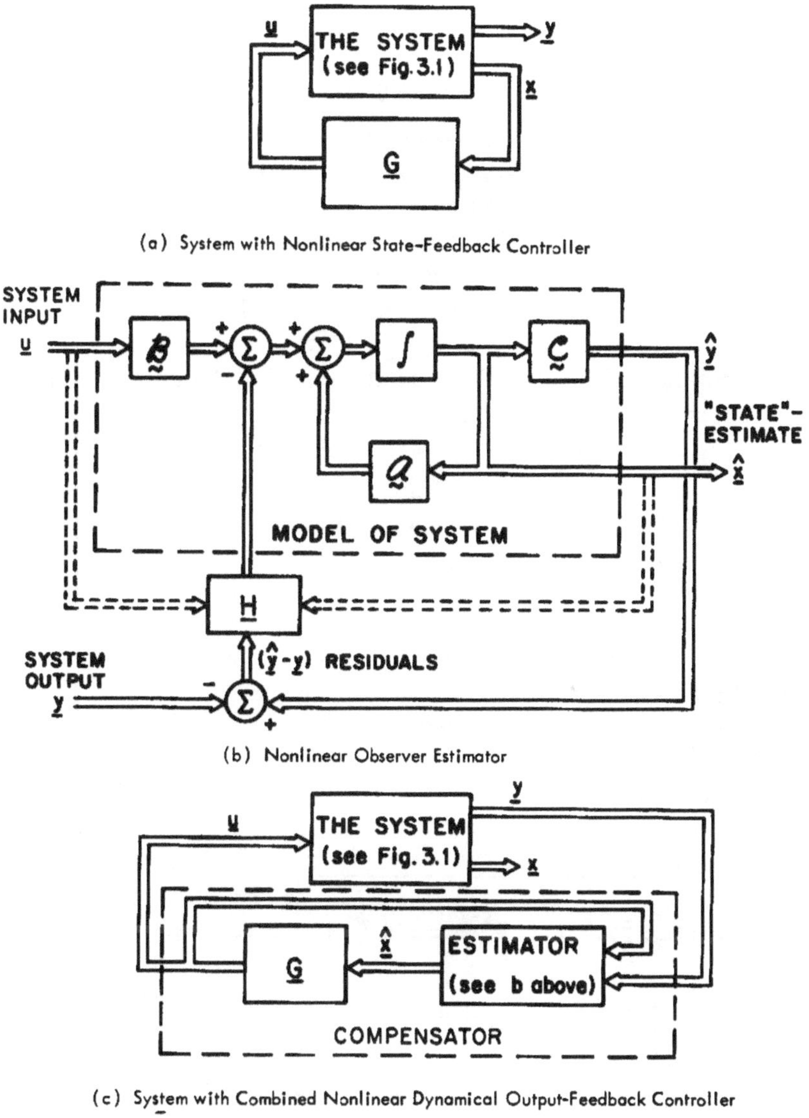

(a) System with Nonlinear State-Feedback Controller

(b) Nonlinear Observer Estimator

(c) System with Combined Nonlinear Dynamical Output-Feedback Controller

Figure 3.2 Controller and estimator structures.

where $H(v)$ is an n × p matrix whose elements are dependent on u and on the current "state" estimate $\hat{x}(t)$.

(iii) *Combined Nonlinear Dynamical Output-Feedback Controller* (figure 3.2c):

$$u = -G(\text{v})\hat{x}$$

$$\frac{\text{d}}{\text{dt}}\hat{x} = \mathbf{A}\hat{x} + \mathbf{B}u - H(\text{v})(\hat{y} - y); \qquad \hat{x}(0^-) = 0 \tag{3.3.4}$$

$$\hat{y} = \mathbf{C}\hat{x},$$

where $G(\cdot)$ and $H(\cdot)$ are as above.

The stability margins and robustness properties of suboptimal nonlinear linear-quadratic-Gaussian estimator and controller designs are addressed as special cases or results pertaining to the structures (3.3.2)–(3.3.4).

A useful method for describing the dynamical evolution of the nonlinear observer's error

$$e \triangleq \hat{x} - x,$$

is by the feedback equations (see figure 3.3):

$$\left.\begin{aligned} \frac{\text{d}}{\text{dt}}e &= \tilde{\mathbf{A}}(x)e + v; \qquad e(0^-) = 0 \\ r &= \tilde{\mathbf{C}}(x)e - \theta \end{aligned}\right\} \tag{3.3.5}$$

$$v \triangleq -H(\text{v})r - \xi, \tag{3.3.6}$$

where

$$r \triangleq \hat{y} - y \tag{3.3.7}$$

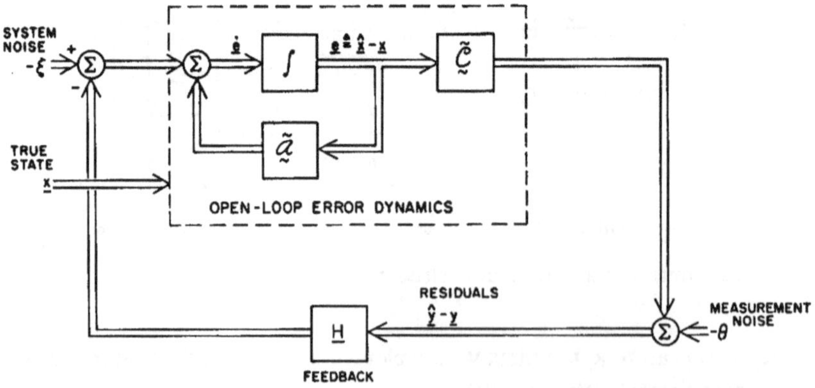

Figure 3.3 Feedback representation of the error dynamics of the nonlinear observer.

and $\tilde{\mathbf{A}}(x)$ and $\tilde{\mathbf{C}}(x)$ are dynamical nonlinear operators defined by

$$\tilde{\mathbf{A}}(x)\delta x \triangleq \mathbf{A}(x + \delta x) - \mathbf{A}x \tag{3.3.8}$$

$$\tilde{\mathbf{C}}(x)\delta x \triangleq \mathbf{C}(x + \delta x) - \mathbf{C}x \tag{3.3.9}$$

for all $\delta x \in \mathscr{M}_2(\mathrm{R}_+, \mathrm{R}^n)$. From this feedback representation of the nonlinear observer estimator (figure 3.3), it is immediately evident that the problem of choosing a residual gain $H(\cdot)$ so as to make the estimator nondivergent is equivalent to the problem of choosing a stabilizing feedback for the system (3.3.5).

In order to facilitate the selection of suitable state-feedback-gain and residual-gain matrices ($G(\cdot)$ and $H(\cdot)$, respectively), it is assumed that, given any given value of v (e.g., $\mathrm{v} = \mathrm{v}_0$), the system (3.3.1) admits a nominal constant linearization approximating its behavior for v near v_0:

$$\begin{aligned} \frac{\mathrm{d}}{\mathrm{dt}}\delta x &= A(\mathrm{v})\delta x + B(\mathrm{v})\delta u + \xi; \qquad \delta x(0^-) = 0 \\ \delta y &= C(\mathrm{v})\delta u + \theta, \end{aligned} \tag{3.3.10}$$

where $A(\mathrm{v})$, $B(\mathrm{v})$, and $C(\mathrm{v})$ are constant matrices of appropriate dimensions whose entries in general depend on v_0. The idea is to design the gains $G(\cdot)$ and $H(\cdot)$ assuming v_0 is fixed; the nonlinear control and estimation problem is thus reduced to a linear time-invariant problem for which a variety of methods is available for designing $\mathrm{G}(\cdot)$ and $H(\cdot)$, e.g., pole-assignment, linear-quadratic-Gaussian optimization, etc. As with **A, B, C,** the v-dependence of A, B, C, G, and H is suppressed in the sequel, except where clarity mandates its presence. Clearly, the simplest controller and estimator structures (3.3.2)–(3.3.4) result when A, B, C, and hence G and H, are chosen to be independent of their arguments.

3.4 State-Feedback Stability Margins

In this section, we characterize the stability margins of the closed-loop system resulting when the nonlinear state feedback (3.3.2) is applied to the system (3.3.1). The margins are with respect to the nominal linearization of (3.3.1) and (3.3.2):

$$\dot{x} = A(\mathrm{v}) + B(\mathrm{v}) + \xi; \qquad x(0^-) = 0 \tag{3.4.1}$$

$$u = -G(\mathrm{v})x, \tag{3.3.2}$$

where $A(\cdot)$ and $B(\cdot)$ are as in (3.3.10). Following development of general results in section 3.4.1, we will consider the special case of optimal LQSF compensators in section 3.4.2, showing that such compensator designs have a certain inherent robustness as a consequence of their optimality, including infinite gain margin and at least $\pm 60°$ phase margins in each control input channel.

3.4.1 General Results

The following result gives stability margins for the linearized state-feedback system (3.4.1), (3.3.2); the result provides a sufficient condition for the actual nonlinear state-feedback system (3.3.1), (3.3.2) to be closed-loop stable.

LEMMA 3.1 (State-Feedback Stability Margins) Let the constant matrix $P \in \mathrm{R}^{n \times n}$ and the ν-dependent matrix $S(\nu) \in \mathrm{R}^{n \times n}$ be symmetric, uniformly positive-definite solutions of the Lyapunov equation

$$P[A - B\,G] + [A - B\,G]^{\mathrm{T}} P + S = 0. \tag{3.4.2}$$

If uniformly for all ν either

(i) $$P\{[A - \mathbf{A}] + [B - \mathbf{B}][-G]\} + \frac{1}{2} S > 0 \tag{3.4.3a}$$

or

(ii) $$P[(A - \nabla \mathbf{A}(x)) - (B - \nabla \mathbf{B}(u)) \cdot G] + S > 0, \tag{3.4.3b}$$

then the system (3.3.1) with nonlinear state feedback (3.3.2) is closed-loop finite-gain stable. Condition (3.4.3a) is implied by condition (3.4.3b).[3]

PROOF See appendix A.

The condition (3.4.2) is not a severe restriction; it specifies, in essence, that the matrix P must be chosen such that $x^{\mathrm{T}}(t)Px(t)$ is a positive-definite Lyapunov function ensuring closed-loop stability for the ideal situation in which the linearization (3.4.1) exactly models the actual system (3.3.1)

3 Note that the ν-dependence of S, like that of $\mathbf{A}$, $\mathbf{B}$, $\mathbf{C}$, A, B, C, G, and H has been suppressed in equations (3.4.2) and (3.4.3). The matrix P, which is by hypothesis constant, is the *only* operator in this theorem that may not in general be ν-dependent.

[18, p. 25]. For example, when A, B, and G are constant matrices and G stabilizes the linearization (3.4.1), a constant matrix P satisfying (3.4.2) can easily be found by simply picking any constant positive-definite S and solving (3.4.2) for the (unique!) positive-definite solution P satisfying (3.4.2) [18, p. 341].

The interesting part of lemma 3.1 is the condition (3.4.3). It characterizes a class of operators **A** and **B** in (3.3.1) for which the feedback gain G is assured of being stable. An important feature of the condition (3.4.3) is that it is expressed in terms of the *deviation* of the open-loop system (3.3.1) from its linearization (3.4.1). When the deviation is zero (i.e., when $\mathbf{A} = A$, $\mathbf{B} = B$), then the condition (3.4.3) is always satisfied, since S is positive definite. The condition (3.4.3) is much easier to verify than may be apparent at first inspection; this is due to the fact that a positively weighted sum of positive operators is positive. Consider, for example, the case where the operators **A** and **B** are nondynamical; suppose that there are constants $a_{ij}^{(\ell)}$, $b_{jk}^{(\ell)}$ ($\ell = 1, 2$; $i, j = 1, \ldots, n$; $k = 1, \ldots, m$) such that for all $x \in R^n$ and all $u \in R^m$

$$0 \geq a_{ij}^{(1)} \leq [A - \nabla\mathbf{A}(x)]_{ij} \leq a_{ij}^{(2)} \geq 0, \tag{3.4.4}$$

$$0 \geq b_{jk}^{(1)} \leq [B - \nabla\mathbf{B}(u)]_{jk} \leq b_{jk}^{(2)} \geq 0. \tag{3.4.5}$$

(The notation $[M]_{ij}$ denotes the ij-th element of the matrix M.) Then, as may be readily verified, sufficient conditions for (3.4.3b) to hold are

$$a_{ij}^{(\ell)}(e_j e_i^T P + P e_i e_j^T) + S > 0 \tag{3.4.6}$$

$$b_{jk}^{(\ell)}(G^T e_k e_j^T P + P e_j e_k^T G) + S > 0 \tag{3.4.7}$$

where e_i denotes the i-th standard basis vector, i.e., the vector whose elements are all zero except the i-th, which is one. To verify conditions (3.4.6) and (3.4.7) requires that we check the positive definiteness of as many $n \times n$-matrices as there are nonzero elements in the set

$$\{a_{ij}^{(\ell)}, b_{jk}^{(\ell)} \mid \ell = 1, 2; i, j = 1, \ldots, n; k = 1, \ldots, m\}$$

(which can be done, e.g., by checking that the principal leading minors of each matrix are positive [18, p. 341]). So if the linear model (3.4.1) of the actual system (3.3.1) is exact except for, say, N nonlinearities or imprecisely modeled parameters, then we need check only the positive definiteness of at most $2N$ $n \times n$ matrices to verify (3.4.3b). At the expense of somewhat more complicated analysis, it can be demonstrated that (3.4.3a) may be verified directly by an analogous procedure.

3.4.2 Linear-Quadratic State Feedback (LQSF)

Consider now the special case of exponentially weighted optimal LQSF. This corresponds to the state-feedback gain matrix G being chosen to minimize the quadratic performance index

$$J = \int_0^\infty e^{2\alpha t}[x^T(t)Qx(t) + u^T(t)Ru(t)]\,dt, \tag{3.4.8}$$

where Q and R are positive-definite weighting matrices, and $\alpha \geq 0$ is an exponential weighting constant, subject to the constraints on x and u imposed by the linear model (3.4.1):

$$\dot{x} = Ax + Bu + \xi; \qquad x(0^-) = 0.$$

For simplicity, attention is restricted to the case where A, B, Q, and R are constant matrices—i.e., independent of v. For design purposes, the disturbance input ξ is presumed to consist of a single impulse $\xi(t) = x_0\delta(t)$ ($x_0 \in \mathrm{R}^n$; $\delta(\cdot) \triangleq$ Dirac delta function). Provided the system (3.4.1) is controllable, then the optimal state feedback G is completely specified by the design parameters $Q \in \mathrm{R}^{n\times n}$ and $R \in \mathrm{R}^{m\times m}$ and is given by [5, p. 50–59]:

$$G = R^{-1}B^TK, \tag{3.4.9}$$

where $K = K^T > 0$ is the unique positive-definite solution of the time-invariant matrix Riccati equation

$$K(A + \alpha I) + (A + \alpha I)^TK - KBR^{-1}B^TK + Q = 0. \tag{3.4.10}$$

The LQSF stability margins are characterized by the following theorem, which gives sufficient conditions for the closed-loop stability of the actual nonlinear system (3.3.1), under optimal LQSF. Also, as will be shown, the result proves that the LQSF design procedure is inherently robust, in that even a crude linear model will lead to a stabilizing feedback design for the actual system; specifically, the theorem shows that the LQSF design procedure automatically ensures that the deviation from the linear design model admissible under the conditions of lemma 3.1 is always quite large.

THEOREM 3.1 (LQSF Stability Margins and Robustness) If either

(i) uniformly for all v

$$K[\alpha I + (A - \mathrm{A}) - (B - \mathrm{B})G] + \frac{1}{2}[Q + KBR^{-1}B^TK] > 0 \tag{3.4.11a}$$

or

(ii) uniformly for all v, x

$$K[\alpha I + (A - \nabla\mathrm{A}(x)) - (B - \nabla\mathrm{B}(u))G] + \frac{1}{2}[Q + KBR^{-1}B^{\mathrm{T}}K] > 0, \tag{3.4.11b}$$

where G, K are as in (3.4.9) and (3.4.10), then the system (3.3.1) with LQSF (3.4.7) is closed-loop finite-gain stable.

PROOF Let

$$S = Q + KBR^{-1}B^{\mathrm{T}}K + 2\alpha K, \tag{3.4.12}$$

$$P = K. \tag{3.4.13}$$

Then (3.4.10) and (3.4.11) ensure that (3.4.2) and (3.4.3) respectively are satisfied. The result follows from lemma 3.1. ▮

To fully appreciate the LQSF robustness implications of theorem 3.4.2 and in particular the implications of theorem 3.1 regarding the gain and phase margins of optimal LQSF designs, it is instructive to consider the special case in which, for all x, u, v,

$$\mathrm{A}x = Ax \tag{3.4.14}$$

and

$$\mathrm{B}u = B\mathrm{N}u \tag{3.4.15}$$

and

$$\mathrm{N}u = \begin{bmatrix} \mathrm{N}_1 \mathrm{u}_1 \\ \vdots \\ \mathrm{N}_m \mathrm{u}_m \end{bmatrix} \tag{3.4.16}$$

so that all differences between the open-loop dynamics of the actual system (3.3.1) and the linear model (3.4.1) are lumped into m dynamical nonlinear perturbations N_i in series with the system inputs, e.g., unmodeled actuator dynamics (figure 3.4). It is stressed that this does not mean we are restricting our attention to systems with only actuator perturbations; rather, we are merely stipulating that the actual system's *open-loop* dynamics have the same input-output behavior as some such system; in practice,

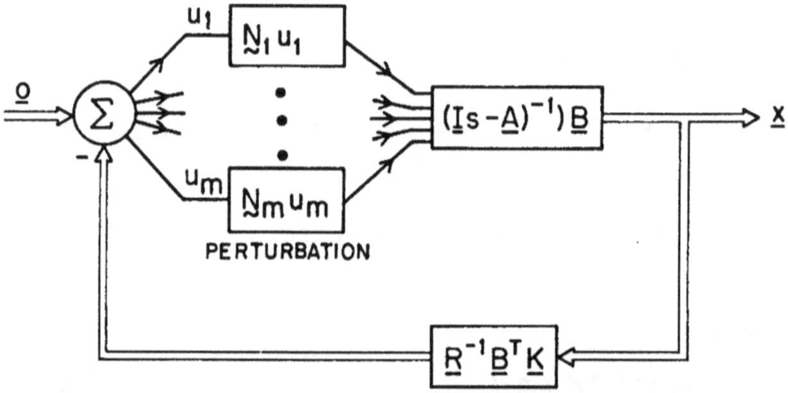

Figure 3.4 Linear-quadratic state-feedback regulator with perturbations in each control loop.

experimental input-output data would normally be used to deduce system input perturbations N producing the open-loop input-output behavior of the actual system. For simplicity, it is further assumed that

$$R = \mathrm{diag}(r_1, \ldots, r_m) \triangleq \begin{bmatrix} r_1 & 0 & 0 \\ 0 & r_2 & 0 \\ \cdots & \cdots & \cdots \\ 0 & 0 & r_m \end{bmatrix}. \tag{3.4.17}$$

With (3.4.14)–(3.4.17) satisfied, the stability condition (3.4.11a) of theorem 3.1 reduces to

$$KB\left\{\mathrm{diag}\left(\left[N_1 - \frac{1}{2}\right]r_1^{-1}, \ldots, \left[N_m - \frac{1}{2}\right]r_m^{-1}\right)\right\}B^TK + \frac{1}{2}Q \geq 0, \tag{3.4.18}$$

which is satisfied if

$$N_i - \frac{1}{2} \geq 0 \qquad (i = 1, \ldots, m). \tag{3.4.19}$$

The condition (3.4.19) characterizes the inherent robustness of optimal LQSF designs by establishing a lower bound on the stability margins associated with every LQSF design—every LQSF design can tolerate *at least* perturbations N_i satisfying (3.4.19). For example, if the N_i are non-dynamical nonlinearities $(N_iu_i)(t) = f_i[u_i(t)]$, then condition (3.4.19) is satisfied if the graphs of the N_i lie in the conic sector lying between the lines

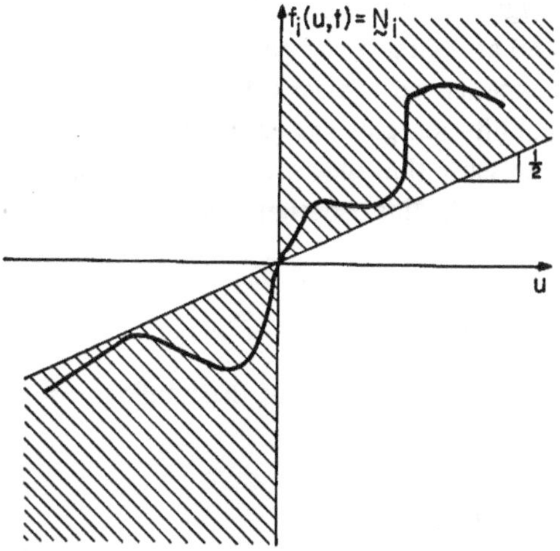

Figure 3.5 Nondynamical actuator nonlinearity that will not destabilize an optimal linear-quadratic state-feedback system.

of slope 1/2 and slope ∞ (figure 3.5). Alternatively, if the N_i are open-loop stable linear time-invariant dynamical elements with respective transfer functions $L_i(s)$ $(i = 1, \ldots m)$, then condition (3.4.17) becomes[4] (as a consequence of Parseval's theorem)

$$\mathrm{Re}[L_i(j\omega)] \geq \frac{1}{2} \qquad (i = 1, \ldots, m), \tag{3.4.20}$$

i.e., the Nyquist locus of each $L_i(j\omega)$ must lie to the right of the vertical line in the complex plane passing through the point $\frac{1}{2} + j0$. For example, if $L_i(s)$ $(i = 1, \ldots, m)$ are nondynamical linear gains $L_i(j\omega) = h_i$, then (3.4.20) becomes

$$k_i \geq \frac{1}{2}. \tag{3.4.21}$$

Alternatively, if $L_i(s) = \exp(j\phi_i)$, corresponding to a pure phase shift of angle ϕ_i $(i = 1, \ldots, m)$ in the m respective control input channels, then condition (3.4.20) becomes

$$|\phi_i| \leq \frac{\pi}{3} \text{radians} = 60° \qquad (i = 1, \ldots, m). \tag{3.4.22}$$

4 See lemma 2.6.

This shows that every LQSF design has an infinite gain margin, at least a 50% gain reduction tolerance, and at least a $\pm 60°$ phase margin in each control input channel. Engineers experienced in classical servomechanism design will recognize that these stability margins are quite large, ensuring that LQSF designs are robust in the sense that they are closed-loop stable despite substantial differences between the linear design model (3.4.1) and the actual system (3.3.1).

3.5 Nonlinear Observer Stability Margins

In this section we characterize the stability margins of the nonlinear observer

$$\frac{d}{dt}\hat{x} = \mathbf{A}\hat{x} + \mathbf{B}u - H\cdot(\hat{y} - y); \qquad \hat{x}(0^-) = 0$$
$$\hat{y} = \mathbf{C}\hat{x}. \tag{3.3.3}$$

The margins are relative to the ideal situation in which the linear design model (3.3.10) is exact—i.e., $(\mathbf{A}, \mathbf{B}, \mathbf{C}) = (A, B, C)$. Also, stability margins are determined for the error-dynamics feedback representation (3.3.5) and (3.3.6) of the nonlinear observer (3.3.3); provided that the deviation of the system operators $\mathbf{A}$, $\mathbf{C}$ from the linear design model matrices A, C is within these margins, then the nonlinear observer is assured of being nondivergent with finite gain.

Following the development of some results of general applicability to nonlinear observers in section 3.5.1, we consider in 3.5.2 the special case of the suboptimal CGEKF. The results demonstrate that the CGEKF, besides being suboptimally accurate, is inherently robust in that its stability margins are always large. The results developed in this chapter are mathematically dual to the state-feedback control results of chapter 4.

3.5.1 General

I now state a basic result concerning the stability margins of the nonlinear observer (3.3.3) and of its associated error-dynamics feedback system (3.3.5) and (3.3.6).

LEMMA 3.2 (Nonlinear Observer Stability Margins and Nondivergence): Let the constant matrix $P \in \mathrm{R}^{n\times n}$ and the ν-dependent matrix $S \in \mathrm{R}^{n\times n}$ be symmetric, uniformly positive-definite solutions of the Lyapunov equation

$$[A - HC]P + P[A - HC]^{T} + S = 0. \tag{3.5.1}$$

(a) If

$$[(A - \nabla \mathbf{A}(x)) - H\cdot(C - \nabla \mathbf{C}(x)]P + \frac{1}{2}S > 0 \tag{3.5.2}$$

uniformly for all ν, x, then the nonlinear observer (3.3.3) is nondivergent with finite gain; i.e., the mapping of ξ, θ into $e \triangleq \hat{x} - x$ has finite gain.

(b) If

$$[(A - \mathbf{A}) - H\cdot(C - \mathbf{C})]P + \frac{1}{2}S > 0 \tag{3.5.3}$$

uniformly for all ν, then the nonlinear observer (3.3.3) is finite-gain stable; i.e., the mapping of (y, u) into $\hat{x}$ defined by (3.3.3) has finite gain. Condition (3.5.3) is implied by condition (3.5.2).[5]

PROOF See appendix B.

Comments The condition (3.5.1), like the analogous condition (3.4.2) of lemma 3.1, is not a severe restriction; it merely specifies that $x^{T}(t)Px(t)$ must be a positive-definite Lyapunov function ensuring stability for the ideal situation in which the linear design model (3.3.1) is exact.

The interesting part of lemma 3.2 is the condition (3.5.2). It characterizes a class of nonlinearities for which the nonlinear observer (3.3.3) is assured of being nondivergent. An important feature of lemma 3.2 is the *form* of condition (3.5.2)—it is expressed in terms of the *deviation* of the system (3.3.1) from the linearization (3.3.10) used in selecting the residual gain. When the deviation is zero [i.e., when $(\mathbf{A}, \mathbf{C}) \equiv (A, C)$], then the condition (3.5.2) is always satisfied, since S is positive definite.

The question naturally arises: How difficult is it to verify condition (3.5.2)? The fact that the left-hand side of (3.5.2) is linear in **A** and **C** and the fact that a positively weighted sum of positive operators is positive make (3.5.2) much easier to verify than may be apparent at first inspection.

5 Because equations (3.5.2)–(3.5.3) are required to hold *uniformly* for all ν, it follows that if **A** and **C** are not ν-dependent then allowing A, C, H to be dependent on ν offers no advantage in satisfying the conditions (3.5.2) and (3.5.3), though it may be possible to improve the error statistics in some situations by allowing such dependence.

For example, (3.5.2) holds if **A** and **C** are memoryless, and if there are constants $c_{ij}^{(\ell)}$, $a_{jk}^{(\ell)}$ ($\ell = 1, 2; i = 1, \ldots, p; j, k = 1, \ldots, n$) such that for all $x \in R^n$

$$0 \geq c_{ij}^{(1)} \leq [C - \nabla C(x)]_{ij} \leq c_{ij}^{(2)} \geq 0 \tag{3.5.4}$$

$$0 \geq a_{jk}^{(1)} \leq [A \quad \nabla A(x)]_{jk} \leq a_{jk}^{(2)} \geq 0. \tag{3.5.5}$$

Since $[M]_{ij}$ denotes the ij-th element of the matrix M, then it may be readily verified that sufficient conditions for (3.5.2) to hold are

$$c_{ij}^{(\ell)}(Pe_j e_i^T H^T + He_i e_j^T P) + S > 0 \tag{3.5.6}$$

$$a_{jk}^{(\ell)}(Pe_k e_j^T + e_j e_j^T P) + S > 0, \tag{3.5.7}$$

where e_i denotes the i-th standard basis vector, i.e., the vector whose elements are zero except the i-th, which is a one. To verify conditions (3.5.6)–(3.5.7) requires checking the positive definiteness of as many $n \times n$ matrices as there are nonzero elements in the set

$$\{c_{ij}^{(\ell)}, a_{jk}^{(\ell)} \mid \ell = 1, 2; 1 = 1, \ldots, p; j, k = 1, \ldots, n\},$$

which can be done, for example, by checking that the principal leading minors of each matrix are positive [118, p. 341]. So, if the nonlinear system (3.3.1) is identical to the linearization (3.3.1) except for N memoryless nonlinearities, then the positive definiteness of at most 2N $n \times n$ matrices need be checked in order to verify (3.5.2).

3.5.2 Constant-Gain Extended Kalman Filter (CGEKF)

Intuitively, it is clear that if the linearization (3.3.1) is sufficiently faithful to the nonlinear system (3.3.1), then the error response of the nonlinear observer will be close to the error response obtained in the ideal situation in which the linearization is exact. This intuition is validated by the error-bounding results of [35] and [87]. Consequently, if the disturbances ξ and θ are reasonably well approximated by zero-mean white noise, then it is reasonable to expect that a good suboptimal minimum-variance estimator can be obtained by choosing the residual gain H to be the minimum-variance optimal gain for the linearized system (3.3.10), i.e., the Kalman filter gain [46, p. 214]:

$$H = \Sigma C^T \Theta^{-1} \tag{3.5.8}$$

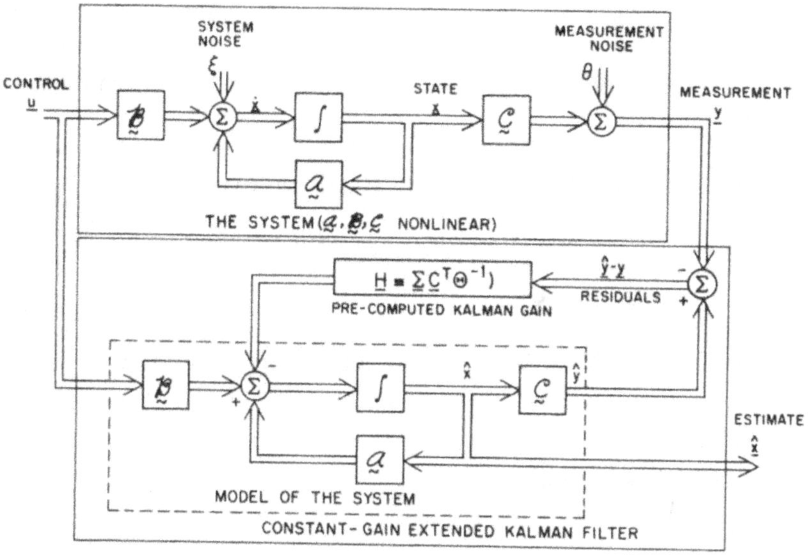

Figure 3.6 The system with constant-gain extended Kalman filter (CGEKF).

where $\Sigma = \Sigma^{T} > 0$ satisfies the matrix Riccati equation[6,7]

$$0 = \Sigma(A + \alpha I)^{T} + (A + \alpha I)\Sigma - \Sigma C^{T}\Theta^{-1}C\Sigma + \Xi \tag{3.5.9}$$

and where Ξ and Θ are the positive definite covariance matrices of the disturbances ξ and θ, respectively. For simplicity, we restrict our attention to the case where A, C, Ξ, and Θ are constant matrices.[8] The resultant estimator is the CGEKF depicted in figure 3.6.

A surprising and important consequence of the CGEKF approach to nonlinear observer design is that, in addition to yielding a suboptimally accurate estimator design, the CGEKF design procedure is inherently robust in the sense that even a crude linearization will suffice for residual-

6 We assume that the required controllability and observability conditions are satisfied so that there is a unique positive-definite solution of (2.5.9) [41, pp. 234–243].

7 An "exponential-weighting factor" $\alpha \geq 0$ has been included; in the Kalman filter, α is usually taken to be $\alpha = 0$. The interpretation of the constant α is discussed in [70] and [104, p. 215], but only for the special case $\Xi = 0$. The case $\Xi \neq 0$ has evidently not been considered in the literature.

8 Insofar as nondivergence and stability are concerned, this does not appear to be a serious restriction.

gain design. The CGEKF design procedure automatically ensures that the deviation from the design linearization admissible under the conditions of lemma 3.2 can be quite large. The extent of this robustness is quantified in the following result:

THEOREM 3.2 (CGEKF Robustness): If uniformly

$$\{\alpha I + [A - \nabla \mathrm{A}(x)] - H[C - \nabla \mathrm{C}(x)]\}\Sigma + \frac{1}{2}(\Xi + \Sigma C^{\mathrm{T}}\Theta^{-1}C\Sigma) > 0, \tag{3.5.10}$$

then the CGEKF is nondivergent with finite gain.

PROOF Let

$$\begin{aligned} S &= \Xi + \Sigma C^{\mathrm{T}}\Theta^{-1}C\Sigma + 2\alpha\Sigma \\ P &= \Sigma. \end{aligned} \tag{3.5.11}$$

Then (3.5.9) and (3.5.10) ensure that (3.5.1) and (3.5.2) respectively are satisfied. The result follows from lemma 3.2.

To fully appreciate the implications of theorem 3.2 with regard to the robustness of the CGEKF design procedure, it is instructive to consider the situation in which

$$\mathrm{A}(x) = A \tag{3.5.12}$$

$$\mathrm{C}(x) = [\mathrm{diag}(\mathrm{N}_1, \ldots, \mathrm{N}_p)]C \tag{3.5.13}$$

for all x, so that all the nonlinearities in the open-loop error dynamics system (3.3.5) and the design linearization are lumped into the p dynamical nonlinearities N_i (i = 1, . . . , p) that are in series with the system outputs. This is equivalent to all nonlinearity in the system (3.3.1) being lumped in the actuators and sensors (figure 3.7). It is emphasized that this does not mean that we are restricting our attention to systems with only actuator and sensor nonlinearity; rather, we are merely stipulating that the actual system's open-loop error dynamics have the same input-output behavior as such a system.

For simplicity, we further assume that Θ is of the form

$$\Theta = \mathrm{diag}(\theta_{11}, \theta_{22}, \ldots, \theta_{pp}). \tag{3.5.14}$$

With (3.5.11)–(3.5.14) satisfied, the nondivergence condition (3.5.10) of

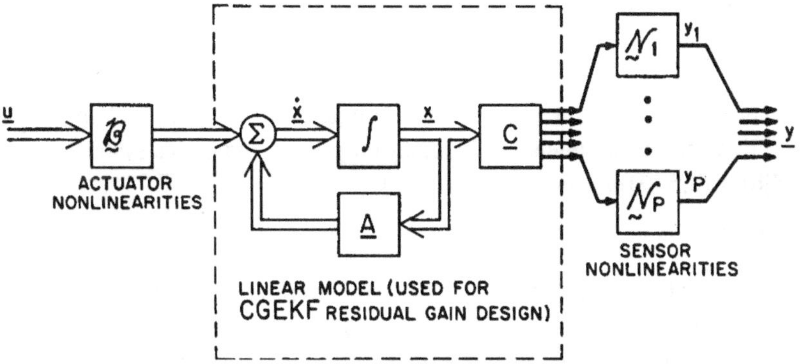

Figure 3.7 System with all nonlinearity lumped in actuators and sensors.

theorem 3.2 reduces to

$$\Sigma C^{T}\,\mathrm{diag}\left[\theta_{11}^{-1}\left(\nabla N_1(x) - \frac{1}{2}\right), \ldots, \theta_{pp}^{-1}\left(\nabla N_p(x) - \frac{1}{2}\right)\right] C\Sigma + \frac{1}{2}\Xi > 0, \tag{3.5.15}$$

which is satisfied if

$$\nabla N_i(x) \geq \frac{1}{2} \qquad (i = 1, \ldots, p). \tag{3.5.16}$$

The condition (3.5.16) establishes a "lower bound," the inherent robustness of the CGEKF design procedure—every CGEKF design can tolerate *at least* nonlinearities satisfying (3.5.16). This inherent robustness can be interpreted in terms of the *gain and phase margin* of the feedback representation (see figure 3.3) of the CGEKF error dynamics as follows: Suppose that the N_i ($i = 1, \ldots, p$) are linear dynamical elements with respective transfer functions $L_i(s)$ ($i = 1, \ldots, p$). Then, condition (3.5.16) becomes

$$\mathrm{Re}[L_i(j\omega)] \geq \frac{1}{2} \qquad (i = 1, \ldots, p), \tag{3.5.17}$$

i.e., the Nyquist locus of each $L_i(j\omega)$ must lie to the right of the vertical line in the complex plane passing through the point $\frac{1}{2} + j0$. For example, if $L_i(s)$ ($i = 1, \ldots, p$) are nondynamical linear gains, that is, if $L_i(j\omega) = k_i$, then (3.5.17) becomes

$$k_i \geq \frac{1}{2}. \tag{3.5.18}$$

Alternatively, if

$$L_i(s) = \exp(j\phi_i) \qquad (i = 1, \ldots, p),$$

corresponding to a pure phase shift of angle ϕ_i ($i = 1, \ldots, p$) in the p respective output channels of the open-loop error dynamics system, then condition (3.5.17) becomes

$$|\phi_i| \leq 60°. \tag{3.5.19}$$

The conditions (3.5.18) and (3.5.19) can be interpreted as saying the CGEKF design procedure leads to an infinite gain margin, at least 50% gain reduction tolerance, and at least ±60° phase margin in each output channel of the error-dynamics feedback system (figure 3.3)—the margins being relative to the ideal situation in which the linearization (3.3.10) is exact. Engineers experienced in classical servomechanism design will recognize that these minimal stability margins are actually quite large, ensuring that the nonlinear-observer error-dynamics feedback system of figure 3.3 will be stable despite substantial differences between the design linearization (3.3.10) and the system (3.3.1). Consequently, the CGEKF design procedure is assured of yielding a nondivergent nonlinear observer design for systems with a good deal of nonlinearity.

This surprisingly large robustness of the CGEKF design procedure is mathematically dual to the robustness of LQSF regulators discussed in section 3.4, wherein full-state feedback linear optimal regulators are shown to have infinite gain margin, 50% gain reduction tolerance, and ±60° phase margin in each input channel. This duality is a consequence of the symmetry between the equations governing the regulation error of linear optimal regulators and the equations governing the estimate error of the CGEKF.

3.6 Nonlinear Dynamical Output-Feedback Controllers

In this section, I develop a fundamental result concerning the use of the nonlinear observer (3.3.3) for state reconstruction in the synthesis of nonlinear output-feedback controllers having the general structure (see figure 3.2c)

$$u = -G(v)\hat{x}$$

$$\frac{d}{dt}\hat{x} = \mathbf{A}\hat{x} + \mathbf{B}u - H(v)\cdot(\hat{y} - y); \qquad \hat{x}(0^-) = 0 \tag{3.3.4}$$

$\hat{y} = Cx.$

The result implies that substitution of the estimates generated by a *non-divergent* nonlinear observer for true values in an otherwise stable feedback control system can never destabilize the closed-loop system; the result has obvious implications regarding the *practical* utility of the controller structure (3.3.4). A simple, practical nonlinear extension of the celebrated LQG design procedure emerges as a promising method for designing the gains G and H in (3.3.4).

3.6.1 Separation of Estimation and Control

The fundamental result concerning the controller structure (3.3.4) is now stated.

THEOREM 3.3 (Separation of Estimation and Control) Let $\mathbf{G}$ be a non-anticipative nonlinear dynamical operator with finite incremental gain; let $\hat{x}$ be any estimate of x that is nondivergent (with *finite gain*).[9] Suppose that the system (3.3.1) is closed-loop bounded (finite-gain stable) with feedback $u = \mathbf{G}x$. Then the system (3.3.1) with feedback $u = \mathbf{G}\hat{x}$ is also closed-loop bounded (finite-gain stable).

PROOF See appendix C.

The practical importance of the simple result embodied in theorem 3.3 is immediate: stable output-feedback controllers can be designed for *nonlinear* systems by designing *separately*:

(i) a stable state-feedback controller, and

(ii) a nondivergent nonlinear observer.

This result, though evidently new (see [107]), is not entirely surprising. In linear control, it has long been recognized that a stable *linear* observer can be employed for state reconstruction in an otherwise-stable *linear* state-feedback system to yield a stable closed-loop output-feedback system [62]. Indeed, in LQG stochastic control problems [9], the separation theorem of estimation and control ensures that the *optimal* output feedback is the cascade of the optimal state feedback and the optimal observer (the Kalman filter).

9 Note that we do *not* stipulate what estimator or state-feedback control is used; in particular, x need *not* be generated by the nonlinear observer (3.3.3) and $\mathbf{G}$ need not be of the form (3.3.2).

3.6.2 Suboptimal Nonlinear Output-Feedback Controllers

A logical suboptimal method for choosing the gains G and H in (3.3.4) is to use the LQSF and CGEKF gains respectively. The separation theorem of estimation and control assures that this choice is actually optimal in the ideal situation in which the linear design model (3.3.10) coincides with the actual system (3.3.1). The resultant suboptimal nonlinear output-feedback controller, depicted in figure 3.8, is completely specified by the following formula (see sections 3.4 and 3.5):

$$u = -R^{-1}B^{\mathrm{T}}K\hat{x}$$

$$\frac{\mathrm{d}}{\mathrm{dt}}\hat{x} = \mathbf{A}\hat{x} + \mathbf{B}u - \Sigma C^{\mathrm{T}}\Theta^{-1}(\hat{y} - y); \qquad \hat{x}(0^{-}) = 0 \tag{3.6.1}$$

$$\hat{y} = \mathbf{C}\hat{x},$$

where K and Σ are the unique positive-definite solutions of the exponentially weighted matrix Riccati equations

$$0 = K(A + \alpha_1 I) + (A + \alpha_1 I)^{\mathrm{T}}K - KBR^{-1}B^{\mathrm{T}}K + Q \tag{3.6.2}$$

$$0 = \Sigma(A + \alpha_2 I)^{\mathrm{T}} + (A + \alpha_2 I)\Sigma - \Sigma C^{\mathrm{T}}\Theta^{-1}C\Sigma + \Xi, \tag{3.6.3}$$

where the exponential weighting constants α_1, $\alpha_2 \leq 0$ and the positive-definite weighting matrices Q, R, Ξ, and Θ are selected by the designer and where A, B, C are the matrices from the linear model (3.3.10) of the actual system (3.3.1). As in sections 3.4.2 and 3.5.2, we restrict our attention to the case where A, B, C, Q, R, Ξ, and Θ are constant matrices.

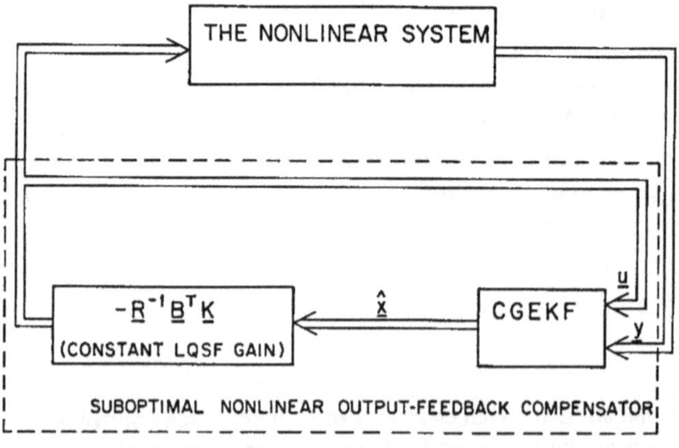

Figure 3.8 Suboptimal nonlinear output-feedback controller.

This approach to suboptimal nonlinear output-feedback control design is similar in spirit to the approach outlined in [19], wherein an extended Kalman filter is cascaded with a time-varying suboptimal feedback gain; however, the precomputed constant gains in the control law (3.6.1) make it drastically simpler to implement from the standpoint of real-time computational burden. The remarkable robustness of the CGEKF design procedure and of LQSF control design assure that this approach will produce a stabilizing feedback control law for systems with even substantial nonlinearity. The extent of this robustness is quantified in the following result:

THEOREM 3.4 (Suboptimal Nonlinear Output-Feedback Robustness) If uniformly

$$\{\alpha_1 I + [A - \nabla \mathrm{A}(x)] + [-\Sigma C^{\mathrm{T}}\Theta^{-1}][C - \nabla \mathrm{C}(x)]\}\Sigma + \frac{1}{2}[\Xi + \Sigma C^{\mathrm{T}}\Theta^{-1}C\Sigma] > 0 \tag{3.6.4}$$

and if

$$K[\alpha_2 I + (A - \mathrm{A}) + (B - \mathrm{B})(-R^{-1}B^{\mathrm{T}}K)] + \frac{1}{2}(Q + KBR^{-1}B^{\mathrm{T}}K) > 0, \tag{3.6.5}$$

then the system (3.3.1) with output feedback (3.6.1), as depicted in figure 3.8, is finite-gain stable.

PROOF Theorem 3.2 ensures that the CGEKF is nondivergent with finite gain. Theorem 3.1 ensures that the feedback $u = -R^{-1}B^{\mathrm{T}}Kx$ leads to closed-loop finite-gain stability. The result follows from theorem 3.3. ∎

3.7 Design Considerations in Suboptimal Estimation and Control for Nonlinear Systems

In this section, I discuss how the LQSF/CGEKF results of sections 3.4 and 3.6 can be of use in the computer-aided design of LQSF/CGEKF estimators and compensators for nonlinear systems.

It is explained how the stability properties of suboptimal gain-scheduled nonlinear controller designs can be assessed *and* improved using the results.

Analogous results are developed regarding residual gain design and "scheduling" for robustly nondivergent nonlinear CGEKF design.

3.7.1 General

The result of theorem 3.6.1 ensures that any nondivergent estimate $\hat{x}$ of the state x can be used by a state-feedback controller for the nonlinear system (3.3.1) without inducing instability. Consequently, the design of a feedback controller for (3.3.1) can naturally be separated into two distinct tasks.

TASK 1 Design a nondivergent estimator for the "state" x. Under appropriate conditions (viz., (3.5.10)), this can be done suboptimally using the CGEKF, but it should be kept in mind that the nondivergence conclusion of theorem 3.2 holds rigorously *only when exact copies of the actual system's* **A, B, C** *operators are incorporated into the internal system model of the CGEKF.*

TASK 2 Design a stabilizing "state" feedback for the system. Under appropriate conditions [viz., (3.6.4)], this can be simply an LQSF gain matrix designed for an approximate linear time-invariant model [viz., (3.3.10)] of the actual system.

The following sections 3.7.2 and 3.7.3 are devoted to elaborations of the specifics of these two design tasks.

3.7.2 Practical CGEKF Synthesis

The following procedure shows how theorem 3.5.2 might be employed in the computer-aided design of practical, nondivergent CGEKF estimators for *nonlinear* systems:

STEP 1 Pick constant values for A, C, Ξ, and Θ. The values of A and C should be initially chosen to reflect as closely as possible the derivatives $\nabla\mathbf{A}(x)$ and $\nabla\mathbf{C}(x)$, respectively, i.e., so that $\|A - \nabla\mathbf{A}(x)\|$ and $\|C - \nabla\mathbf{C}(x)\|$ are small, at least for those values of x which are most probable—statistical linearization methods [34, ch. 7] may be helpful in this regard. The matrices Θ and Ξ should be initially chosen to reflect the covariances of the disturbances θ and ξ, respectively. If the input-output relations of the operators **A**, **B**, and **C** are not precisely known, then the designer may wish to consider compensating for this by using state augmentation following the spirit of [8] in order to reduce bias errors.

STEP 2 Compute Σ and H from (3.5.8) and (3.5.9). This can be done with the aid of a digital computer using available software for solving the Riccati equation.

STEP 3 Test the resultant CGEKF design for nondivergence. This can be done any of the following ways:
(a) By checking the conditions of theorem 3.2;
(b) By direct digital Monte Carlo simulation;
(c) By approximate describing-function simulation [33, sec. 6.4].
If the estimator is divergent, go to step 4; otherwise, proceed to step 5.

STEP 4 Take the divergent CGEKF and, assisted by a computer, determine the values of x for which the condition (3.5.10) is not satisfied. Modify the constant matrices A and C so as to reduce the magnitudes $\|A - \nabla A(x)\|$ and $\|C - \nabla C(x)\|$ at these values of x. If necessary, adjust the Ξ and Θ matrices. Return to step 2.

STEP 5 Check the nondivergent CGEKF for satisfactory performance, i.e., for acceptable error statistics. This can be done using one or more of the following approaches:
(a) By direct digital Monte Carlo simulation;
(b) By approximate describing-function simulation [33, sec. 6.4];
(c) By using the error-bounding results in [35] or [87].
If performance is acceptable, stop. Otherwise, further adjust the values of the constant matrices A, B, C, Ξ, and Θ as in step 4 and return to step 2. (end of procedure)

Comments For systems that are not "too nonlinear," this procedure can be expected to converge rapidly to an acceptable CGEKF design. However, for highly nonlinear systems, the procedure may not lead easily to a satisfactory design, even when such a design exists. A noteworthy limitation of the procedure is that no explicit method is provided for selecting the "best" modifications of A, C, Ξ, and Θ as required in step 4—though further research may demonstrate the utility of numerical optimization methods (see, e.g., [84] or [85]).

Even in cases where a nondivergent CGEKF estimator is not practical, it may be possible to exploit theorem 3.2 to construct a CGEKF estimator which, if properly initialized and if not subjected to excessively large disturbances, has satisfactory performance. This is accomplished by using estimate-dependent matrices $A(\hat{x})$, $C(\hat{x})$, $\Theta(\hat{x})$, and $\Xi(\hat{x})$ so that the residual gain $H \equiv H(\hat{x})$ becomes estimate dependent. That is, $H(\hat{x})$ is "scheduled" according to $\hat{x}$. For each fixed value of $\hat{x}$—i.e., $\hat{x}(t) \equiv x_0 =$ constant—condition (3.5.10) of theorem 3.2 defines a subset of R^n having the property that, provided the true state trajectory remains for all future time within that set, the CGEKF with constant residual gain matrix $H(x_0)$ is stable and nondivergent. Thus, theorem 3.2 serves to determine the number and location of fixed values—viz., $x = x_0$—at which it is necessary to compute values for H in order to cover the entire reachable state space with stabilizing constant residual gain matrices. This information is useful in assessing whether a gain-scheduled design is practical and how complicated the gain-scheduling algorithm must be. It should be emphasized, however, that such gain-scheduled estimators may require careful initialization and may not be able to recover from large disturbances without re-initialization, much like the EKF which in general has similar limitations.

3.7.3 Practical LQSF Synthesis

A procedure analogous to the CGEKF design procedure can be employed for the computer-aided design of practical, stabilizing, constant LQSF gains for nonlinear systems:

STEP 1 Pick constant values for A, B, Q, and R. The values of A and B should initially be chosen to reflect as closely as possible $\mathbf{A}$ and $\mathbf{B}$, respectively; i.e., choose A and B so that $\|(A - \mathbf{A})x\|$ and $\|(B - \mathbf{B})u\|$ are small, at least for those values of x, u in the vicinity of the equilibrium values $x = 0$, $u = 0$. The matrices Q and R should initially be chosen so that the resultant state feedback gain produces acceptable performance under the ideal situation $\mathbf{A} = A$, $\mathbf{B} = B$. If the actual system is known to contain "offsets" (i.e., $\mathscr{A}0 \neq 0$, $\mathscr{B}0 \neq 0$), the designer may wish to consider using state augmentation to introduce compensating integral action in the LQSF controller using the state augmentation methods of [47], [99], or [117].

STEP 2 Compute K and G from (3.4.9) and (3.4.10). This can be done using a digital computer with the aid of available software for solving the Riccati equation.

STEP 3 Test the resultant feedback system (i.e., the nonlinear system

(3.3.1) with feedback G) for closed-loop stability. This can be done either of the following ways:

(a) By checking the conditions of theorem 3.1;

(b) By simulation, digital or analog.

If the closed-loop system is not stable, go to step 4; otherwise, go to step 5.

STEP 4 Take the unstable LQSF feedback design and, assisted by a computer, determine the values of x, u for which condition (3.4.11) is not satisfied. Modify the constant matrices of A and B so as to reduce the magnitude of $\|(A - \mathbf{A})x\|$ and $\|(B - \mathbf{B})u\|$ at these values of x, u. (If necessary, adjust Q and R as well—the designer must use his intuition in changing Q, R since theorem 3.2 does not provide any explicit guidance). Return to step 2.

STEP 5 Check the stable LQSF design for satisfactory performance, i.e., for acceptable transient response, etc. This will normally be done by simulation. If performance is acceptable, stop. Otherwise, make further adjustments in A, B, Q, and R as in step 4, and return to step 2. (end of procedure)

Comments As with CGEKF design, the LQSF design procedure can be expected to converge rapidly to an acceptable suboptimal LQSF state feedback design for (3.3.1), provided system (3.3.1) is not "too nonlinear." But, in highly nonlinear systems where it may be necessary to carefully optimize the choice of the design parameters A, B, Q, and R, the procedure (because it relies partially on intuition and chance in selecting A, B, Q, and R,) may fail. Further research may prove that numerical optimization methods can be of use here [84, 85].

Even in cases in which it is not possible to design a globally stable constant-gain LQSF controller, it may be possible to exploit theorem 3.1 to aid in the design of a locally stable gain-scheduled nonlinear feedback design using state- and control-dependent matrices $A(x, u)$, $B(x, u)$, $Q(x, u)$, and $R(x, u)$. Given a fixed value of x, u (i.e., $(x(t), u(t)) = (x_0, u_0) =$ constant), the conditions (3.4.1a, b) can be used to determine for what region of the state space each constant feedback matrix $G(x, u)|_{(x_0, u_0)}$ is stabilizing. Theorem 3.1 thus serves to determine the number and location of fixed values—viz., x_0, u_0—at which it is necessary to compute values for G in order to cover the entire reachable state space with stabilizing constant feedback gain matrices; this information is useful in assessing whether a gain-scheduled design is practical and in assessing how complicated the gain scheduling algorithm must be. Such gain-scheduled designs are especially attractive for adjustable set-point nonlinear-regulator designs, where it may be desirable to modify the feedback law according to the system's operating point.

3.8 State-Augmented LQSF/CGEKF Designs

Methods have been proposed in the literature for using state-augmentation to improve the performance of LQSF designs and *linear* Kalman filter designs. For example, by appending integrators to the linear design model, it is possible to give the resultant designs proportional-integral feedback; this has made it possible to apply LQG theory to design linear estimators with a zero-mean residual error signal, and to design adjustable set-point regulators that track with zero steady-state error despite mismatching between the nonlinear design model and the dynamics of the actual physical system, provided the overall system is stable.

More generally, by appending a suitable linear time-invariant system to the design model, it has been established that linear LQSF controller and linear Kalman filter designs can be produced which are capable of optimally attenuating colored-noise disturbances (as contrasted with the white-noise optimality of designs obtained without state augmentation). The state augmentation design methods extend mutatis mutandis to suboptimal LQSF and CGEKF designs for *nonlinear* systems. In this section, the state-augmentation procedures are outlined and it is demonstrated that the stability margin and nondivergence results of the preceding sections (and this includes the robust gain and phase margin results) extend directly to state-augmented LQSF/CGEKF designs.

3.8.1 Proportional-Integral LQSF Stability Margins

A *proportional-integral* (PI) feedback law is, as its name suggests, a feedback law incorporating both a memoryless linear gain (the proportional gain) and a gain acting on the time integral of the *output* to be regulated (the integral gain); i.e., a feedback law of the form

$$u = G_1 x + G_2 \frac{1}{s} y, \tag{3.8.1}$$

where

1/s is the integral operator;
x is the system state vector;
y is the system output vector to be regulated;
u is the control input vector.
Such feedback laws can be synthesized using LQSF techniques by either of two methods, a direct method [117] or an indirect method [47, 48, 99].

The direct method involves appending to the system an output integrator (figure 3.9) so that in place of (3.3.10), we use the augmented linear design model

$$\begin{bmatrix} \dot{x} \\ \dot{z} \end{bmatrix} = \begin{bmatrix} A & 0 \\ C & 0 \end{bmatrix} \begin{bmatrix} x \\ z \end{bmatrix} + \begin{bmatrix} B \\ 0 \end{bmatrix} u; \tag{3.8.2}$$

since $z = (1/s)y$, the optimal LQSF control for (3.8.2) is the proportional-integral feedback

$$u = G \begin{bmatrix} x \\ z \end{bmatrix} = G \begin{bmatrix} x \\ \frac{1}{s}y \end{bmatrix} \triangleq G_1 x + G_2 \frac{1}{s} y. \tag{3.8.3}$$

Because the augmented system is an optimal LQSF system, the stability margin results of theorem 3.1 apply directly. In particular, the robustness properties of the LQSF design are retained; i.e., nonlinear dynamical

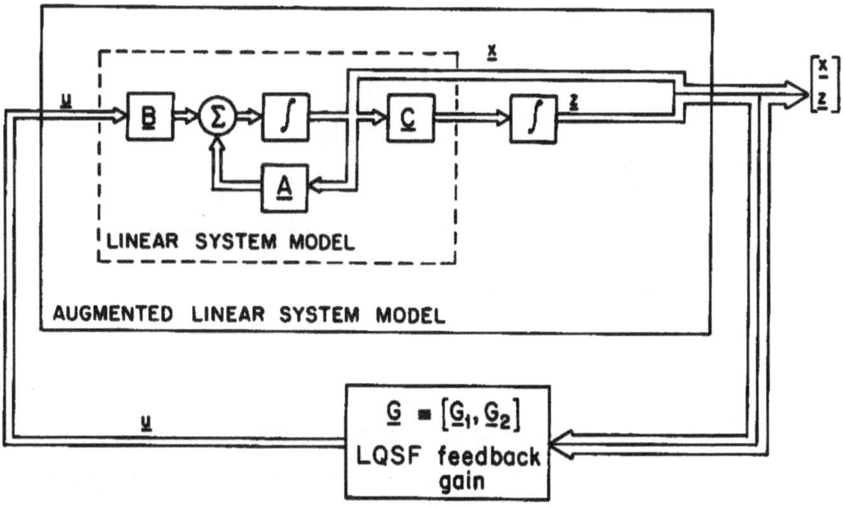

Figure 3.9 Proportional-integral feedback by the direct method.

perturbations N_i (i = 1, . . . , m) can be inserted in series with the inputs of the augmented system, and, provided that

$$N_i - \frac{1}{2} \geq 0 \qquad (i = 1, \ldots, m) \tag{3.4.19}$$

and that R is of the form $R = \text{diag}(r_1, \ldots, r_m)$, the closed-loop system will be stable. Consequently, proportional-integral LQSF compensator designs obtained by the direct method of [117] retain the robustness properties of infinite gain margin, ±60° phase margin, and 50% gain reduction tolerance.

In the indirect method [47, 48, 99], we augment the system with an integrator inserted in series with the system *input* (figure 3.10). The optimal LQSF feedback for the system is then of the form

$$\dot{u} = G_1 x + G_2 u \equiv G\begin{bmatrix} x \\ u \end{bmatrix}, \tag{3.8.4}$$

which, though *not* a proportional-integral feedback law, can be transformed into one via certain manipulations. By a clever choice of the matrix $G' \equiv [G_1' \vdots G_2']$, the open-loop LQSF system (figure 3.11a)

$$v_{out} = [G_1 \vdots G_2]\begin{bmatrix} x \\ u \end{bmatrix} = [G_1 \vdots G_2]\begin{bmatrix} (I_s - A)^{-1}B \\ I \end{bmatrix}\frac{1}{s}v_{in} \tag{3.8.5}$$

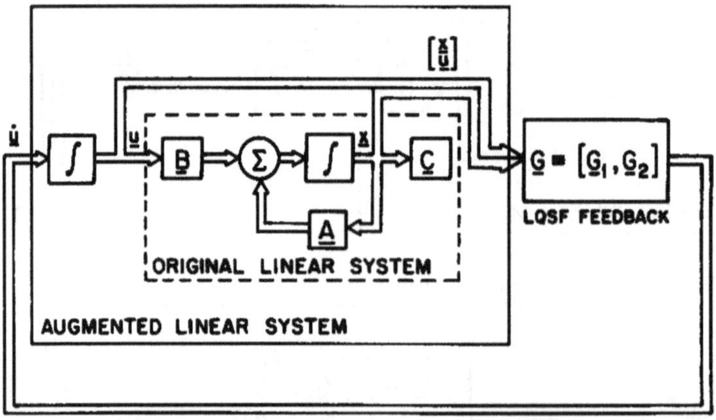

Figure 3.10 State-augmentation employed in indirect method of LQSF proportional-integral feedback design. (Note that the feedback is *not* proportional-integral.)

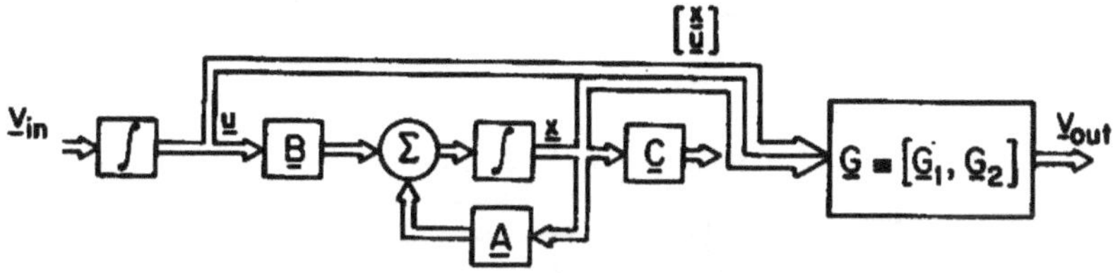

(a) Augmented-state LQSF System with Feedback-loop Opened

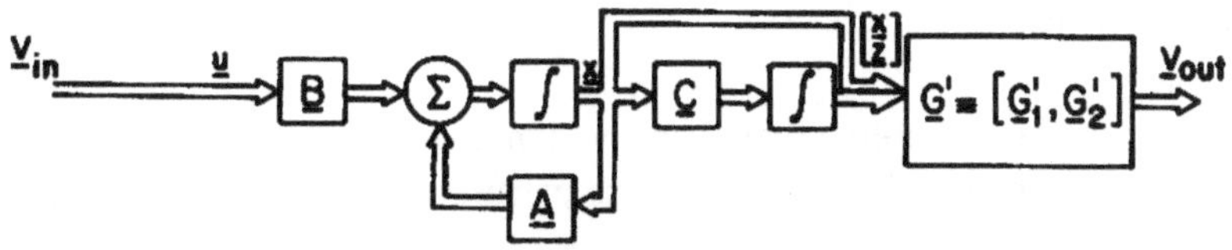

(b) Transformed Augmented-state LQSF System with Feedback-loop opened

Figure 3.11 Two linear systems having identical input-output behavior (from input v_{in} to output v_{out}).

and the transformed open-loop system (figure 3.11b)

$$v_{out} = [G_1' \vdots G_2'] \begin{bmatrix} x \\ \frac{1}{s} Cx \end{bmatrix} = [G_1' \vdots G_2'] \begin{bmatrix} I \\ \frac{1}{s} C \end{bmatrix} (I_s - A)^{-1} B v_{in} \tag{3.8.6}$$

have the same input-output behavior. Consequently, proportional-integral feedback

$$u = G_1' x + G_2' \frac{1}{s} Cx \tag{3.8.7}$$

can be substituted for the feedback law (3.8.4) without any change in the closed-loop system performance.[10]

To show why the robustness of the LQSF design procedure is retained with the feedback law (3.8.7), we parallel the argument used by Anderson [5] in discussing the robustness of single-input PI designs obtained by the

10 For the two feedback laws to yield identical closed-loop performance, we must assume linear model $\dot{x} = Ax + Bu$ *exactly* describes the system dynamics, e.g., there can be no internal noise disturbances or unmodeled dynamics.

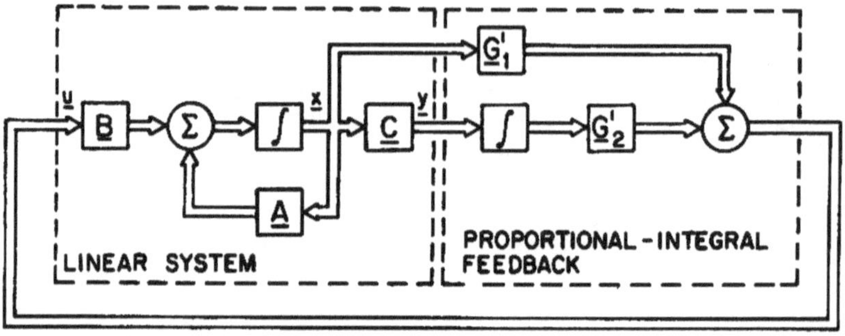

Figure 3.12 Transformed augmented-state LQSF system having proportional-integral feedback.

indirect method. Observe that since the dynamics of (3.8.5) and (3.8.6) are identical, both are tolerant of the same perturbations in the feedback loop when the loop is closed (figure 3.12). As the former system is an LQSF system and therefore [taking $R = \text{diag}(r_1, \ldots, r_m)$] is not distabilized by perturbations N satisfying (3.4.16) and (3.4.19), it follows that the latter system has the same tolerances. We conclude that the robustness properties of the LQSF design procedure are retained when proportional-integral feedback is designed using the indirect method [47, 48, 99]—in particular the resultant PI control system has infinite gain margin, at least a $\pm 60°$ phase margin, and at least a 50% gain reduction tolerance.

3.8.2 Compensated CGEKF

A compensated linear Kalman filter has been proposed in [8] in which the internal system model incorporated in the filter is augmented with integrators, thereby introducing integral feedback (in addition to proportional feedback) into the residual-error feedback loop of the filter. The procedure extends mutatis mutandis to the CGEKF, leading to the compensated CGEKF structure depicted in figure 3.13.

The compensated CGEKF is simply a state-augmented CGEKF having additional states arising from additional noise-driven integrators appended to the stochastic nonlinear system model (figure 3.14). The integrators are positioned such that the residual feedback loop of the resulting augmented CGEKF contains *integral* feedback—so, provided the CGEKF is non-divergent, its steady-state residual bias error $\bar{y} - y$ *must* have a time-average value of zero.

Evidently, the compensated CGEKF is itself a CGEKF—it is a CGEKF

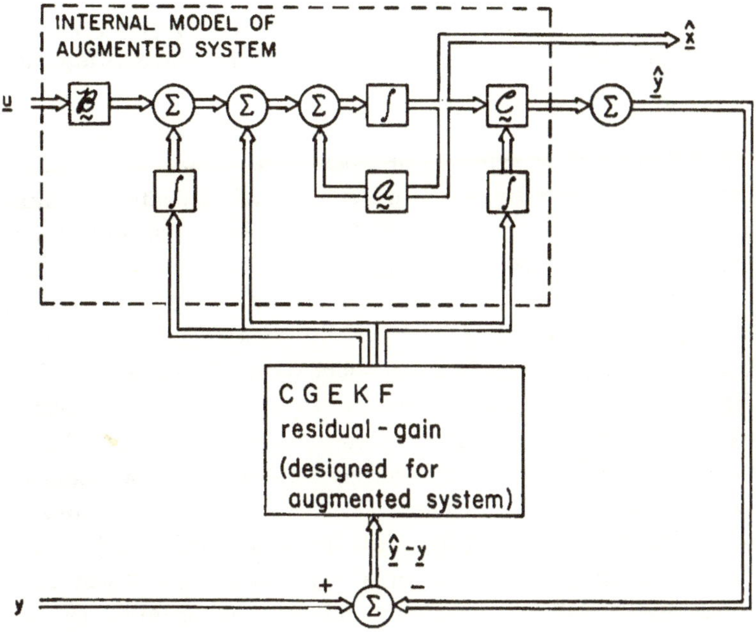

Figure 3.13 Compensated CGEKF. (Compare with CGEKF of figure 3.6.)

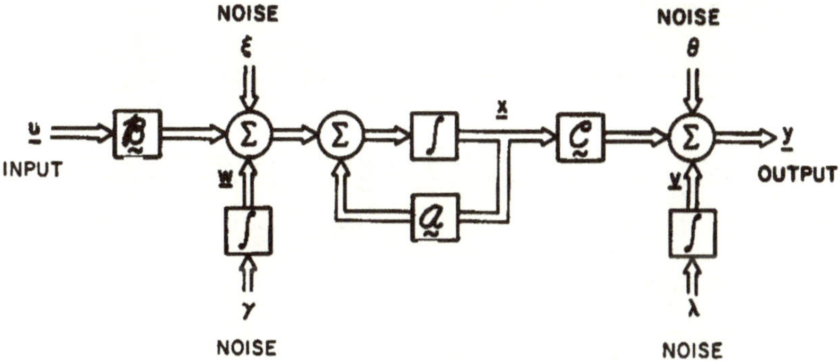

Figure 3.14 Augmented system model employed in compensated CGEKF design. (Compare with the unaugmented model of figure 3.1.)

for the augmented system of figure 3.14; therefore the nondivergence tests of section 3.5 can be applied directly to the compensated CGEKF. Moreover, the compensated CGEKF, being a CGEKF, has the inherent robustness properties associated with all CGEKF designs—e.g., infinite gain margin, at least $\pm 60°$ phase margin, and at least 50% gain reduction tolerance in each output channel of its augmented error-dynamics feedback system.

3.8.3 LQSF General Servomechanism Robustness

A generalization of the direct method of [117] of PI control synthesis concerns the use of state augmentation for the rejection of disturbances generated by an arbitrary linear time-invariant (LTI) system. In this context, a PI compensator can be regarded as a special case in which the closed-loop system is required to reject disturbances generated by the simple LTI system consisting of a single integrator. To synthesize a feedback design capable of rejecting disturbances generated by an arbitrary LTI system, we simply augment the system state by appending to the system output a model of the LTI disturbance process and then design a stabilizing feedback [29] (see figure 3.15). If the stabilizing feedback is designed using the LQSF method, then the resultant feedback design, being an LQSF design, has the inherent robustness characteristic of all LQSF designs, viz., infinite gain margin, at least $\pm 60°$ phase margin, and at least 50% gain reduction tolerance. Moreover, the results of theorem 3.1 can be directly applied to assess the additional stability margins of particular augmented LQSF designs.

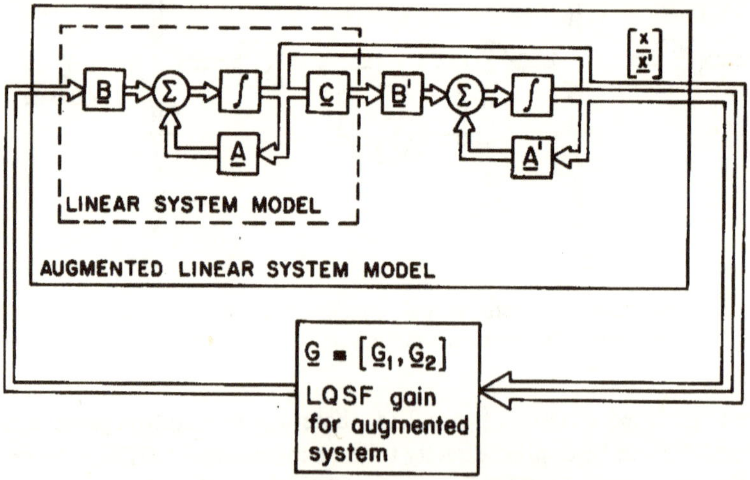

Figure 3.15 Augmented system employed in LQSF general servomechanism design.

3.8.4 Colored-Noise CGEKF

The estimation dual of the LQSF general servomechanism is the "colored noise" CGEKF, in which the residual gain is designed using a state-

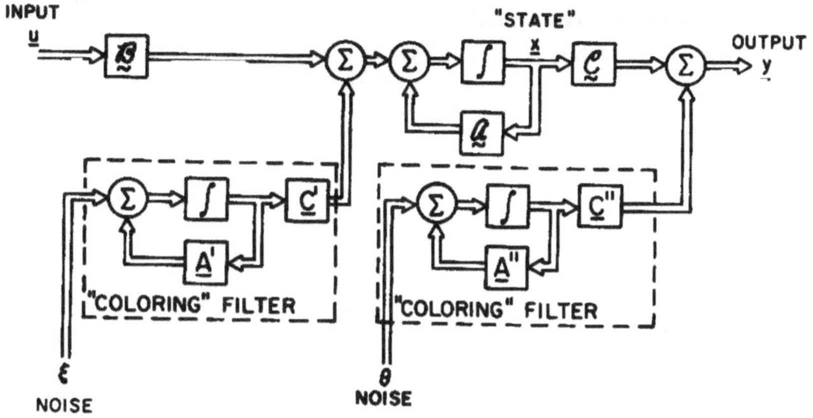

Figure 3.16 Augmented system model employed in colored-noise CGEKF design.

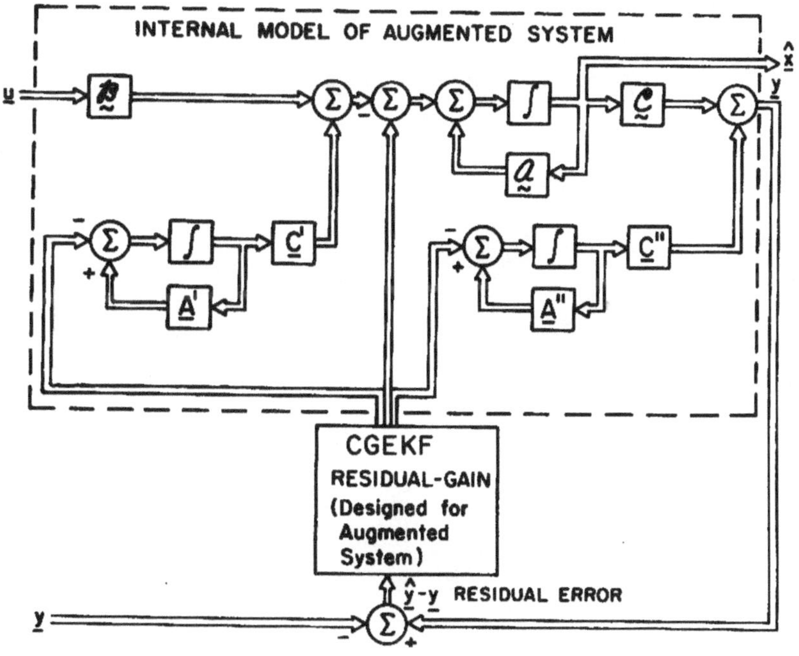

Figure 3.17 Colored-noise CGEKF.

augmented stochastic system model in which the white noises ξ and θ are passed through linear time-invariant "coloring filters" prior to being injected into the system (figure 3.16). This leads to an augmented CGEKF design incorporating the augmented system model in place of the usual nonlinear internal system model (figure 3.17). Because the augmented colored-noise CGEKF is itself a CGEKF, the results of section 3.5 apply directly, including the robust gain and phase margin results.

4

LQG Robustness and Stability: The Discrete-Time/ Sampled-Data Case

4.1 Introduction

Like the continuous-time LQG design procedure discussed in chapter 3, the discrete-time/sampled-data procedure for estimator and controller design (e.g., [10; 28; 55, ch. 6; 68]) has a limitation in that it fails to explicitly incorporate consideration of the stability margins of the resultant designs. That is, the design procedure overlooks the possible destabilizing effects of modeling errors. In this chapter, results are developed which explicitly characterize the stability margins of discrete-time/sampled-data LQG designs. The structure of this chapter and the results presented parallel the structure and results of chapter 3.

There are only minor qualitative differences between the continuous-time results of chapter 3 and the discrete-time/sampled-data results which follow. This is as expected since, in the limit as sampling time decreases to zero, the sampled-data results must coincide with the continuous-time results.

Except for the proofs (which are based on the results of chapter 2), and for the notation (which is explained in section 3.2), the present chapter is logically independent of chapters 2 and 3 and may be read independently.

4.2 Notation and Terminology

The conventions of notation and the terminology employed in this chapter are explained in section 3.2, to which the reader is referred for details.

4.3 Problem Formulation

The results that follow concern the problems of estimation and control for the discrete-time nonlinear dynamical system (figure 4.1a)

$$zx = A(v)\cdot x + B(v)\cdot u + \xi; \qquad x(0) = 0$$
$$y = C(v)\cdot x + \theta, \tag{4.3.1}$$

where
z is the "one-step advance" operator defined by $zx(t) \triangleq x(t + 1)$ for all x;
v is a vector of functions including y, u, t as well as all other *known* or

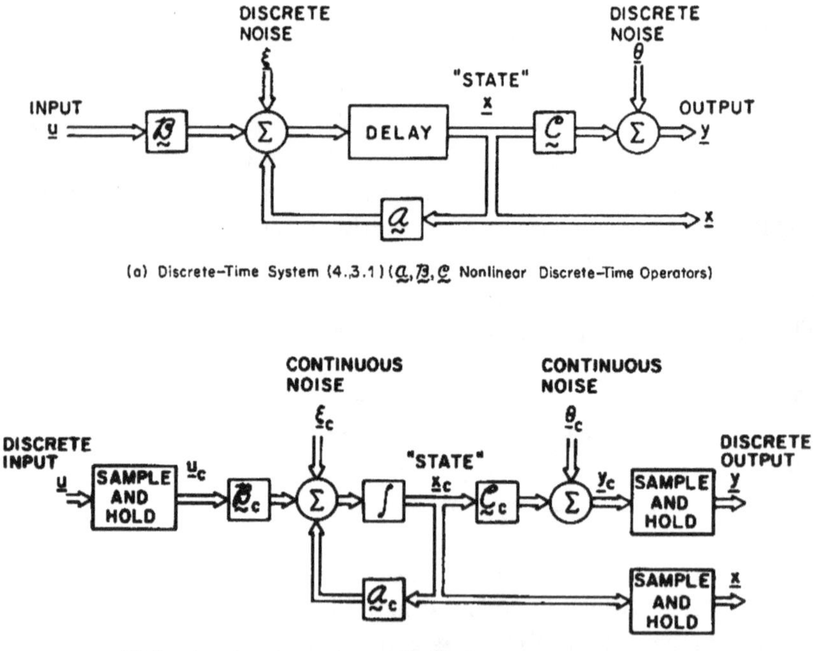

(a) Discrete-Time System (4.3.1) ($\mathcal{A}, \mathcal{B}, \mathcal{C}$ Nonlinear Discrete-Time Operators)

(b) Sampled-Data System (4.3.2) ($\mathcal{A}_c, \mathcal{B}_c, \mathcal{C}_c$ Nonlinear Continuous-Time Operators)

Figure 4.1 The discrete-time system and the sampled-data system which it models.

observed functions (e.g., estimates $\hat{x}$ of x generated from observations and known exogenous inputs to the system);
A, B, C are nonanticipative, differentiable, dynamical nonlinear operators which have finite incremental gain and which may in general be nonanticipatively dependent on v;
$\xi \in m_{2e}(Z_+, R^n)$, $\theta \in m_{2e}(Z_+, R^p)$ are disturbance input (noise) functions;
$y: Z_+ \to R^p$ is an observed output function;
$u: Z_+ \to R^m$ is a control input function;
$x: Z_+ \to R^n$ is a function which is to be estimated and/or controlled, depending on the problem specifications.
For simplicity, it is further assumed that $\mathbf{A}0 = 0$, $\mathbf{B}0 = 0$, and $\mathbf{C}0 = 0$. This system is the discrete-time analogue of the continuous time system considered in chapter 3. As in chapter 3, the v-dependence of **A, B, C** is suppressed for brevity of notation in the following.

Relation to Sampled-Data Systems The discrete-time system (4.3.1) is of practical interest primarily because it models the input-output behavior of sampled-data continuous-time systems such as (figure 4.1b)

$$\begin{aligned}
\dot{x}_c &= \mathbf{A}_c x_c + \mathbf{B}_c u_c + \xi_c \\
y_c &= \mathbf{C}_c x_c + \theta_c \\
u_c(t/k\Delta) &= u(k), \qquad k\Delta \leq t \leq (k+1)\Delta \qquad (4.3.2) \\
x(k) &= x_c(t)|_{t=k\Delta} \\
y(k) &= y_c(t)|_{t=k\Delta},
\end{aligned}$$

where Δ is the sampling interval and $k \in Z_+$, $t \in R_+$ (the subscript "c" indicates continuous time—ξ_c, θ_c, u_c, x_c, and y_c are functions on R_+, rather than on Z_+). Such systems arise, for example, when a digital computer is employed in the estimation and control of continuous-time systems, since the digital computer must interface with the continuous-time system through some sort of sample-and-hold device.

In general, with appropriately chosen **A, B, C** operators, the discrete-time system exactly models the input-output behavior of the sampled-data system (4.3.2) from input u to output y. Consequently, provided the sampled system does not have any unstable internal modes of behavior which are not detectable through the output sampler and/or not stabilizable with discrete inputs (e.g., resonances at the sampling frequency), then it is evident that the discrete model (4.3.1) should be adequate for the purpose of designing stabilizing digital feedback laws for the sampled system (4.3.2).

In the simple case in which $\mathbf{A}_c, \mathbf{B}_c, \mathbf{C}_c$ are constant matrices, the discrete-time system operators $\mathbf{A}$, $\mathbf{B}$, $\mathbf{C}$ are likewise constant matrices and are given explicitly by

$$\mathbf{A} = \exp(\Delta \mathbf{A}_c) = I + \Delta \mathbf{A}_c + o(\Delta)$$

$$\mathbf{B} = \int_0^{\Delta} \exp[(\Delta - t)\mathbf{A}_c]\mathbf{B}_c \, dt = \Delta t \mathbf{B}_c + o(\Delta)$$

$$\mathbf{C} = \mathbf{C}_c,$$

where $o(\Delta)$ is a term depending on Δ with the property

$$\lim_{\Delta \to 0} o(\Delta)/\Delta = 0.$$

This generalizes easily to the case where $\mathbf{A}_c$, $\mathbf{B}_c$, $\mathbf{C}_c$ are time-varying matrices [28].

Controller and Estimator Structures For estimation and control of the system (4.3.1), three structures are considered:

(i) *Nonlinear State-Feedback Controller* (figure 4.2a)

$$u = -G(v)x, \tag{4.3.3}$$

where $G(\cdot)$ is an $m \times n$ matrix whose elements are dependent on v.

(ii) *Nonlinear Observer Estimator* (figure 4.2b)

$$\begin{aligned} z\hat{x}^{(-)} &= \mathbf{A}\hat{x}^{(-)} + \mathbf{B}u - H(v)[\hat{y}^{(-)} - y]; \qquad \hat{x}^{(-)}(0) = 0 \\ \hat{y}^{(-)} &= \mathbf{C}\hat{x}^{(-)} \\ \hat{x}^{(+)} &= \hat{x}^{(-)} - F(v)(\hat{y}^{(-)} - y), \end{aligned} \tag{4.3.4}$$

where $H(v)$ is an $n \times p$ matrix whose elements are dependent on v:[1]

(iii) *Combined Nonlinear Output-Feedback Controller* (figure 4.2c)

$$\begin{aligned} u &= -G(v)\hat{x}^{(+)} \\ z\hat{x}^{(-)} &= \mathbf{A}\hat{x}^{(-)} + \mathbf{B}u - H(v)[\hat{y}^{(-)} - y]; \qquad \hat{x}^{(-)}(0) = 0 \\ \hat{y}^{(-)} &= \mathbf{C}\hat{x}^{(-)} \end{aligned} \tag{4.3.5}$$

1 $x^{(-)}(t)$ is an estimate of $x(t)$ based on observations $\{y(i) \mid i \leq t - 1\}$, but ignoring the current measurement $y(t)$; $x^{(+)}(t)$ is an adjusted estimate incorporating the measurement $y(t)$.

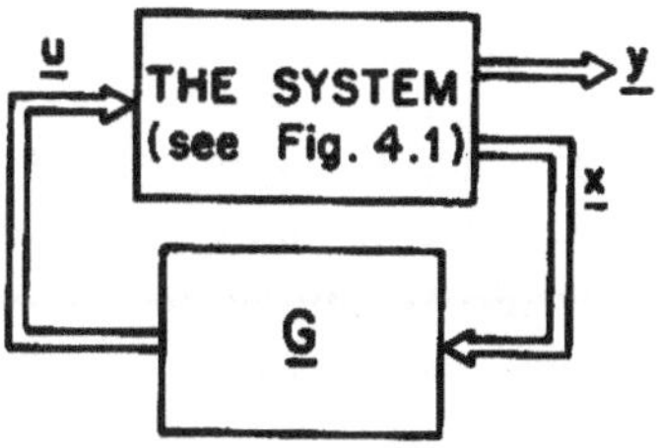

(a) System and Nonlinear State-Feedback Controller

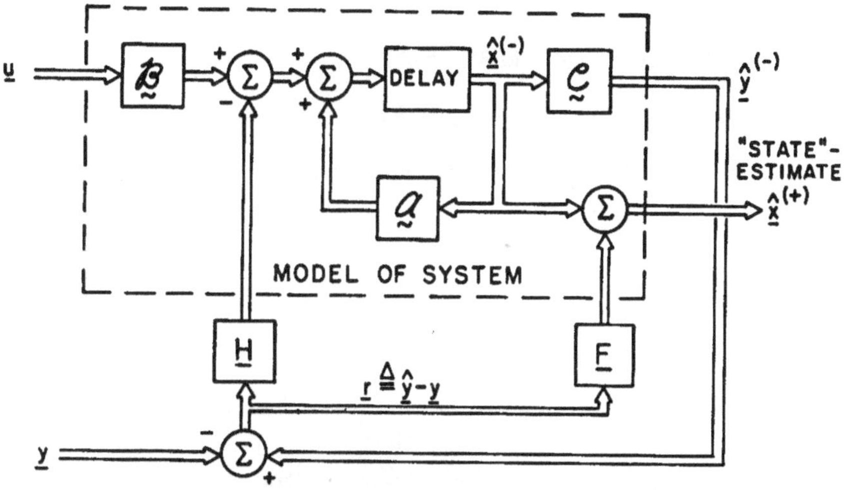

(b) Nonlinear Observer Estimator

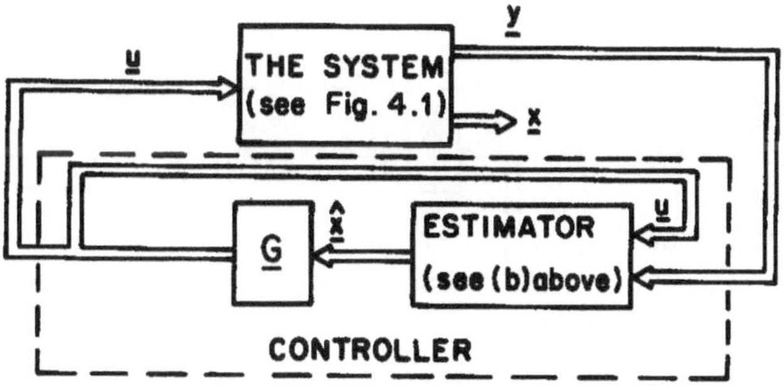

(c) System with Combined Nonlinear Output-Feedback Controller

Figure 4.2 Controller and estimator structures.

$$\hat{x}^{(+)} = \hat{x}^{(-)} - F(\mathrm{v})(\hat{y}^{(-)} - y),$$

where $F(\cdot)$, $G(\cdot)$, and $H(\cdot)$ are as above. The stability margins of suboptimal nonlinear LQG estimator and controller designs are addressed as special cases of the results pertaining to the structures (4.3.3)–(4.3.5) above.

Comments A useful method describing the dynamical evolution of the nonlinear observer's error sequences,

$$e^{(-)} \triangleq \hat{x}^{(-)} - x, \qquad e^{(+)} \triangleq \hat{x}^{(+)} - x,$$

is by the feedback equations (figure 4.3)

$$\left.\begin{aligned} ze^{(-)} &= \tilde{\mathbf{A}}(x)e^{(-)} + v - \xi; \qquad e(0) = 0 \\ e^{(+)} &= e^{(-)} - F(\mathrm{v})r \\ r &= \tilde{\mathbf{C}}(x)e^{(-)} - \theta \end{aligned}\right\} \tag{4.3.6}$$

$$v \triangleq -H(\mathrm{v})r, \tag{4.3.7}$$

where

$$r \triangleq \hat{y}^{(-)} - y, \tag{4.3.8}$$

and $\tilde{\mathbf{A}}(x)$ and $\tilde{\mathbf{C}}(x)$ are dynamical nonlinear operators defined by

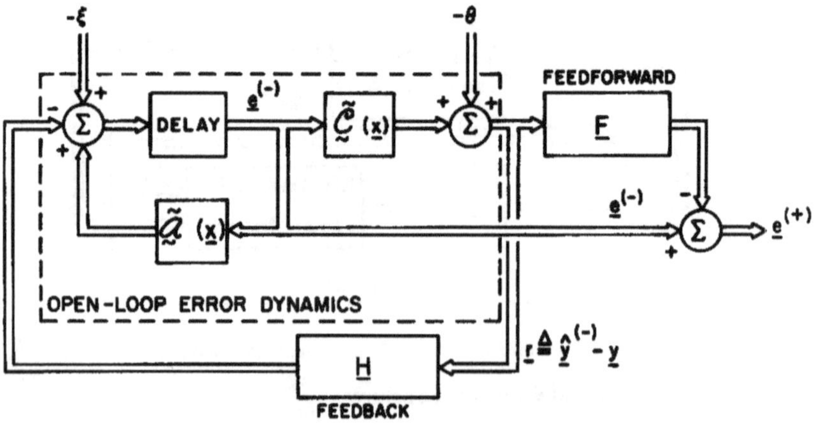

Figure 4.3 Feedback representation of nonlinear-observer dynamics.

$$\tilde{A}(x)\delta x \triangleq A(x + \delta x) - Ax \tag{4.3.9}$$

$$\tilde{C}(x)\delta x \triangleq C(x + \delta x) - Cx, \tag{4.3.10}$$

for all $\delta x \in m_2(Z_+, R^n)$. From this feedback representation of the nonlinear observer estimator (4.3.4), it is immediately evident that the problem of choosing a residual gain $H(\cdot)$ so as to make the estimator nondivergent is equivalent to the problem of choosing a stabilizing feedback for the system (4.3.6).

In order to facilitate the selection of suitable state-feedback-gain and residual-gain matrices ($G(\cdot)$ and $H(\cdot)$, respectively), it is assumed that given *any* fixed v (e.g., $v = v_0$), the system (4.3.1) admits a nominal linearization approximating[2] its behavior for v near v_0:

$$\begin{aligned} z\delta x &= A(v_0)\delta x + B(v_0)u + \xi \\ \delta y &= C(v_0)\delta u + \theta, \end{aligned} \tag{4.3.11}$$

where $A(v_0)$, $B(v_0)$, and $C(v_0)$ are constant matrices of appropriate dimensions whose entries depend in general on v_0. The idea is to design the gains $F(\cdot)$, $G(\cdot)$, and $H(\cdot)$ assuming v_0 is fixed; as in the continuous-time case discussed in chapter 3, this reduces the problem to a linear time-invariant problem for which a variety of methods are available for designing $G(\cdot)$ and $H(\cdot)$, e.g., pole-assignment, LQG optimization, etc. For brevity of notation the arguments of A, B, C, G, and H are suppressed in the following, except where clarity mandates their presence. Clearly, A, B, C, F, G, and H may be chosen to be independent of their arguments; this results in the simplest controller and estimator structures.

4.4 State-Feedback Stability Margins

In this chapter, we characterize the stability margins of discrete-time state-feedback systems of the type shown in figure 4.2a (see equations (4.3.1) and (4.3.3)). The margins are with respect to the nominal linear model

$$zx = Ax + Bu + \xi; \qquad x(0) = 0 \tag{4.4.1}$$

$$u = -Gx, \tag{4.3.3}$$

where $A(\cdot)$ and $B(\cdot)$ are as in (4.3.11).

2 The term "approximating" is intentionally vague; what constitutes a satisfactory approximation in a given application is the subject of the subsequent sections of this chapter.

The basic result, lemma 4.1 below, characterizes a convex set of nondestabilizing deviations of the actual system dynamics (4.3.1), (4.3.3) from the nominal linear model (4.4.1), (4.3.3). The implications of this result regarding LQSF designs are addressed by theorem 4.1. It is shown that LQSF sampled-data designs approach infinite gain margin, at least $\pm 60°$ phase margin, and at least 50% gain reduction tolerance as the sampling rate increases; a test for whether the sampling rate is sufficiently high to approximate these margins is developed.

4.4.1 General Results

The following result gives stability margins for the linearized state-feedback system (4.4.1), (4.3.3); the result gives a sufficient condition for the actual nonlinear state-feedback system (4.3.1), (4.3.3) to be closed-loop stable.

LEMMA 4.1 (State-Feedback Stability Margins) Let the constant matrix $P \in R^{n \times n}$ and the v-dependent matrix $S(v) \in R^{n \times n}$ be symmetric, uniformly positive-definite solutions of the discrete Lyapunov equation

$$P = [A - B \quad G]^T P [A - B \quad G] + S. \tag{4.4.2}$$

If uniformly for all (x, u) either

(i) $\text{Graph}(P^{1/2}[\mathbf{A} + \mathbf{B} \circ (-G)])$ strictly inside $\text{Cone}(0, P^{1/2})$ (4.4.3a)

or

(ii) $\text{Graph}(P^{1/2}[\nabla \mathbf{A}(x) + \nabla \mathbf{B}(u) \circ (-G)])$ strictly inside $\text{Cone}(0, P^{1/2})$, (4.4.3b)

then the system (4.3.1) with nonlinear state feedback (4.3.3) is closed-loop finite-gain stable. Condition (4.4.3a) is implied by condition (4.4.3b).

PROOF See appendix D.

The condition (4.4.2) is not a severe restriction; it specifies in essence that the matrix P must be chosen so that $x^T(t)Px(t)$ is a positive-definite Lyapunov function ensuring closed-loop stability for the ideal situation in which the linearization (4.4.1) exactly models the actual system (4.3.1). For example, when A, B, and G are constant matrices and G stabilizes the linearization (4.4.1), a constant matrix P satisfying (4.4.2) can easily be found by simply picking any positive-definite S and solving (4.4.2) for the unique positive-definite solution P satisfying (4.4.2) [112, p. 175].

The interesting part of lemma 4.1 is the condition (4.4.3). It characterizes a class of operators **A** and **B** in (4.3.1) for which the feedback gain G is assured of being stable. In view of (4.4.2), the condition (4.4.3a) can be expressed equivalently in terms of the deviation $(\Delta\mathbf{A}, \Delta\mathbf{B})$ between $(\mathbf{A}, \mathbf{B})$ and (A, B), as

$$\begin{aligned}&\operatorname{Graph}(P^{1/2}[A - BG + \Delta\mathbf{A} + (\Delta\mathbf{B})(-G)])\\ &\qquad \text{strictly inside } \operatorname{Cone}(0, [(A - BG)^{\mathrm{T}}P(A - BG) + S]^{1/2}),\end{aligned} \tag{4.4.4}$$

where

$$\begin{aligned}\Delta\mathbf{A} &\triangleq \mathbf{A} - A\\ \Delta\mathbf{B} &\triangleq \mathbf{B} - B.\end{aligned} \tag{4.4.5}$$

Equation (4.4.3b) can be analogously expressed in terms of the deviation $(\Delta\mathbf{A}, \Delta\mathbf{B})$. Since S is positive definite, it is immediately evident that (4.4.4) and, hence, (4.4.3) are satisfied when the deviation $(\Delta\mathbf{A}, \Delta\mathbf{B})$ is zero, i.e., when the linear model (4.4.1) is exact. Thus, condition (4.4.3) defines a set of deviations of the actual system (4.3.1) from the linear model (4.4.1) within which the feedback G is assured of stabilizing the system (4.3.1). Moreover, since conic sectors are convex, it follows that this set of nondestabilizing deviations $(\Delta\mathbf{A}, \Delta\mathbf{B})$ is convex, i.e., if the pairs $(\Delta\mathbf{A}_i, \Delta\mathbf{B}_i)$ $(i = 1, \ldots, N)$ are in the set then for every N-vector λ such that $\sum_{i=1}^{N} \lambda_i = 1$ the pair $(\sum_{i=1}^{N} \lambda_i \Delta\mathbf{A}_i, \sum_{i=1}^{N} \lambda_i \Delta\mathbf{B}_i)$ is in the set too.[3]

As a consequence of the convexity of the set of nondestabilizing deviations $(\Delta\mathbf{A}, \Delta\mathbf{B})$, the condition (4.4.3) is much easier to verify than might be apparent at first inspection; one need only find some polygonal region containing the set of possible $(\Delta\mathbf{A}, \Delta\mathbf{B})$ and then simply check that (4.4.3) holds at the vertices of the region. For example, suppose that the matrix S is a constant matrix and the operators **A** and **B** are nondynamical and that there are constants $a_{ij}^{(\ell)}$, $b_{jk}^{(\ell)}$ $(\ell = 1, 2;\ i, j = 1, \ldots, n;\ k = 1, \ldots, m)$ such that for all $x \in \mathrm{R}^n$ and all $u \in \mathrm{R}^m$

$$0 \geq a_{ij}^{(1)} \leq [A - \nabla\mathbf{A}(x)]_{ij} \leq a_{ij}^{(2)} \geq 0 \tag{4.4.6a}$$

$$0 \geq b_{jk}^{(1)} \leq [B - \nabla\mathbf{B}(u)]_{jk} \leq b_{ij}^{(2)} \geq 0 \tag{4.4.6b}$$

3 This follows by induction from lemma 2.2.

(the notation $[M]_{ij}$ denotes ij-th element of the matrix M). Then, as one may readily verify, the convexity of conic sectors implies that sufficient conditions for (4.4.3) to be satisfied are

$$\text{Graph}\,(P^{1/2}[A - BG + \text{N}a_{ij}^{(\ell)} e_i e_j^{\text{T}}]) \text{ strictly inside Cone}\,(0, P^{1/2}), \tag{4.4.7a}$$

$$\text{Graph}\,(P^{1/2}[A - BG - \text{N}b_{ij}^{(\ell)} e_j e_k^{\text{T}} G]) \text{ strictly inside Cone}\,(0, P^{1/2}) \tag{4.4.7b}$$

($\ell = 1, 2$; i, j = 1, . . . , n; k = 1, . . . , m), where e_i denotes the i-th standard basis vector (i.e., e_i is the vector where elements are all zero except the i-th, which is one), and where N is the number of nonzero elements in the set[4]

$$\{(a_{ij}^{(1)}, a_{ij}^{(2)}), (b_{jk}^{(1)}, b_{jk}^{(2)}) \mid \text{i, j} = 1, \ldots, \text{n}; \text{k} = 1, \ldots, \text{m}\}.$$

So, if the linear model (4.4.1) of the discrete system (4.3.1) is exact except for N nonlinearities and/or imprecisely modeled parameters, then one need only check the conicity of at most 2N n × n matrices to verify (4.4.3); this involves checking the positive definiteness of the 2N quadratic forms corresponding to (4.4.7a, b), which can be done, e.g., by checking that the leading minors of 2N n × n matrices are positive.[5]

4.4.2 Linear-Quadratic State Feedback (LQSF)

Consider now the case of exponentially-weighted optimal LQSF. This corresponds to the state feedback G being chosen so as to minimize the quadratic performance index

$$\text{J} = \sum_{t=0}^{\infty} \alpha^{2t}[x^{\text{T}}(t)Qx(t) + 2u^{\text{T}}(t)Mx(t) + u^{\text{T}}(t)Ru(t)]$$

(where Q, R, M are weighting matrices having the property that $\begin{bmatrix} Q & M^{\text{T}} \\ M & R \end{bmatrix}$

4 The word *sufficient* is emphasized because it appears that (4.4.7) is far from a *necessary* condition for (4.4.3) to be satisfied. Whereas (4.4.6) defines a polygonal region in parameter space with 2^{N} vertices, the condition (4.4.7) tests conicity of a somewhat larger polygonal region with only 2N vertices containing the former polygonal region—the use of the larger 2N-vertex region keeps the number of conicity checks down to 2N vice 2^{N}.

5 For R, M matrices, Graph (M) strictly inside Cone (0, R) iff $R^{\text{T}}R - M^{\text{T}}M > 0$.

is positive definite, and $\alpha \geq 1$ is an exponential weighting constant; α is commonly taken to be unity) subject to the constraint on x and u imposed by the linear model (4.4.1):

$$zx = Ax + Bu + \xi; \qquad x(0) = 0.$$

For simplicity, attention is restricted to the case where A, B, Q, R, and M are constant matrices, i.e., ones that are independent of x, u. For design purposes the disturbance ξ is presumed to consist of a single pulse $\xi(t) = \delta_{t,0}x_0$ ($x_0 \in R^n$; δ_{t_1,t_2} is the Kronecker delta). Provided that the system is controllable, then the optimal state feedback is given by [28]

$$G = (R + B^T KB)^{-1}(B^T KA + M), \tag{4.4.8}$$

where K is the unique symmetric positive-definite solution of the discrete Riccati equation[6]

$$K = \alpha^2[A^T KA + Q - (B^T KA + M)^T \cdot (R + B^T KB)^{-1}(B^T KA + M)]. \tag{4.4.9}$$

Relation to Sampled-Data Linear-Quadratic State Feedback It is known [28] that with $\alpha = 1$ and with appropriately specified (Q, R, M, A, B) the discrete-time optimal state feedback (4.4.8) is also the optimal state feedback for the sampled-data optimal control problem

$$\min \int_0^\infty x_c^T(t)Q_c x_c(t) + u_c^T(t)R_c u_c(T)\, dt \tag{4.4.10}$$

subject to

$$\begin{aligned} \dot{x}_c &= A_c x_c + B_c u_c \\ u_c(t/\Delta) &= u(k), \qquad k\Delta \leq t \leq (k+1)\Delta \\ x(k) &= x_c(t)|_{t=k\Delta} \end{aligned} \tag{4.4.10'}$$

(see figure 4.1b). Formulas relating (Q, R, M, A, B) to (Q_c, R_c, A_c, B_c) can be found in [28].

Stability Margins of Optimal State Feedback The following theorem

6 The exponentially-weighted discrete-time optimal linear-quadratic control law has not previously been published. Equations (4.4.8) and (4.4.9) are found by substituting $Q(t) = Q\alpha^{2t}$, $R(t) = R\alpha^{2t}$, $M(t) = M\alpha^{2t}$, and $K(t) = K\alpha^{2(t-1)}$ into the well-known time-varying optimal-feedback equations [28, eqs. (23)–(24)].

characterizes the stability margins of discrete-time optimal LQSF designs. Also, as will be shown, the result proves that the discrete-time linear-quadratic design procedure is inherently robust, though in general not as robust as continuous-time optimal designs.

THEOREM 4.1 (LQSF Stability Margins and Robustness) Let K, G be as in (4.4.8) and (4.4.9). Then,

$$K^{1/2} = \alpha\left((A - BG)^{\mathrm{T}}K(A - BG) + [I, -G^{\mathrm{T}}]\begin{bmatrix} Q & M^{\mathrm{T}} \\ M & R \end{bmatrix}\begin{bmatrix} I \\ -G \end{bmatrix}\right)^{1/2} \tag{4.4.11}$$

If either

(i) Graph$(K^{1/2}[\mathbf{A} + \mathbf{B}(-G)])$ strictly inside Cone$(0, K^{1/2})$ (4.4.12a)

or

(ii) uniformly
Graph$(K^{1/2}[\nabla\cdot\mathbf{A}(x) + (\nabla\mathbf{B}(u))\cdot(-G)])$
strictly inside Cone$(0, K^{1/2})$, (4.4.12b)

then the system (4.3.1) with LQSF (4.4.8) is closed-loop finite-gain stable.

PROOF Equation (4.4.11) follows from (4.4.9). Let

$$S = [I, -G^{\mathrm{T}}]\begin{bmatrix} Q & M^{\mathrm{T}} \\ M & R \end{bmatrix}\begin{bmatrix} I \\ -G \end{bmatrix} + (1 - 1/\alpha^2)K \tag{4.4.13}$$

$$P = K; \tag{4.4.14}$$

then (4.4.11) and (4.4.12) ensure that (4.4.2) and (4.4.3) respectively are satisfied. The result follows from lemma 4.1. ∎

To fully appreciate the implications of theorem 4.1 with regard to the inherent robustness of discrete LQSF designs and, in particular, to demonstrate the gain and phase margin interpretation of this robustness, it is instructive to consider the special case in which all the deviation between the actual system (4.3.1) and the linear model (4.4.1) is "lumped" into a single nonlinear dynamical perturbation $\mathbf{N}$ inserted in the feedback loop at the point indicated in figure 4.4; this corresponds to the case

$$\mathbf{A} = A \tag{4.4.15}$$

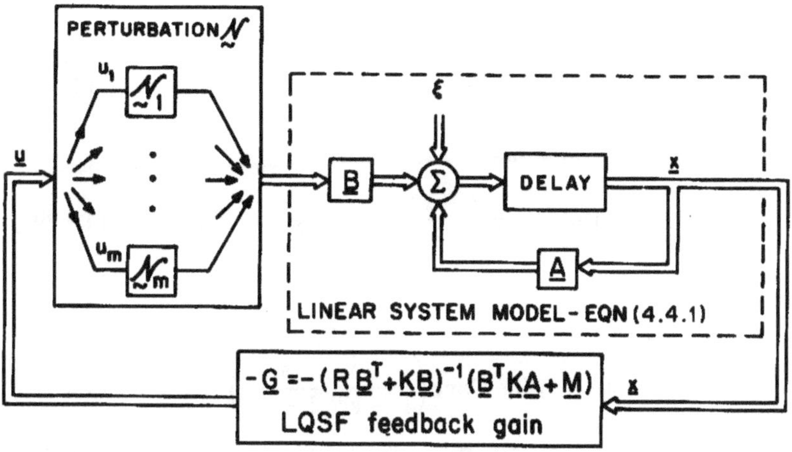

Figure 4.4 Discrete LQSF design with perturbation in feedback loop.

$$\mathrm{B} = B\mathrm{N}, \tag{4.4.16}$$

where N has finite incremental gain and N0 = 0. It is emphasized that we are *not* restricting attention to systems with only perturbations originating physically at the point indicated in figure 4.4; rather, we are merely stipulating that the *open-loop* dynamics of the actual LQSF design [equations (4.3.1), (4.3.8)] have the same input-output behavior as such a system—in practice, one would normally use experimental input-output data to deduce system input perturbation N producing the open-loop input-output behavior of the actual system. For simplicity, it is further assumed that

$$\mathrm{R} = \operatorname{diag}(\mathrm{r}_1, \ldots, \mathrm{r}_m) \equiv \begin{bmatrix} \mathrm{r}_1 & 0 \cdots 0 \\ 0 & \mathrm{r}_2 \cdots 0 \\ \cdots & \cdots \\ 0 & 0 \cdots \mathrm{r}_m \end{bmatrix} \tag{4.4.17}$$

and that the perturbation N satisfies

$$\mathrm{N}u = \begin{bmatrix} \mathrm{N}_1 \mathrm{u}_1 \\ \vdots \\ \mathrm{N}_m \mathrm{u}_m \end{bmatrix} \tag{4.4.18}$$

One is led to the following corollary to theorem 4.1.

COROLLARY 4.1 (Multiloop Gain and Phase Margin) Let (4.4.15)–(4.4.18) be satisfied; let $M = 0$; let

$$a_i \triangleq \sqrt{\frac{r_i}{r_i + \lambda_{max}(B^T K B)}} \qquad (i = 1, \ldots, m). \tag{4.4.19}$$

If for all $t = 1, \ldots, m$ either

(i) $\quad \text{Graph}(N_i) \text{ inside Cone}\left(\frac{1}{1 - a_i^2}, \frac{a_i}{1 - 1_i^2}\right)$ (4.4.20a)

or

(ii) uniformly

$$\text{Graph}(\nabla N_i(u_i)) \text{ inside Cone}\left(\frac{1}{1 - a_i^2}, \frac{a_i}{1 - 1_i^2}\right) \tag{4.4.20b}$$

Then the system (4.3.1) with linear-quadratic state feedback (4.4.8) is closed-loop finite-gain stable.

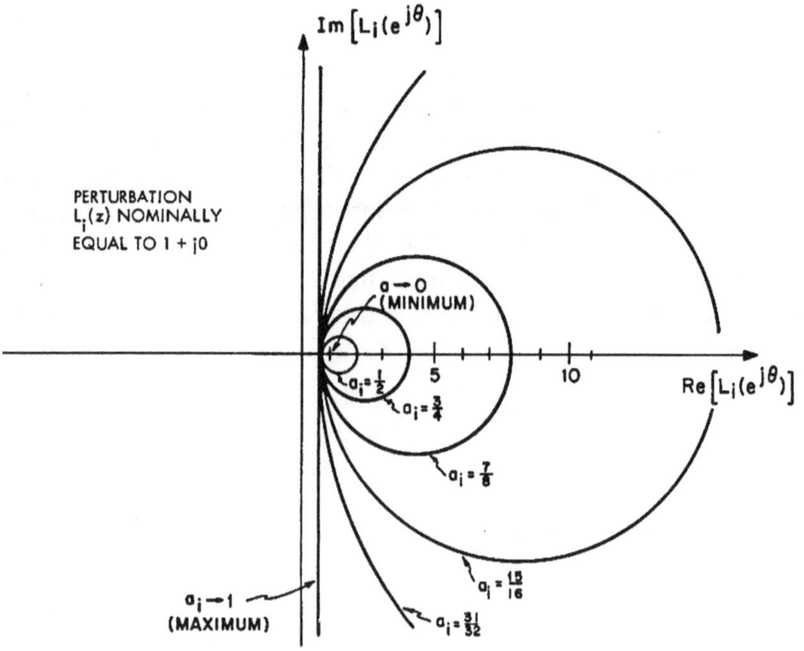

Figure 4.5 Circles in complex plane of radius $(a_i/(1 - a_i^2))$ centered at $(1/(1 - a_i^2)) + j0$ for several values of a_i; stability is assured by corollary 4.1 if the Nyquist locus of each perturbation $L_i(z)$ lies inside the appropriate circle.

PROOF See appendix E.

Comment It can be shown that[7]

$$\text{Cone}\left(\frac{1}{1-a_i^2}, \frac{a_i}{1-a_i^2}\right) = \{(x, y) \mid (y, x) \in \text{Cone}(1, a_i)\}; \tag{4.4.21}$$

Consequently if $N^{-1}([\nabla \mathcal{N}_a(\cdot)]^{-1})$ exists, then (4.4.20a) and (4.4.20b) can be replaced respectively by the equivalent expressions

(i) Graph(N_i^{-1}) inside Cone$(1, a_i)$, (4.4.22a)

(ii) uniformly
Graph$([\nabla N_i(u_i)]^{-1})$ inside Cone$(1, a_i)$. (4.4.22b)

To see the gain and phase margin interpretation of corollary 4.1, consider the case in which each N_i is a finite-gain linear time-invariant operator with z-transform transfer function $L_i(z)$ $(i = 1, \ldots, m)$. Then, (4.4.20a, b) holds if for each $i = 1, \ldots, m$, the z-transform Nyquist locus of $L_i(z)$,

$$\{L_i(e^{j\theta}) \in C \mid \theta \in [0, \pi]\} \qquad (i = 1, \ldots, m), \tag{4.4.23}$$

lies entirely inside the circle of radius $a_i/(1 - a_i^2)$ centered at the point $1/(1 - a_i^2) + j\theta$ in the complex plane C (figure 4.5).[8] For example, if $L_i(z)$ are nondynamical nonlinear gains $L_i(z) = k_i$ $(i = 1, \ldots, m)$, then (4.20a, b) is satisfied if

$$\frac{1}{1+a_i} \le k_i \le \frac{1}{1-a_i} \qquad (i = 1, \ldots, m). \tag{4.4.24}$$

Alternatively, if $L_i(z) = \exp(j\phi_i)$ corresponding to a pure phase shift of angle ϕ_i $(i = 1, \ldots, m)$ in the respective input channels, then condition (4.4.20a, b) becomes

$$|\phi_i| \le 2 \arcsin\left(\frac{a_i}{2}\right). \tag{4.4.25}$$

7 This is shown as part of the proof of corollary 4.1 in appendix E (see eqs. E.1, E.2).
8 This is a consequence of lemma 2.8.

Inequalities (4.4.24)–(4.4.25) specify the minimal gain- and phase-margins associated with each of the m input channels of a discrete LQSF design.

It is noteworthy that when $\lambda_{max}(B^TKB) \ll r_i$—this will be the case for example when (4.3.1) models a sampled-data system with vanishing small sampling interval Δ—then $a_i \to 1$ $(i = 1, \ldots, m)$; it follows immediately from (4.4.24)–(4.4.25) that in the limit as the sampling interval Δ in a sampled LQSF system approaches zero, then the system gain margin becomes infinite; its phase margin approaches (at least!) $\pm 60°$, and it has a gain reduction tolerance approaching (at least!) 50% in each control input channel. These are precisely the stability margins associated with continuous-time LQSF designs (cf. section 3.4.2). Evidently, if

$$\lambda_{max}(B^TKB) \ll r_i \qquad (i = 1, \ldots, m), \tag{4.4.26}$$

then $a_i \to 1$. So for LQSF sampled-data designs, a good indication of whether the sampling interval Δ is small enough to preserve the minimal robustness properties of continuous-time designs is provided by the condition

$$\lambda_{max}(B^TKB) \ll \lambda_{min}(R), \tag{4.4.27}$$

where $\lambda_{min}(R)$ and $\lambda_{max}(B^TKB)$ denote the minimum and maximum eigenvalues of R and B^TKB, respectively.

4.5 Nonlinear Observer Stability Margins

In this section we characterize the stability margins of the discrete-time nonlinear observer

$$\begin{aligned} z\hat{x}^{(-)} &= \mathbf{A}\hat{x}^{(-)} + \mathbf{B}u - H[\hat{y}^{(-)} - y]; \qquad \hat{x}^{(-)}(0) = 0 \\ \hat{y}^{(-)} &= \mathbf{C}\hat{x}^{(-)} \\ \hat{x}^{(+)} &= \hat{x}^{(-)} - F(\hat{y}^{(-)} - y), \end{aligned} \tag{4.3.4}$$

the margins being relative to the ideal situation in which the linear-design model (4.3.11) is exact, i.e., $\mathbf{A} = A$, $\mathbf{B} = B$. Also, stability margins are determined by the error-dynamics feedback representation (4.3.6) and (4.3.7) of the nonlinear observer (4.3.4); these margins characterize a convex set of deviations $(\Delta\mathbf{A}, \Delta\mathbf{C}) \equiv (\mathbf{A} - A, \mathbf{C} - C)$ within which the nonlinear observer is assured of being *nondivergent with finite gain.*

The implications of these results regarding the stability margins and nondivergence of constant-gain extended Kalman filter (CGEKF) designs are addressed by theorem 4.2 below. It is shown that under certain conditions the discrete CGEKF designs approach infinite gain margin, at least $\pm 60°$ phase margin, and at least 50% gain reduction tolerance, the margins being measured at the p inputs to the residual-gain matrix H; this ensures that such designs will be stable and nondivergent despite substantial deviation between the linear-design model (4.3.11) and the nonlinear system (4.3.1).

4.5.1 General

We now state a basic result concerning the stability margins of the nonlinear observer (4.3.4) and its associated error-dynamics feedback system (4.3.6), (4.3.7).

LEMMA 4.2 (Nonlinear Observer Stability Margins and Nondivergence) Let the constant matrix $P \in R^{n \times n}$ and the v-dependent matrix $S(\mathrm{v})$ be symmetric, uniformly positive-definite solutions of the discrete Lyapunov equation

$$P = [A - HC]P[A - HC]^{\mathrm{T}} + S. \tag{4.5.1}$$

(a) If uniformly for all v, x

$$\mathrm{Graph}\,(P^{-1/2}[\nabla A(x) - H \cdot \nabla C(x)]) \text{ strictly inside Cone}\,(0, P^{-1/2}), \tag{4.5.2}$$

then the nonlinear observer (4.3.4) is nondivergent with finite gain; i.e. the mapping of (ξ, θ) into $(e^{(-)}, e^{(+)})$ is finite-gain stable.

(b) If uniformly for all v

$$\mathrm{Graph}\,(P^{-1/2}[\mathrm{A} - H \cdot \mathrm{C}) \text{ strictly inside Cone}\,(0, P^{-1/2}), \tag{4.5.3}$$

then the nonlinear observer (4.3.3) is finite-gain stable; i.e., the mapping of y, u into $(\hat{x}^{(-)}, \hat{x}^{(+)})$ defined by the nonlinear observer has finite gain. Condition (4.5.3) is implied by condition (4.5.2).

PROOF See appendix F.

Comments The condition (4.5.1) of lemma 4.2, like the analogous condition (4.4.2) of lemma 4.1, is not a severe restriction; it merely specifies that $x^{\mathrm{T}}(t)P^{-1}x(t)$ must be a positive-definite Lyapunov function ensuring stability for the ideal situation in which the linear design model (4.3.11) is exact.

The interesting parts of lemma 4.2 are the conditions (4.5.2) and (4.5.3).[9] When the linearization (4.3.11) is exact, the conditions (4.5.2) and (4.5.3) are automatically satisfied as a consequence of (4.5.1).[10] Analogously to condition (4.4.3) of lemma 4.1, conditions (4.5.2), (4.5.3) characterize a *convex* set of nondestabilizing deviations $(\Delta\mathbf{A}, \Delta\mathbf{C}) \equiv (\mathbf{A} - A, \mathbf{C} - C)$ of the actual system (4.3.1) from the linearization (4.3.11). As with condition (4.4.3), conditions (4.5.2), (4.5.3) can be verified (using conditions analogous to (4.4.6), (4.4.7)) by checking the positive definiteness of at most 2N matrices where N is the number of nonlinearities in **A** and **C**.

4.5.2 Constant-Gain Extended Kalman Filter (CGEKF)

Intuitively, it is clear that if the linearization (4.3.11) is sufficiently faithful to the nonlinear system (4.3.1), then the error response of the nonlinear observer (4.3.4) will be close to the error response one would get in the ideal situation in which the linearization is exact. This intuition is validated by the error-bounding results of [38]. Consequently, if the disturbances ξ and θ are reasonably well approximated by zero-mean white noise, then it is reasonable to expect that a good suboptimal minimum variance estimator can be obtained by choosing the residual gain matrices F and H to be the minimum-variance optimal gains for the linearized system (4.3.11), i.e., the discrete-time Kalman filter gains [33, p. 110]

$$F = \Sigma C^{\mathrm{T}}(C\Sigma C^{\mathrm{T}} + \Theta)^{-1} \tag{4.5.4}$$

$$H = AF, \tag{4.5.5}$$

9 Because equations (4.5.2) and (4.5.3) are required to hold uniformly for all $(x^{(-)}, z^{-1}u)$, allowing A, C, H to be dependent on $(x^{(-)}, z^{-1}u)$ offers no advantage in satisfying the conditions (4.5.2), (4.5.3); though it may be possible to improve the error statistics in some situations by allowing such dependence.

10 To see this, let $\mathcal{A} \equiv (A - HC)$ be a stable matrix. Then from (4.5.1),

$$\begin{aligned} I &= (P - S)^{-1/2}\mathcal{A}P\mathcal{A}^{\mathrm{T}}(P - S)^{-1/2} \\ &= [(P - S)^{-1/2}\mathcal{A}P^{1/2}][(P - S)^{-1/2}\mathcal{A}P^{1/2}]^{\mathrm{T}} \\ &= [(P - S)^{-1/2}\mathcal{A}P^{1/2}]^{\mathrm{T}}[(P - S)^{-1/2}\mathcal{A}P^{1/2}] = P^{1/2}\mathcal{A}^{\mathrm{T}}(P - S)^{-1}\mathcal{A}P^{1/2}. \end{aligned}$$

So, pre- and post-multiplying by $P^{-1/2}$, we have

$$P^{-1} = \mathcal{A}^{\mathrm{T}}(P - S)^{-1}\mathcal{A} > \mathcal{A}^{\mathrm{T}}P^{-1}\mathcal{A} \equiv (A - HC)^{\mathrm{T}}P^{-1}(A - HC),$$

from which the conclusion follows.

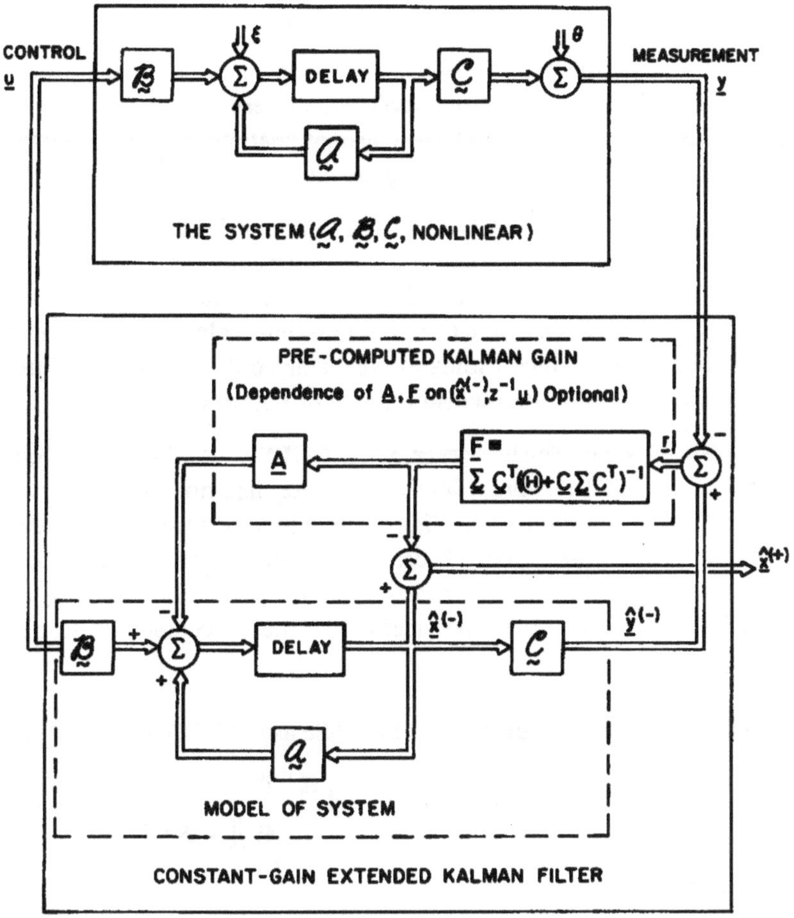

Figure 4.6 System and constant-gain extended Kalman filter (CGEKF).

where $\Sigma = \Sigma^{\mathrm{T}} > 0$ satisfies the discrete-time Riccati equation[11,12]

11 We assume that the required controllability and observability conditions are satisfied so that there is a unique positive-definite solution of (4.5.6) [46, pp. 234–243].

12 An "exponential-weighting factor" $\alpha \geq 1$ has been included—in the Kalman filter α is normally taken to be one. I shall not attempt to provide a rigorous statistical interpretation of α—though intuitively it appears that large values of α lead to increased weighting of recent measurements by the estimator [104, pp. 151–154].

$$\Sigma = \alpha^2[A\Sigma A^{\mathrm{T}} + \Xi - A\Sigma C^{\mathrm{T}}(C\Sigma C^{\mathrm{T}} + \Theta)^{-1}C\Sigma A]^{\mathrm{T}}, \tag{4.5.6}$$

where Ξ and Θ are the *positive-definite* covariance matrices of the disturbances ξ and θ, respectively. For simplicity, we restrict our attention to the case where A, C, Ξ, and Θ are constant matrices.[13] The resultant estimator is the CGEKF depicted in figure 4.6.

Relation to Sampled-Data Estimation The relation of discrete-time minimum-variance estimation to sampled-data minimum-variance estimation is discussed by, e.g., [104, pp. 174–177] wherein it is shown that with appropriately specified Ξ, Θ, A, and C the discrete-time Kalman filter provides optimal minimum-variance estimates for sampled-data systems subject to continuous-time white-noise disturbances of known covariance.

Stability Margins and Nondivergence of the CGEKF An important consequence of the CGEKF procedure for discrete-time nonlinear observer design is that, in addition to yielding a suboptimally accurate estimator design, the discrete-time CGEKF design procedure is inherently robust in the sense that even a crude linearization will suffice for residual-gain design. The following theorem provides a quantitative characterization of this robustness.

THEOREM 4.2 **(CGEKF Robustness)** Let H be as in (4.5.5), (4.5.6). Then

$$\Sigma = \alpha^2\left((A - HC)\Sigma(A - HC)^{\mathrm{T}} + [I, -H]\begin{bmatrix}\Xi & 0\\ 0 & \Theta\end{bmatrix}\begin{bmatrix} I \\ -H^{\mathrm{T}}\end{bmatrix}\right). \tag{4.5.7}$$

(a) If uniformly

$$\mathrm{Graph}\,(\Sigma^{-1/2}(\nabla \mathrm{A}(x) - H\nabla \mathrm{C}(x)) \text{ strictly inside Cone}\,(0, \Sigma^{-1/2}), \tag{4.5.8}$$

then the CGEKF is nondivergent with finite gain.

(b) If

$$\mathrm{Graph}\,(\Sigma^{-1/2}(\mathrm{A} - H\mathrm{C})) \text{ strictly inside Cone}\,(0, \Sigma^{-1/2}), \tag{4.5.9}$$

then the CGEKF is closed-loop finite-gain stable.

PROOF Equation (5.7) follows from (4.5.5), (4.5.6). Let

13 Insofar as nondivergence and stability are concerned, this does not appear to be a serious restriction. See note 9.

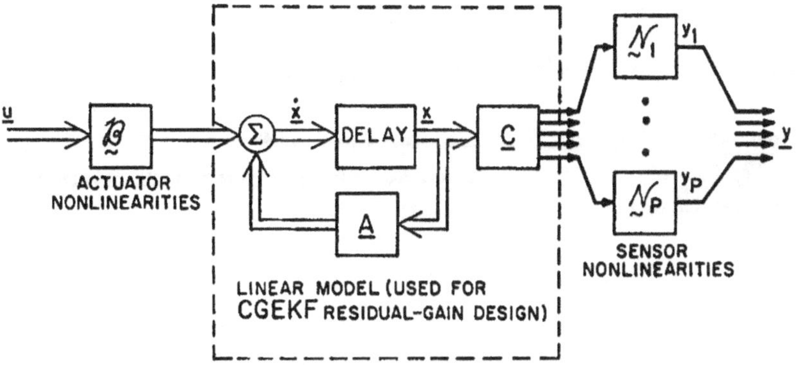

Figure 4.7 System with all nonlinearity lumped in actuators and sensors.

$$S = [I, -H]\begin{bmatrix} \Xi & 0 \\ 0 & \Theta \end{bmatrix}\begin{bmatrix} I \\ -H^{T} \end{bmatrix} + (1 - 1/\alpha^{2})\Sigma \tag{4.5.10}$$

$$P = \Sigma. \tag{4.5.11}$$

Then (4.5.7)–(4.5.9) ensure respectively that (4.5.1)–(4.5.3) are satisfied. The result follows from lemma 4.5.1. ∎

To fully appreciate the implications of theorem 4.2 with regard to the inherent robustness of discrete-time CGEKF designs and in particular to the gain and phase margin interpretation of this robustness, it is instructive to consider the situation in which

$$\mathrm{A}(x) = A \tag{4.5.12}$$

$$\mathrm{C}(x) = [\operatorname{diag}(\mathrm{N}_1, \ldots, \mathrm{N}_p)]C, \tag{4.5.13}$$

for all x, so that all the differences between the open-loop error dynamics system (4.3.6) and the design linearization (4.3.11) are lumped into the nonlinearities N_i (i = 1, . . . , p), which are in series with the system outputs. This is equivalent to all nonlinearity in the system (4.3.1) being lumped in the actuators and sensors (figure 4.7). It is emphasized that this does not mean that we are restricting our attention to systems with only actuator and sensor nonlinearity; rather, we are merely stipulating that the actual system's open-loop error dynamics have the same input-output behavior as such a system.

For simplicity, we further assume that the N_i (i = 1, . . . , p) are linear and time-invariant and that Θ is of the form

$$\Theta = \text{diag}(\theta_{11}, \theta_{22}, \ldots, \theta_{pp}). \tag{4.5.14}$$

One is led to the following corollary to theorem 4.2.

COROLLARY 4.2 (CGEKF Multiloop Gain and Phase Margins) Let (4.5.12)–(4.5.14) be satisfied; let N_i be finite-gain linear time-invariant[14] operators with transfer function $L_i(z)$ (i = 1, . . . , p); let

$$a_i = \sqrt{\frac{\theta_i}{\theta_i + \lambda_{max}(C\Sigma C^T)}} \quad (i = 1, \ldots, p). \tag{4.5.15}$$

If

$$|[L_i(e^{j\theta})]^{-1} - 1| \leq a_i \tag{4.5.16}$$

for each i = 1, . . . , p and all $\theta \in [0, \pi]$, then the CGEKF is closed-loop finite-gain stable and is nondivergent with finite gain.

PROOF See appendix G.

So, by analogy with the discussion of gain and phase-margin in section 4.4 the CGEKF is nondivergent and stable if the z-transform Nyquist locus of $L_i(z)$, viz., $\{L_i(e^{j\theta}) \mid \theta \in [0, \pi]\}$ (i = 1, . . . , p), lies entirely inside the circle of radius $a_i/1 - a_i^2$ centered at $1/(1 - a_i^2) + j0$ in the complex plane C (see figure 4.5). If $L_i(e^{j\theta}) = k_i$, corresponding to the insertion of a scalar gain k_i into each of the p output channels (figure 4.7), then (4.5.16) is satisfied if

$$\frac{1}{1 + a_i} \leq k_i \leq \frac{1}{1 - a_i} \quad (i = 1, \ldots, p); \tag{4.5.17}$$

alternatively, if $L_i(e^{j\theta}) = \exp(j\phi_i)$ (i = 1, . . . , p) corresponding to a pure phase shift of ϕ_i degrees in each output channel, then (4.5.16) is satisfied if

$$|\phi_i| \leq 2 \arcsin\left(\frac{a_i}{2}\right) \quad (i = 1, \ldots, p). \tag{4.5.18}$$

14 It seems probable that the linear time-invariant assumption can be relaxed; though some refinements in the stability results employed in the proof will probably be required if one is to preserve the duality between the proofs of corollaries 4.1 and 4.2.

Inequalities (4.5.17) and (4.5.18) respectively specify the minimal gain and phase margin associated with each of the p output channels of the error-dynamics feedback system (4.3.6), (4.3.7) of a discrete-time CGEKF design.

These minimal stability margins approach the continuous-time CGEKF stability margins (see section 3.5) as $a_i \to 1$, viz.,

$$|\phi_i| \leq \pm 60^\circ \tag{4.5.19}$$

$$\frac{1}{2} < k_i < \infty. \tag{4.5.20}$$

Engineers experienced with classical servomechanism design will recognize these limiting stability margins (4.5.19), (4.5.20) as quite large, ensuring that for $a_i \to 1$ a CGEKF design will be stable and nondivergent despite substantial nonlinearity. Since $a_i \to 1$ when $\lambda_{max}(C\Sigma C^T) \ll \theta_i$, a good indication of whether a given discrete CGEKF design approximately attains the continuous-time robustness limits (4.5.19), (4.5.20) is provided by the condition

$$\lambda_{max}(C\Sigma C^T) \ll \lambda_{min}(\Theta). \tag{4.5.21}$$

In the case of sampled-data designs employing a sampler which averages data over each sampling interval [68], condition (4.5.21) is always satisfied when the sampling interval is sufficiently small. Condition (4.5.21) provides a quantitative test which can be used to judge whether or not the sampling interval is small enough for such a sampled-data CGEKF design to provide the large stability margins associated with continuous-time CGEKF designs.

4.6 Nonlinear Dynamical Output-Feedback Controllers

In this section I develop a fundamental result concerning the use of the discrete-time nonlinear observer (4.3.4) for nonlinear output-feedback controllers having the general structure (see figure 3.2c)

$$\begin{aligned}
&u = G\hat{x}^{(+)} \\
&zx^{(-)} = Ax^{(-)} - Bu - H\cdot[\hat{y}^{(-)} - y] \\
&\hat{x}^{(-)}(0) = 0 \\
&\hat{y}^{(-)} = C\hat{x}^{(-)} \\
&\hat{x}^{(+)} = \hat{x}^{(-)} - F\cdot(\hat{y}^{(-)} - y).
\end{aligned} \tag{4.3.5}$$

The result, which is completely parallel to the continuous-time result developed in section 3.6, implies that the substitution of the estimates generated by a *nondivergent* nonlinear observer for true values in an otherwise-stable feedback-control system can never destabilize the closed-loop system; the result has obvious implications regarding the practical merit of the controller structure (4.3.5). A simple, practical, nonlinear extension of the linear-quadratic Gaussian design procedure emerges as a promising method for designing the gain matrices F, G, and H in (4.3.5).

4.6.1 Separation of Estimation and Control

The fundamental result concerning the controller structure (4.3.5) is now stated.

THEOREM 4.3 (Separation of Estimation and Control) Let **G** be a non-anticipative nonlinear dynamical operator with finite incremental gain; Let $\hat{x}$ be any estimate of x that is nondivergent (with finite gain).[15] Suppose that the system (4.3.1) with feedback $u = \mathbf{G}x$ is closed-loop bounded (finite-gain stable). Then, the system (4.3.1) with feedback $u = \mathbf{G}\hat{x}$ is also closed-loop bounded (finite-gain stable).

PROOF The proof follows mutatis mutandis the proof for the continuous-time case in appendix C.

The practical importance of the result embodied in theorem 4.3 is immediate: stable output-feedback controllers can be designed for nonlinear systems by designing *separately*

(i) a stable state-feedback controller, and

(ii) a nondivergent nonlinear observer.

4.6.2 Suboptimal Nonlinear Output-Feedback Controllers

A logical suboptimal method for choosing the gains F, G, and H of (4.3.5) is to use the LQSF/CGEKF gains. The LQG theorem concerning the separation of estimation and control for discrete-time systems [10, 68] assures that this choice is actually optimal in the ideal situation in which the linear design model (4.3.11) coincides with the actual system (4.3.1).

15 Note that we do *not* stipulate what estimator or what state-feedback control **G** is used; in particular, x need not be generated by the nonlinear observer and **G** need not be of the form (4.3.3).

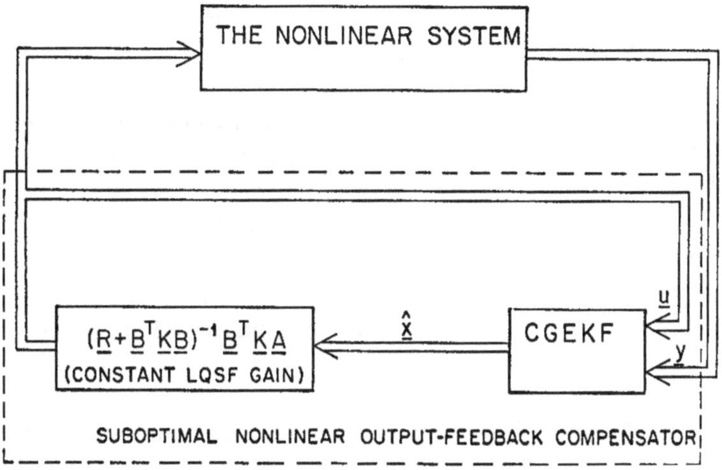

Figure 4.8 Suboptimal nonlinear output-feedback compensator.

The resultant suboptimal feedback controller depicted in figure 4.8 is completely specified by the following formula (cf. sections 4.4 and 4.5):

$$
\begin{aligned}
&u = -(R + B^{\mathrm{T}}KB)^{-1}B^{\mathrm{T}}KA\hat{x}^{(+)}\\
&z\hat{x}^{(-)} = \mathbf{A}\hat{x}^{(-)} + \mathbf{B}u - A\Sigma C^{\mathrm{T}}(\Theta + C\Sigma C^{\mathrm{T}})^{-1}[\hat{y}^{(-)} - y]; \quad \hat{x}^{(-)}(0) = 0\\
&\hat{y}^{(-)} = \mathbf{C}\hat{x}^{(-)} \qquad\qquad (4.6.1)\\
&\hat{x}^{(+)} = \hat{x}^{(-)} - \Sigma C(\Theta + C\Sigma C^{\mathrm{T}})^{-1}[\hat{y}^{(-)} - y],
\end{aligned}
$$

where K and Σ are positive-definite solutions of the (exponentially weighted) discrete-time matrix Riccati equations (sections 4.4 and 4.5)

$$K = \alpha_1^2[A^{\mathrm{T}}KA + Q - A^{\mathrm{T}}KB(R + BKB)^{-1}(B^{\mathrm{T}}KA] \qquad (4.6.2)$$

$$\Sigma = \alpha_2^2[A\Sigma A^{\mathrm{T}} + \Xi - A\Sigma C^{\mathrm{T}}(\Theta + C\Sigma C^{\mathrm{T}})^{-1}C\Sigma A^{\mathrm{T}}], \qquad (4.6.3)$$

where the exponential-weighting constants α_i, $\alpha_2 \geq 1$ and the positive-definite weighting matrices Q, R, Ξ, and Θ are chosen by the designer; and where A, B, C are the matrices from the linear model (4.3.11).[16] As in sections 4.4.2 and 4.5.2, we restrict our attention to the case where A, B, C, Q, R, Ξ, and Θ are constant matrices.

This approach to suboptimal nonlinear output-feedback controller

16 The (u, x) "cross-weighting" term M has in (4.6.2) been taken to be $M = 0$ for simplicity (see section 4.4.2).

design is similar in spirit to the approach outlined in [10], wherein an extended Kalman filter is cascaded with a time-varying suboptimal feedback gain; however the pre-computed constant gains F, G, and H of the feedback law (4.6.1) make it considerably simpler to implement from the standpoint of real-time computational burden than suboptimal feedback laws with time-varying gains. The inherent robustness of the LQSF/CGEKF design procedures ensure that the feedback law (4.6.1) is stabilizing for systems with even substantial nonlinearity. The extent of this robustness is quantified by the following result, which characterizes a set of tolerable deviations between the linear model (4.3.11) and the actual system (4.3.1).

THEOREM 4.4 (Suboptimal Nonlinear Output-Feedback Robustness) If uniformly

$$\text{Graph}\,(\Sigma^{-1/2}(\nabla \mathbf{A}(x) - H\nabla \mathbf{C}(x))) \text{ strictly inside Cone}\,(0, \Sigma^{-1/2}) \tag{4.6.4}$$

and if

$$\text{Graph}\,(K^{1/2}(\mathbf{A} + \mathbf{B}(-G))) \text{ strictly inside Cone}\,(0, K^{1/2}), \tag{4.6.5}$$

then the system (4.3.1) with suboptimal nonlinear output-feedback (4.6.1) is closed-loop finite-gain stable.

PROOF Theorem 4.2 ensures that the CGEKF is nondivergent with finite gain. Theorem 4.1 ensures that the feedback $u = -(R + B^TKB)^{-1}B^TKA$ leads to closed-loop finite-gain stability. The result follows from theorem 4.3. ∎

4.7 Design Considerations in Suboptimal Estimation and Control for Nonlinear Systems

In this section I will discuss briefly how the results of sections 4.4–4.6 can be of use in the computer-aided-design of LQSF/CGEKF estimators and controllers for *nonlinear* systems. The ideas presented are essentially identical to those of section 3.7; so, in the interest of avoiding excessive redundancy, only the main points will be repeated.

The separation result embodied in theorem 4.3 ensures that *any nondivergent estimate* $\hat{x}$ of the state x can be used by a state-feedback controller for (4.3.1) without causing instability. This has the important practical

implication that nonlinear output feedback controller design can be separated into two distinct tasks:
(i) state-estimator design, and
(ii) state-feedback design.
These two design tasks can be accomplished suboptimally using the CGEKF/LQSF design procedure; this leads under appropriate conditions[17] to a closed-loop finite-gain stable nonlinear controller whose dynamics consist only of a nonlinear internal model of the system.

Insofar as the actual design of a stable LQSF state-feedback and a nondivergent CGEKF estimator is concerned, the computer-aided-design methodology outlined in sections 3.7.2 and 3.7.3 can be applied mutatis mutandis to discrete-time designs. The discrete-time/sampled-data robustness results of sections 4.4 and 4.5 provide the basis for constructive modification and improvement of such LQSF/CGEKF designs and can be used in gain-scheduled controller and estimator design to determine the region of the state-space in which nondivergence and closed-loop stability are assured for each value of the gains.

4.8 State-Augmented LQSF/CGEKF Designs

As with continuous-time LQSF/CGEKF designs, it is possible with the aid of state augmentation to improve the performance of the designs. The design of proportional-integral discrete LQSF control laws and of discrete Kalman filters which are compensated with integral feedback has been addressed in several technical reports [17, 57, 58]; the methods involve a relatively straightforward modification of the methods employed for continuous-time systems.[18] It is possible to employ state augmentation methods for the design of discrete Kalman filters for linear systems with nonwhite disturbances [109] and for the design of dynamical LQSF feedback laws for discrete systems which are capable of zero-error tracking in the presence of disturbances satisfying an arbitrary differential equation; again this involves a straightforward modification of ideas which have been developed for continuous systems.[19] Such state-augmentation

17 Viz., the conditions of theorems 4.1 and 4.2.

18 Note, however, there are some subtle differences involving the necessity of set-point feedforward gains in adjustable set-point LQSF proportional-integral designs for discrete systems [17].

19 State-augmented continuous LQSF/CGEKF designs are discussed in section 3.8.

methods evidently extend directly to the design of discrete CGEKF estimators for nonlinear systems; this leads to CGEKF designs having a dynamical residual gain, identical to the continuous-time state-augmented CGEKF designs introduced in section 3.8.4 but with the delay operator $1/z$ substituted for the integral operator $1/s$.

With regard to the stability margins of state-augmented discrete LQSF/CGEKF designs, the key point to remember is that a state-augmented discrete LQSF (or discrete CGEKF) design is itself a discrete LQSF (or discrete CGEKF) design and consequently all of the stability margin results developed in sections 4.4–4.6, as well as the computer-aided-design methodology suggested in section 4.7, apply directly, exactly as has been demonstrated for continuous-time state-augmented designs. In particular, state-augmented discrete LQSF/CGEKF designs retain the large gain and phase margins associated with all discrete LQSF/CGEKF designs—the gain margins approaching infinity and the phase margins approaching at least $\pm 60°$ in sampled-data designs having a sufficiently small sampling interval, as is shown in sections 4.4.2 and 4.5.2.

5

Conclusion

5.1 Conclusions

The *main stability theorem* (theorem 2.1) provides an abstract yet simple conceptual framework for stability theory, a framework sufficiently general to encompass classical Lyapunov theory and Zames's conic relation theorem. The main stability theorem shows that, subject to certain conditions, a multiloop feedback system consisting of a multivariable plant in its forward loop and a multivariable feedback in its backward loop is stable if the dynamical input-output relation of the feedback is disjoint from the inverse of the plant's dynamical relation. Stability analysis is thus only a little more complicated than determining whether or not two sets intersect, a relation being merely a particular type of set. The main practical difficulties in testing for stability of specific systems arise because dynamical relations are in general subsets of infinite-dimensional function spaces; though these difficulties can be overcome either by restricting attention to relations which are relatively simply structured (such as, e.g., nondynamical relations or linear time-invariant relations) or by containing the relations within larger but more simply structured bounding sets. In this monograph, I have focused attention principally on the use of bounding sets:[1] sectors, including conic sectors, are examples of such bounding

1 Restricting attention to linear time-invariant relations (i.e., transfer functions)

sets; and (as is demonstrated by corollaries 2.1a, b) Lyapunov functions also may be viewed as defining such bounding sets. In the case of conic sectors having matrix-valued frequency-dependent center and radius, it has been found that the main stability theorem leads directly to multivariable frequency-domain stability criteria generalizing the circle criterion (section 2.5).

The possibility of using bounding sets, especially conic sectors having matrix-valued frequency-dependent centers and radii, is what makes the main stability theorem ideal for the characterization of stability margins and robustness for multivariable feedback systems. When conic sectors are employed in establishing the nonintersection of sets required by the theorem, a *convex* set (see lemma 2.3) of nondestabilizing variations in the multivariable plant dynamics is established, much in the same spirit as the Nyquist theorem is employed in classical feedback theory to establish the gain and phase margins of single-loop feedback systems.[2] As is explained in section 2.6, the results provide a constructive basis for the synthesis of robustly stable feedback systems.

The new theory has been applied to the characterization of the stability margins and the robustness of modern multivariable feedback systems and estimators. Design-specific stability margins of multivariable LQSF designs and Kalman filters, both continuous- and discrete-time, have been characterized as convex sets of dynamical nonlinear deviations from the linear design model parameterized by the Riccati equation solution. Additionally, continuous-time LQSF and Kalman filter designs have been found to have a certain inherent robustness including an infinite gain margin, at least a $\pm 60°$ phase margin, and at least a 50% gain reduction tolerance—the margins being relative to the linear-design model and measured, in the LQSF case, at each plant input channel and, for the Kalman filter, at each output channel of the filter's internal model of the process dynamics.[3] Discrete-time/sampled-data designs have been found

would have led to results such as the multivariable Nyquist theorem [89, p. 199], or more precisely the sufficiency part of the multivariable Nyquist theorem.

2 Note that specifying a feedback design's gain and phase margins does not specify a *convex* set of tolerable variations; so in this regard conic sectors provide a better measure of stability margin than classical gain and phase margin.

3 Strictly speaking, the results which have been proved require that the open-loop system's dynamical relation lie within these margins for *all* frequencies in order to conclude closed-loop stability; however, for most engineering purposes,

to approximate this inherent robustness under the conditions

$$\lambda_{min}(R) \gg \lambda_{max}(B^T K B),$$
$$\lambda_{min}(\Theta) \gg \lambda_{max}(C \Sigma C^T);$$

these conditions are always satisfied in the case of sampled-data designs for which the sampling interval is chosen to be sufficiently small.

In arriving at these characterizations of stability margins for LQSF and Kalman filter designs, we employed the sector conditions induced by the respective Lyapunov functions

$$x^T K x,$$
$$x^T \Sigma^{-1} x,$$

where K and Σ are the respective solutions of the LQSF and Kalman filter Riccati equations. As pointed out in section 2.7, the optimal solution of the Hamilton-Jacobi equation is normally a Lyapunov function for the optimal closed-loop system[4] and, as demonstrated by the results in section 2.3, a Lyapunov function establishes a sector condition that can be used to determine stability margins. That $x^T K x$ is a Lyapunov function assuring the stability of the optimal LQSF design is a consequence of the fact that $x^T K x$ is the optimal solution of the Hamilton-Jacobi equation for the linear-quadratic optimal-control problem; that $x^T \Sigma^{-1} x$ is a Lyapunov function assuring the stability of the Kalman filter follows indirectly by the mathematical duality between Kalman filters and LQSF optimal designs.

The interpretation of the stability margins of the Kalman filter differs in a subtle, but significant, way from the interpretation of the LQSF stability margins. The LQSF stability margins define a set of variations in open-loop dynamics of the actual physical plant that can be tolerated without closed-loop instability of the plant. The Kalman filter stability margins pertain to the amount of unmodeled nonlinearity that can be tolerated in the filter itself without instability of the filter. So, for example, the Kalman filter margins can be used to assess the stability of an estimator, such as the CGEKF, having a residual-gain matrix designed for an approximate linear-

it should be sufficient for the actual system to lie within these margins throughout the bandwidth of the open-loop system.

4 The system must be "cost-observable" for the Hamilton-Jacobi equation solution to be a Lyapunov function for the optimal closed-loop system.

process model but employing a more precise nonlinear internal model of the process for actually generating the residuals. However, in order to conclude that a CGEKF is *nondivergent* the results require that, in addition to being stable, the CGEKF must incorporate an *accurate* nonlinear internal model of the process dynamics. This latter fact supports the intuition that the choice of residual gain in a model-reference estimator is not very critical so long as the estimator is stable and so long as it incorporates an accurate nonlinear internal model of the process dynamics.

A simple, almost obvious, but very important separation theorem (theorems 3.3 and 4.3) has been established for nonlinear systems: nondivergent estimates can, unconditionally, be substituted for true values in an otherwise stable nonlinear feedback system without ever causing instability. This separation result, unlike the other results in stated in this monograph, does *not* depend for its proof on theorem 2.1; rather, the result follows almost immediately from the definition of stability once the problem has been put in the right frame of coordinates (viz., (x, e) rather than $(x, \hat{x})$). The principal practical implication of the result is that the design of stabilizing dynamical output-feedback controllers for nonlinear systems can with complete mathematical rigor be split into two separate tasks:

Task 1 Design a *nondivergent* state estimator (e.g., a CGEKF).

Task 2 Design a stabilizing full-state feedback controller (e.g., an LQSF controller).

Of course, because this separation of estimation and control holds rigorously only when a *nondivergent* estimator is employed and because nondivergence can be assured only when an accurate internal model of the process dynamics is incorporated in the CGEKF, the engineer is obliged to ensure that the internal model employed in the CGEKF is accurate, at least throughout the bandwidth of the open-loop CGEKF (e.g., with the internal feedback loop of the CGEKF opened at, say, the input to the residual-gain matrix H).

As explained in sections 3.7 and 4.7, the LQSF/CGEKF stability-margin/nondivergence results combine via the nonlinear separation theorem to provide a theoretical basis for the design of *gain-scheduled* nonlinear output-feedback controllers. The separation theorem permits the design to be split as explained above and the stability margin conditions of theorems 3.1, 3.2 and 4.1, 4.2 serve to define a region in the state space for which each constant LQSF gain matrix (respectively, CGEKF residual-gain matrix) is stable (respectively, nondivergent); this provides insight useful in assessing whether a gain-scheduled design is feasible and, if it is feasible, in assessing how complicated the gain-scheduling algorithm must be.

Proportional integral LQSF designs, compensated CGEKF designs, and other modifications of the LQSF and CGEKF designs involving state augmentation present no difficulties to the theory: the stability margin, the nondivergence, and the separation results all apply directly.

5.2 Perspective

A point which should be emphasized is that the stability margin and robustness results developed in this monograph are not primarily nonlinear system results; rather, the results are most appropriately viewed as approximation results. The results provide a theoretical framework within which quantitative bounds on the imprecision in an engineering model may be used to test whether or not the model is sufficiently precise to be of use in assessing the actual system's behavior with any given feedback law. In this framework, nonlinear systems emerge as a special case in which one is typically interested in either

(i) testing the validity of a *linear* approximation to or linearization of the system, or

(ii) testing the validity of a first-order differential-equation approximation (such as is done in classical Lyapunov theory wherein the dynamics of a system are approximated by a first-order differential equation which bounds the rate of decrease of a scalar Lyapunov function).

In the approximation results that have been developed in this monograph, *closed-loop stability* is the criterion for whether or not a given approximation is satisfactory: the modeling imprecision must not be so great as to permit the possibility of instability. This, it might be argued, is the least common denominator of all possible criteria since stability is virtually always a design requirement. Of course, in specific applications the engineer is nearly always faced with design specifications in addition to closed-loop stability; on the other hand, as is well known to engineers experienced in classical servomechanism design, much about a feedback system's transient response, attenuation of noise, and general robustness can be learned from detailed knowledge of its stability margins. Also, some important feedback properties, such as the zero steady-state tracking error property of a proportional-integral controller, are dependent only on the closed-loop stability of the overall system.

Potential applications of the theory of approximations developed in this monograph include virtually every dynamical system engineering problem, since approximations are a fact of life in virtually every practical problem. The testing of the validity of linearization is but one application of the results.

Another potential application is in testing the validity of time-scale decomposition in hierarchical control designs: for this, conic sectors might be used to approximate the dynamics of the various subsystems at each level of the hierarchy; to keep the system model appropriately simple one would employ progressively lower-bandwidth models at successively higher levels in the hierarchy, bounding the ensuant modeling imprecision at each level using conic sectors centered at the design models and having frequency-dependent radii which increase rapidly at frequencies outside the models' bandwidths. The use of such sectors could substantially reduce the design engineer's dependence on intuition and simulation in assessing the validity of the time-scale-decomposition modeling approximation.[5]

Hierarchical feedback theory might also be applied to the design of simplified model-reference estimators (e.g., suboptimal Kalman filters, CGEKFs, etc.) for complex, possibly nonlinear, large-scale systems. For nondivergence, one would of course require that the estimator incorporate a complete accurate model of the process dynamics, but the theory does provide a theoretical basis for simplifying the structure of the estimator's residual gain. A residual gain which is designed in stages employing a time-scale-decomposed process model will be sparse except near the diagonal (assuming the states are appropriately labeled); this may have significant advantages in some applications.

More generally, the approximation results are potentially applicable to the very basic engineering problem of *model simplification*; this includes as special cases the practices of linearization and time-scale decomposition. The results provide a theoretical framework that may be useful in assessing how much a model can be simplified. Since with most modern feedback synthesis techniques, the complexity of the system model is closely related to the complexity of the feedback law that results by applying the synthesis

5 Of course, classical control theory has provided much insight to engineers by making clear the tradeoffs between modeling uncertainty and bandwidth, but this insight is largely qualitative, since the classical theory applies rigorously only to single-loop systems.

technique, the theory has some implications regarding the minimal complexity of the feedback law required to achieve a particular control objective. For example, the results could be helpful in answering questions like: "Is an adaptive controller/estimator necessary?";[6] "Will a two-pole linear time-invariant controller suffice?"; etc.

5.3 Future Directions

Two main areas require further work. First, computer software must be developed for checking multivariable sector conditions using the results of section 2.5.[7] Such computer software is necessary before any really interesting applications of the results are possible. Second, additional theory is needed in order to facilitate the bounding of sectors with larger, more simply structured sectors (such as might be required, for example, in testing the validity of multilevel, hierarchical, time-scale decomposition). The availability of a means for generating simplified sector bounds will facilitate the application of the theory to extremely complex large-scale problems.

A third important area requiring work is the area of synthesis. This monograph is primarily concerned with the analysis of stability margins and robustness for specified feedback designs and provides a method of evaluating stability margins for given systems; as yet there is no clearly defined algorithm for *synthesizing* feedback systems having prescribed stability margins.[8] To more fully automate the robust-feedback design process, robust-feedback synthesis algorithms must be developed.

6 The discussion in sections 3.7 and 4.7 regarding the requisite complexity of an LQSE/CGEKF gain-scheduling algorithm for a nonlinear system can be viewed as a special case of this, a gain-scheduled system being a very simple type of adaptive system.
7 Simple modifications of the software developed for the characteristic locus design procedure may suffice (see theorem 2.3 and the comments following it).
8 However, some not-so-clearly-defined ad hoc methods for synthesis are suggested in this monograph (sections 2.6, 3.7, and 4.7); these rely heavily on the designer's intuition.

Appendix A

Proof of Lemma 3.1

We apply theorem 2.2. The system (3.3.1) with state feedback (3.3.2) is described equivalently by the feedback equations

$$z = \mathbf{G}(\xi)x \equiv [\mathbf{A} + \mathbf{B}\cdot(-G)]x + \xi$$
$$x = \mathbf{H}z \equiv \left(\int_0^t z(t)\,dt\right)_{t\in R_+}, \tag{A.1}$$

which are of the form to which theorem 2.2 is applicable. The relation Graph (H) is not subject to disturbance inputs and hence trivially satisfies the stability stipulation in the sector stability criterion; the mapping taking ξ into the relation Graph (G(ξ)) is clearly finite-gain stable about the set Graph (G(0)) (since ξ enters additively the gain is in fact at most one!).

That (3.4.3a) is implied by (3.4.3b) follows from part (b) of lemma 2.3. Consequently, we may assume (3.4.3a) holds. From (3.4.3a)

$$\text{Graph } P[(A - \mathbf{A}) + (B - \mathbf{B})(-G)] \text{ strictly inside } +\text{-Cone}(\tfrac{1}{2}S). \tag{A.2}$$

Using (3.4.2) we have

$$\begin{aligned} +\text{-Cone}(\tfrac{1}{2}S) &= \{(x, z) \mid \langle \mathbf{P}_\tau(z + \tfrac{1}{2}Sx), \mathbf{P}_\tau(-x)\rangle \le 0 \text{ for all } \tau \in R_+\} \\ &= \{(x, z) \mid \langle \mathbf{P}_\tau(z - \tfrac{1}{2}[P(A - BG) + (A - BG)^T P]x), \mathbf{P}_\tau(-x)\rangle \le 0 \\ &\qquad \text{for all } \tau \in R_+ \\ &= \{(x, z) \mid \langle \mathbf{P}_\tau(z - P(A - BG)x), \mathbf{P}_\tau x\rangle \ge 0 \text{ for all } \tau \in R_+\} \end{aligned}$$

$$= +\text{-Cone}(-P(A - BG))$$

$$= \text{Sector}\begin{bmatrix} 0 & -I \\ I & -P(A - BG) \end{bmatrix}. \tag{A.3}$$

Substituting (A.3) into (A.2) and applying sector properties (iv), (v), and (iii) (2.4.11), (2.4.12), and (2.4.10)),

$$[\text{Graph}(\mathbf{G}(0))]^{\mathrm{I}} \equiv [\text{Graph}(\mathbf{A} + \mathbf{B}\cdot(-\mathbf{G}))]^{\mathrm{I}}$$

$$\text{strictly inside Sector}\left(\begin{bmatrix} 0 & -I \\ I & -P(A - BG) \end{bmatrix}\begin{bmatrix} I & P(A - BG) \\ 0 & I \end{bmatrix} \times \begin{bmatrix} -P & 0 \\ 0 & I \end{bmatrix}\begin{bmatrix} 0 & I \\ I & 0 \end{bmatrix}\right)$$

$$= \text{Sector}\begin{bmatrix} -I & 0 \\ 0 & -P \end{bmatrix}. \tag{A.4}$$

On the other hand, for all $(z, x) \in \text{Graph}(\mathbf{H})$ and all $\tau \in \mathbf{R}_+$,

$$\begin{aligned} \langle \mathbf{P}_\tau(-Ix), \mathbf{P}_\tau(-Pz) \rangle &= \langle \mathbf{P}_\tau x, \mathbf{P}_\tau Pz \rangle \\ &= \langle \mathbf{P}_\tau x, \mathbf{P}_\tau P\dot{x} \rangle \\ &= \frac{1}{\tau}\int_0^\tau x^{\mathrm{T}}(t)P\dot{x}(t)\,dt \\ &= \frac{1}{\tau}\int_0^{x(\tau)} x^{\mathrm{T}}P\,dx \\ &= \frac{1}{2\tau}x^{\mathrm{T}}(\tau)Px(\tau) \geq 0 \end{aligned} \tag{A.5}$$

(since P is positive definite); so,

$$\text{Graph}(\mathbf{H}) \text{ outside Sector}\begin{bmatrix} -I & 0 \\ 0 & -P \end{bmatrix}. \tag{A.6}$$

This proves that (3.4.3) and (3.4.2) together imply that (3.3.1) with feedback (3.4.9) is closed-loop finite-gain stable. ∎

Appendix B

Proof of Lemma 3.2

We apply theorem 2.2, proving first assertion (b) and then assertion (a).

Proof of assertion (b):

The dynamics of the nonlinear observer (3.3.3) are equivalently described by the feedback equations

$$z = \mathbf{G}(y, u)\hat{x} \equiv (\mathbf{A} - HC)\hat{x} + \mathbf{B}u + Hy$$

$$\hat{x} = \mathbf{H}z \equiv \left(\int_0^t z(\mathrm{t})\,\mathrm{dt}_t\right)_{t \in R_+}, \tag{B.1}$$

which are of the form to which theorem 2.2 is applicable. The relation Graph (**H**), being without a disturbance input, is trivially finite-gain stable about the relation Graph (**H**); the mapping taking (y, u) into Graph ($\mathbf{G}(y, u)$) is clearly finite-gain stable about Graph ($\mathbf{G}(0, 0)$) (since **B** and H both have finite gain and the disturbances $\mathbf{B}u$, Hy enter additively, its gain is in fact bounded by $g(\mathbf{B}) + g(H)$).

From (3.5.3), it follows that

$$\text{Graph}\,([(A - \mathbf{A}) - H(C - \mathbf{C})]P) \textit{ strictly inside } +\text{-Cone}\,(\tfrac{1}{2}S). \tag{B.2}$$

Using (3.5.1) it follows (see (A.5)) that

$$+\text{-Cone}\,(\tfrac{1}{2}S) = +\text{-Cone}\,(-(A + HC)P)$$
$$\triangleq \text{Sector}\begin{bmatrix} 0 & -I \\ I & -(A - HC)P \end{bmatrix} \tag{B.3}$$

Substituting (B.3) into (B.2) and applying sector properties (iv), (v), and (iii), it follows that

$$[\text{Graph}\,(\mathbf{G}(0,0))]^{\mathrm{I}} \equiv [\text{Graph}\,(\mathbf{A} - H\mathbf{C})]^{\mathrm{I}}$$

$$\text{strictly inside Sector}\left(\begin{bmatrix} 0 & -I \\ I & -(A-HC)P \end{bmatrix}\begin{bmatrix} I & (A-HC)P \\ 0 & I \end{bmatrix} \times \begin{bmatrix} I & 0 \\ 0 & -P^{-1} \end{bmatrix}\begin{bmatrix} 0 & I \\ I & 0 \end{bmatrix}\right)$$

$$= \text{Sector}\begin{bmatrix} P^{-1} & 0 \\ 0 & I \end{bmatrix}. \tag{B.4}$$

On the other hand (see (A.5), (A.6)),

$$\text{Graph}\,(\mathbf{H}) \text{ outside Sector}\begin{bmatrix} P^{-1} & 0 \\ 0 & I \end{bmatrix}. \tag{B.5}$$

It follows from theorem 2.2 that the nonlinear observer (3.3.3) is closed-loop finite-gain stable.

That (3.5.3) is implied by (3.5.2) follows from lemma 2.3.

Proof of assertion (*a*):

It is sufficient to prove that the relation between (θ, ξ) and $e \triangleq \hat{x} - x$ defined by the error-dynamics feedback system (3.3.5), (3.3.6) is closed-loop finite-gain stable irrespective of the "state trajectory" x. The dynamics of (3.3.5), (3.3.6) are described equivalently by the feedback equations

$$z = \mathbf{G}'_x(\xi, \theta) \equiv (\tilde{\mathbf{A}}(x) - H(\tilde{\mathbf{C}}x))e + H\theta - \xi$$

$$e = \mathbf{H}z \equiv \left(\int_0^t z(\mathrm{t})\,\mathrm{dt}_t\right)_{t\in\mathrm{R}_+}. \tag{B.6}$$

For notational simplicity, let

$$\mathbf{F} \equiv [(A - \mathbf{A}) - H(C - \mathbf{C})]P + \tfrac{1}{2}S \tag{B.7}$$

$$\tilde{\mathbf{F}}(x) \equiv [(A - \tilde{\mathbf{A}}(x)) - H(C - \tilde{\mathbf{C}}(x))]P + \tfrac{1}{2}S. \tag{B.8}$$

Then, for all $\eta \in \mathscr{M}_{2e}(\mathrm{R}_+, \mathrm{R}^n)$ and all $\tau \in \mathrm{R}_+$,

$$\langle \mathbf{P}_\tau \tilde{\mathbf{F}}(x)\eta, \mathbf{P}_\tau\eta\rangle = \langle \mathbf{P}_\tau(\mathbf{F}(x+\eta) - \mathbf{F}\eta), \mathbf{P}_\tau\eta\rangle$$

$$= \left\langle \mathbf{P}_\tau\left(\int_x^{x+\eta} \nabla\mathbf{F}(x+z)\,\mathrm{d}z\right), \mathbf{P}_\tau\eta\right\rangle$$

$$= \left\langle \mathbf{P}_\tau\left(\left(\int_0^1 \nabla\mathbf{F}(x+\rho\eta)\eta\, d\rho\right), \mathbf{P}_\tau\eta\right\rangle\right.$$
$$= \int_0^1 \langle \mathbf{P}_\tau \nabla\mathbf{F}(x+\rho\eta)\eta, \mathbf{P}_\tau\eta\rangle\, d\rho. \tag{B.9}$$

From (B.9) and (3.5.2), it follows that uniformly

$$\text{Graph}\,([(A - \tilde{\mathbf{A}}(x)) - H(C - \tilde{\mathbf{C}}(x))]P) \text{ strictly inside } +\text{-Cone}\,(\tfrac{1}{2}S). \tag{B.10}$$

Hence (see (B.2)–(B.4)), uniformly

$$[\text{Graph}\,(\mathbf{G}_x'(0, 0))]^{\mathrm{I}} \text{ strictly inside Sector}\begin{bmatrix} P^{-1} & 0 \\ 0 & I \end{bmatrix} \tag{B.11}$$

Since

$$\text{Graph}\,(\mathbf{H}) \text{ outside Sector}\begin{bmatrix} P^{-1} & 0 \\ 0 & I \end{bmatrix}$$

it follows from the sector stability criterion that the mapping of (θ, ξ) into e induced by the nonlinear observer (3.3.3) is finite-gain stable irrespective of x; hence the nonlinear observer is nondivergent with finite gain. ∎

Appendix C

Proof of Theorem 3.3

Let **BG** be the operator defined by

$$\mathbf{BG}(x)\delta x = \mathbf{BG}(x + \delta x) - \mathbf{BG}x. \tag{C.1}$$

Then, taking $e \triangleq \hat{x} - x$ we have

$$\mathbf{BG}\hat{x} = \mathbf{BG}(x + e) = \mathbf{BG}x + \mathbf{BG}(x)e. \tag{C.2}$$

Let $\xi' \triangleq \xi + \mathbf{BG}(x)e$. Then the dynamics of the closed-loop system with $u = \mathbf{G}\hat{x}$ satisfy

$$\frac{\mathrm{d}}{\mathrm{dt}}x = (\mathbf{A} + \mathbf{BG})x + \xi', \tag{C.3}$$

whereas the dynamics with $u = \mathbf{G}x$ satisfy

$$\frac{\mathrm{d}}{\mathrm{dt}}x = (\mathbf{A} + \mathbf{BG})x + \xi. \tag{C.4}$$

Since, by hypothesis, (C.4) is bounded (finite-gain stable), it is sufficient to observe that

$$\begin{aligned} \|\xi'\|_t &\triangleq \|\xi + \mathbf{BG}(x)e\|_\tau \le \|\xi\|_\tau + \|\mathbf{BG}(x)e\|_\tau \\ &\le \|\xi\|_\tau + \tilde{g}(\mathbf{B})\tilde{g}(\mathbf{G})\|e\|_\tau < \infty. \quad \blacksquare \end{aligned} \tag{C.5}$$

Appendix D

Proof of Lemma 4.1

We apply theorem 2.2. The system (4.3.1) with state feedback (4.3.3) is described equivalently by the feedback equations

$$\begin{aligned} w &= \mathbf{G}(\xi)x \equiv [\mathbf{A} + \mathbf{B}(-G)]x + \xi \\ x &= \mathbf{H}w \equiv (x(t-1), \text{if } t \geq 1; 0, \text{if } t = 0)_{t \in \mathbf{Z}_+}, \end{aligned} \tag{D.1}$$

which is of the form to which theorem 2.2 is applicable. The relation Graph (**H**) is not subject to disturbances and hence trivially satisfies with finite gain the stability stipulation of the sector stability criterion; the mapping taking ξ into Graph ($\mathbf{G}(\xi)$) is clearly finite-gain stable about Graph ($\mathbf{G}(0)$) (since ξ enters additively, the gain is in fact at most one).

That (4.4.3a) is implied by (4.4.3b) follows from part (a) of lemma 2.3; consequently, we may assume (4.4.3a) holds. From (4.4.3a) and sector properties (v), (iii), (i), and (ii) (see equations (2.4.8)–(2.4.10) and (2.4.12))

$$\begin{aligned} &[\text{Graph}\,(\mathbf{G}(0))]^{\mathrm{I}} \equiv [\text{Graph}\,(\mathbf{A} + \mathbf{B}(-G))]^{\mathrm{i}} \\ &\quad \text{strictly outside Sector}\left(\begin{bmatrix} -I & 0 \\ 0 & -I \end{bmatrix}\begin{bmatrix} I & 0 \\ 0 & -I \end{bmatrix}\begin{bmatrix} I & -P^{1/2} \\ I & P^{1/2} \end{bmatrix}\right. \\ &\qquad\qquad \left. \times \begin{bmatrix} P^{1/2} & 0 \\ 0 & I \end{bmatrix}\begin{bmatrix} 0 & I \\ I & 0 \end{bmatrix}\right) \end{aligned}$$

$$= \text{Sector}\begin{bmatrix} P^{1/2} & -P^{1/2} \\ P^{1/2} & P^{1/2} \end{bmatrix}; \tag{D.2}$$

in (D.2) we have used the definition

$$\text{Cone}(\mathbf{C}, \mathbf{R}) = \text{Sector}\begin{bmatrix} \mathbf{I} & (-\mathbf{C} - \mathbf{R}) \\ \mathbf{I} & (-\mathbf{C} + \mathbf{R}) \end{bmatrix} \tag{D.3}$$

On the other hand, for all $(w, x) \in$ Graph (**H**) and all $\tau \in \mathbf{Z}_+$,

$$\begin{aligned} \langle \mathbf{P}_\tau(P^{1/2}x - P^{1/2}w), \mathbf{P}_\tau(P^{1/2}x + P^{1/2}w)\rangle &= \langle \mathbf{P}_\tau x, P\,\mathbf{P}_\tau x\rangle - \langle \mathbf{P}_\tau w, P\mathbf{P}_\tau w\rangle \\ &\triangleq \frac{1}{\tau}\sum_{t=0}^{\tau}(x^{\mathrm{T}}(t)x(t) - w^{\mathrm{T}}(t)w(t)) \\ &= -\frac{1}{\tau}w^{\mathrm{T}}(\tau)w(\tau) \le 0, \end{aligned} \tag{D.4}$$

which implies

$$\text{Graph}(\mathbf{H}) \text{ inside Sector}\begin{bmatrix} P^{1/2} & -P^{1/2} \\ P^{1/2} & P^{1/2} \end{bmatrix} \tag{D.5}$$

The result follows from theorem 2.2. ∎

Appendix E

Proof of Corollary 4.1

By lemma 2.3, (4.4.20b) implies (4.4.20a); consequently we may assume (4.4.20a) holds. We apply the various properties of sectors (section 2.4) and the definition of a conic sector to prove that the conditions of theorem 4.1 are satisfied. From the definition of a conic sector, from sector property (ii), and from (4.4.20a),

$$\begin{aligned}
&\mathrm{Graph}\,(N_i) \text{ inside Cone}\left(\frac{1}{1-a_i^2}, \frac{a_i}{1-a_i^2}\right) \\
&\quad = \mathrm{Sector}\left(\begin{bmatrix} (1-a_i) & 0 \\ 0 & (1+a_i) \end{bmatrix}\begin{bmatrix} 1 & \left(-\frac{1}{1-a_i^2} - \frac{a_i}{1-a_i^2}\right) \\ 1 & \left(-\frac{1}{1-a_i^2} + \frac{a_i}{1-a_i^2}\right) \end{bmatrix}\right) \\
&\quad = \mathrm{Sector}\begin{bmatrix} (1-a_i) & -1 \\ (1+a_i) & -1 \end{bmatrix}.
\end{aligned} \tag{E.1}$$

So, applying sector properties (ii), (iii), and (iv) to (E.1)

$$\begin{aligned}
&[\mathrm{Graph}\,(N_i)]^I \text{ inside Sector}\left(\begin{bmatrix} -1 & 0 \\ 0 & -1 \end{bmatrix}\begin{bmatrix} (1-a_i) & -1 \\ (1+a_i) & -1 \end{bmatrix}\begin{bmatrix} 0 & 1 \\ 1 & 0 \end{bmatrix}\right) \\
&\quad = \mathrm{Sector}\begin{bmatrix} 1 & (-1-a_i) \\ 1 & (-1+a_i) \end{bmatrix} = \mathrm{Cone}\,(1, a_i).
\end{aligned} \tag{E.2}$$

Applying sector properties (ii) and (iv) to (E.2), the definition (4.4.19) yields

$$([\mathrm{Graph}(N_i)]^I - 1) \text{ inside Sector}\begin{bmatrix}\sqrt{r_i + \lambda} & -\sqrt{r_i} \\ \sqrt{r_i + \lambda} & \sqrt{r_i}\end{bmatrix} \tag{E.3}$$

where

$$\lambda \equiv \lambda_{\max}(B^T KB). \tag{E.4}$$

Hence, applying sector property (vi) to (E.3) and using the fact

$$\langle \mathbf{P}_\tau y, \mathbf{P}_\tau B^T KBy\rangle \leq \lambda \|\mathbf{P}_\tau y\|^2, \tag{E.5}$$

we have

$$\begin{aligned}
&([\mathrm{Graph}(N)]^I - I) \text{ inside Sector}\begin{bmatrix}\mathrm{diag}(\sqrt{r_1 + \lambda}, \ldots, \sqrt{r_m + \lambda}) & -R^{1/2} \\ \mathrm{diag}(\sqrt{r_1 + \lambda}, \ldots, \sqrt{r_m + \lambda}) & +R^{1/2}\end{bmatrix} \\
&\quad = \{(x, y) \mid \langle \mathbf{P}_\tau([\mathrm{diag}(\sqrt{r_1 + \lambda}, \ldots, \sqrt{r_m + \lambda})]y - R^{1/2}x), \\
&\qquad \mathbf{P}_\tau([\mathrm{diag}(\sqrt{r_1 + \lambda}, \ldots, \sqrt{r_m + \lambda})]y + R^{1/2}x)\rangle \leq 0 \\
&\qquad \text{for all } \tau \in \mathbf{Z}_+ \text{ sufficiently large}\} \\
&\quad = \{(x, y) \mid \langle \mathbf{P}_\tau y, \mathbf{P}_\tau Ry\rangle + \lambda\|\mathbf{P}_\tau y\|^2 \leq \langle \mathbf{P}_\tau x, \mathbf{P}_\tau x\rangle \\
&\qquad \text{for all } \tau \in \mathbf{Z}_+ \text{ sufficiently large}\} \\
&\quad \subset \{(x, y) \mid \langle \mathbf{P}_\tau y, \mathbf{P}_\tau(R + B^T KB)y\rangle \leq \langle \mathbf{P}_\tau x, \mathbf{P}_\tau x\rangle \\
&\qquad \text{for all } \tau \in \mathrm{T} \text{ sufficiently large}\} \\
&\quad = \text{Sector}\begin{bmatrix}(R + B^T KB)^{1/2} & -R^{1/2} \\ (R + B^T KB)^{1/2} & R^{1/2}\end{bmatrix};
\end{aligned} \tag{E.6}$$

i.e.,

$$([\mathrm{Graph}(N)]^I - I) \text{ inside Sector}\begin{bmatrix}(R + B^T KB)^{1/2} & -R^{1/2} \\ (R + B^T KB)^{1/2} & R^{1/2}\end{bmatrix}. \tag{E.7}$$

Applying sector properties (iv) and (iii), and using the identity (which follows from the Riccati equation (4.4.9))

$$K \equiv \alpha^2(A^T KA + Q - G^T(R + B^T KB)G); \alpha \geq 1, \tag{E.8}$$

we have

$$(\text{Graph}\,[\mathbf{N}(-G)])\text{ inside Sector}\left(\begin{bmatrix}(R+B^{\mathrm{T}}KB)^{1/2} & -R^{1/2}\\ (R+B^{\mathrm{T}}KB)^{1/2} & R^{1/2}\end{bmatrix}\begin{bmatrix}I & -I\\ 0 & I\end{bmatrix}\times\begin{bmatrix}0 & I\\ I & 0\end{bmatrix}\begin{bmatrix}I & 0\\ 0 & -G\end{bmatrix}\right)$$

$$= \text{Sector}\begin{bmatrix}(-(R+B^{\mathrm{T}}KB)^{1/2}-R^{1/2}) & (-(R+B^{\mathrm{T}}KB)^{1/2}G)\\ (-(R+B^{\mathrm{T}}KB)^{1/2}+R^{1/2}) & (-(R+B^{\mathrm{T}}KB)^{1/2}G)\end{bmatrix}$$

$$= \{(x, y) \mid \langle \mathbf{P}_\tau y, B^{\mathrm{T}}KB\mathbf{P}_\tau y\rangle + 2\langle \mathbf{P}_\tau y, (R+B^{\mathrm{T}}KB)G\mathbf{P}_\tau x\rangle + \langle \mathbf{P}_\tau x, G^{\mathrm{T}}(R+B^{\mathrm{T}}KB)G\mathbf{P}_\tau x\rangle \le 0 \text{ for all } \tau \in \mathbf{Z}_+ \text{ sufficiently large}\}$$

(applying the definition of a sector and rearranging)

$$\subset \{(x, y) \mid \langle \mathbf{P}_\tau y, B^{\mathrm{T}}KB\mathbf{P}_\tau y\rangle + 2\langle \mathbf{P}_\tau y, B^{\mathrm{T}}KA\mathbf{P}_\tau x\rangle + \langle \mathbf{P}_\tau x, (G^{\mathrm{T}}(R+B^{\mathrm{T}}KB)G - Q)\mathbf{P}_\tau x\rangle \le -\varepsilon\|\mathbf{P}_\tau(x, y)\|^2 \text{ for all } \tau \in \mathbf{Z}_+ \text{ sufficiently large}\}$$

(using the identity (4.4.8) and the hypothesis $M = 0$)

$$\subset \{(x, y) \mid \langle \mathbf{P}_\tau y, B^{\mathrm{T}}KB\mathbf{P}_\tau y\rangle + 2\langle \mathbf{P}_\tau y, B^{\mathrm{T}}KAP_\tau x\rangle + \langle \mathbf{P}_\tau x, (A^{\mathrm{T}}KA - K)\mathbf{P}_\tau x\rangle \le \varepsilon\|\mathbf{P}_\tau(x, y)\|^2 \text{ for all } \tau \in \mathbf{Z}_+ \text{ sufficiently large}\}$$

(using the identity (E.8))

$$\text{strictly inside Sector}\begin{bmatrix}K^{1/2}B & (K^{1/2}A - K^{1/2})\\ K^{1/2}B & (K^{1/2}A + K^{1/2})\end{bmatrix}, \tag{E.9}$$

where $\varepsilon = \lambda_{\min}(Q)/(1 + [g(\mathbf{N}(-G))]^2) > 0$. Hence, applying sector properties (v), (iv), and (v),

$$\text{Graph}\,(K^{1/2}[\mathbf{A} + \mathbf{B}\cdot(-G)]) \equiv \text{Graph}\,(K^{1/2}[A + B\cdot\mathbf{N}\cdot(-G)])$$

$$\text{strictly inside Sector}\begin{bmatrix}I & -K^{1/2}\\ I & K^{1/2}\end{bmatrix} = \text{Cone}\,(0, K^{1/2}), \tag{E.10}$$

which establishes that the conditions of theorem 4.1 hold. ∎

Appendix F

Proof of Lemma 4.2

We apply theorem 2.2, proving first assertion (b) and then assertion (a).

Proof of assertion (b):

The dynamics of the nonlinear observer (4.3.4) are equivalently described by the feedback equations

$$\begin{aligned} w &= \mathbf{G}(y, u)\hat{x}^{(-)} \equiv [(\mathbf{A} - HC)\hat{x}^{(-)} + Hy] + \mathbf{B}u \\ \hat{x}^{(-)} &= \mathbf{H}w \equiv (w(\mathrm{t} - 1), \text{if } \mathrm{t} \geq 1; 0, \text{if } \mathrm{t} = 0)_{\mathrm{t} \in \mathbf{Z}_+}, \end{aligned} \tag{F.1}$$

which are of the form to which theorem 2.2 is applicable. The relation Graph (**H**), being without disturbances, is trivially finite-gain stable about Graph (**H**); the mapping taking (y, u) into Graph $(\mathbf{G}(y, u))$ is clearly finite-gain stable about Graph $(\mathbf{G}(0, 0))$ (since **B** and H have finite gain and the disturbances enter additively, the gain is in fact bounded by $g(\mathbf{B}) + g(H)$).

From (4.5.3),

$$\begin{aligned} &\text{Graph}\,(P^{-1/2}(\mathbf{A} - HC)) \text{ strictly inside Cone}\,(0, P^{-1/2}) \\ &= \text{Sector}\begin{bmatrix} I & -P^{-1/2} \\ I & P^{-1/2} \end{bmatrix}. \end{aligned} \tag{F.2}$$

So, applying sector properties (v), (iii), and (i),

$$[\text{Graph}\,(\mathbf{G}(0, 0))]^{\mathrm{I}} \equiv [\text{Graph}\,(\mathbf{A} - HC)]^{\mathrm{I}}$$

$$\text{strictly outside Sector}\left(\begin{bmatrix} -I & 0 \\ 0 & I \end{bmatrix}\begin{bmatrix} I & -P^{-1/2} \\ I & P^{-1/2} \end{bmatrix}\begin{bmatrix} P^{-1/2} & 0 \\ 0 & I \end{bmatrix}\begin{bmatrix} 0 & I \\ I & 0 \end{bmatrix}\right)$$

$$= \text{Sector}\begin{bmatrix} P^{-1/2} & -P^{-1/2} \\ P^{-1/2} & P^{-1/2} \end{bmatrix}. \tag{F.3}$$

On the other hand,

$$\text{Graph (H) inside Sector}\begin{bmatrix} P^{-1/2} & -P^{-1/2} \\ P^{-1/2} & P^{-1/2} \end{bmatrix} \tag{F.4}$$

(see equations (D.5) and (D.6)). It follows from the sector stability criterion that the map of (y, u) into $\hat{x}^{(-)}$ has finite gain; that the map of (y, u) into $\hat{x}^{(+)}$ has finite gain follows since

$$\hat{x}^{(+)} = (I - FC)\hat{x}^{(-)} + Fy, \tag{F.5}$$

and I, F, and **C** have finite gain.

That (4.5.3) is implied by (4.5.2) follows from lemma 2.3.

Proof of assertion (*a*):

It is sufficient to prove that the relation between (ξ, θ) and $(e^{(+)}, e^{(-)})$ defined by the error-dynamics feedback system (4.3.6), (4.3.7) is closed-loop finite-gain stable irrespective of the "state trajectory" x. The dynamics of (4.3.6), (4.3.7) are described equivalently by

$$\begin{aligned} w &= \mathbf{G}'_x(\xi, \theta)e^{(-)} \equiv (\tilde{\mathbf{A}}(x) - H\tilde{\mathbf{C}}(x))e^{(-)} + H\theta - \xi \\ e^{(-)} &= \mathbf{H}w \equiv (w(\mathrm{t}-1), \text{if } \mathrm{t} \geq 1; 0, \text{if } \mathrm{t} = 0)_{\mathrm{t}\in \mathrm{Z}_+}, \end{aligned} \tag{F.6}$$

which is of the form to which theorem 2.2 is applicable.

Consider first Graph $[\mathbf{G}'_x(0, 0)]$. For each $x, \eta \in m_{2e}(\mathrm{Z}_+, \mathrm{R}^n)$,

$$\begin{aligned} \nabla[P^{-1/2}\mathbf{G}'_x(0, 0)](\eta) &- P^{-1/2}[\nabla[\tilde{\mathbf{A}}(x)](\eta) - H\nabla[\tilde{\mathbf{C}}(x)](\eta)] \\ &= \mathrm{P}^{-1/2}[\nabla\mathbf{A}(x + \eta) - H\nabla\mathbf{C}(x + \eta)]. \end{aligned} \tag{F.7}$$

From (4.5.2), (F.7) and lemma 2.3, it follows that uniformly

$$\text{Graph}\,[P^{-1/2}\mathbf{G}'_x(0, 0)] \text{ strictly inside Cone}(0, P^{-1/2})$$

$$= \text{Sector}\begin{bmatrix} I & -P^{-1/2} \\ I & P^{-1/2} \end{bmatrix}. \tag{F.8}$$

So,

$$[\text{Graph}\,(\mathbf{G}'_x(0,0))]^{\mathrm{I}} \text{ strictly outside Sector}\begin{bmatrix} P^{-1/2} & -P^{-1/2} \\ P^{-1/2} & P^{-1/2} \end{bmatrix} \tag{F.9}$$

(see (F.3)). In view of (F.4), it follows from the sector stability criterion that the map of (ξ, θ) into $e^{(-)}$ induced by (F.6) has finite gain. That the map of (ξ, θ) into $e^{(+)}$ has finite gain follows from the identity

$$\begin{aligned} e^{(+)} &\triangleq \hat{x}^{(+)} - x \\ &= [\hat{x}^{(-)} - F(\hat{y}^{(-)} - y)] - x \\ &= [\hat{x}^{(-)} - F(\mathbf{C}\hat{x}^{(-)} - \mathbf{C}x - \theta)] - x \\ &= e^{(-)} - F\tilde{\mathbf{C}}(x)e^{(-)} + F\theta \\ &= [I - F\tilde{\mathbf{C}}(x)]e^{(-)} + F\theta \end{aligned} \tag{F.10}$$

and the fact that $\mathbf{C}$, F have finite gain and finite incremental gain. ▮

Appendix G

Proof of Corollary 4.2

From (4.5.16), for each $i = 1, \ldots, p$

$$([\text{Graph}(L_i(e^{j\theta}))]^I - 1) \text{ inside Cone}(0, a_i) \tag{G.1}$$

for all $\theta \in [0, \pi]$. Hence, for all $\theta \in [0, \pi]$

$$([\text{Graph}(L_{i-}^*(e^{j\theta}))]^I - 1) \text{ inside Cone}(0, a_i). \tag{G.2}$$

Proceeding analogously to the proof (appendix E) of corollary 4.1,

$$([\text{Graph}(L_i^*(e^{j\theta}))]^I - 1) \text{ inside Sector}\begin{bmatrix} \sqrt{\theta_i + \lambda} & -\sqrt{\theta_i} \\ \sqrt{\theta_i + \lambda} & \sqrt{\theta_i} \end{bmatrix}. \tag{G.3}$$

From (G.3) it follows (equations (E.3)–(E.10)) that

$$\text{Graph}(\Sigma^{1/2}[A^T - C^T L^*(e^{j\theta}))H^T]) \text{ strictly inside Cone}(0, \Sigma^{1/2}) \tag{G.4}$$

where $L^* = \text{diag}(L_1^*, \ldots, L_p^*)$. Hence, for some $\varepsilon > 0$,

$$(1 - \varepsilon)I \geq (\Sigma^{1/2}[A^T - C^T L^*(e^{j\theta})H^T])^*(\Sigma^{1/2}[A^T - C^T L^*(e^{j\theta})H^T]) \tag{G.5}$$

from which it follows that

$$(1 - \varepsilon)I \geq (\Sigma^{1/2}[A^T - C^T L^*(e^{j\theta})H^T])(\Sigma^{1/2}[A^T - C^T L^*(e^{j\theta})H^T])^*. \tag{G.6}$$

Hence, for some $\varepsilon' > 0$,

$$-\varepsilon' I + \Sigma^{-1} \geq (A - HL(e^{j\theta})C)^{*}\Sigma^{-1}(A - HL(e^{j\theta})C). \tag{G.7}$$

So, by lemma 2.8,

$$\text{Graph}\,(\Sigma^{-1/2}(A - HNC)) \text{ strictly inside Cone}\,(0, \Sigma^{-1/2}). \tag{G.8}$$

The result follows from theorem 4.2. ▮

References

1. B. D. O. Anderson, "The Inverse Problem of Optimal Control," Stanford Electronics Laboratories Technical Report No. SEL-66-038 (T.R. No. 6560-3), Stanford, Calif., April 1966.

2. B. D. O. Anderson, "The Testing for Optimality of Linear Systems," *Int. J. Control*, vol. 4, no. 1, pp. 29–40, 1966.

3. B. D. O. Anderson, "Sensitivity improvement using optimal design," *Proc. IEE*, vol. 113, no. 6, pp. 1084–1086, June 1966.

4. B. D. O. Anderson, "Stability Results for Optimal Systems," *Electronics Letters*, vol. 5, p. 545, Oct. 1969.

5. B. D. O. Anderson and J. B. Moore, "*Linear Optimal Control.* Englewood Cliffs, N.J.: Prentice-Hall, 1971.

6. M. Araki, "Input-Output Stability of Composite Feedback Systems," *IEEE Trans. on Automatic Control*, vol. AC-21, no. 2, pp. 254–258, April 1976.

7. M. Athans, *Optimal Control.* New York: McGraw-Hill, 1966.

8. M. Athans, "The Compensated Kalman Filter," *Proc. Second Symposium on Nonlinear Estimation Theory and Its Applications*, San Diego, Calif., pp. 10–22, Sept. 13–15, 1971.

9. M. Athans, "The Role and Use of the Stochastic Linear-Quadratic-Gaussian Problem in Control System Design," *IEEE Trans. on Automatic Control*, vol.

AC-16, no. 6, pp. 529–552, Dec. 1971.

10. M. Athans, "The Discrete Time Linear-Quadratic-Gaussian Stochastic Control Problem," *Annals of Economic and Social Measurement*, vol. 1, no. 4, pp. 449–491, 1972.

11. S. Barnett, "Sensitivity of Optimal Linear Systems to Small Variations in Parameters," *Int. J. Control*, vol. 4, no. 1, pp. 41–48, 1966.

12. S. Barnett and C. Storey, "Insensitivity of Optimal Linear Control Systems to Persistent Changes in Parameters," *Int. J. Control*, vol. 4, no. 2, pp. 179–184, 1966.

13. S. Barnett, "Insensitivity of Control Systems," *Int. J. Control*, vol. 10, no. 6, pp. 665–675, 1969.

14. S. Barnett, "Insensitivity of Optimal Linear Discrete-Time Regulators," *Int. J. Control*, vol. 21, no. 5, pp. 843–848, 1975.

15. J. J. Belletrutti and A. G. J. MacFarlane, "Characteristic loci techniques in multivariable-control-system design," *Proc. IEE*, vol. 118, pp. 1291–1296, 1971.

16. H. W. Bode, *Network Analysis and Feedback Amplifier Design*. New York: Van Nostrand, 1945.

17. J. Broussard and M. Safonov, "Design of Generalized Discrete Proportional Integral Controllers by Linear-Optimal Control Theory," Rpt. No. TIM-804–1, The Analytic Sciences Corp., Reading, Mass., 7 Oct. 1976.

18. C. T. Chen, *Introduction of Linear System Theory*. New York: Holt, Rinehart, and Winston, 1970.

19. C. Y. Chong and M. Athans, "On the Stochastic Control of Linear Systems with Different Information Sets," *IEEE Trans. on Automatic Control*, vol. AC-16, no. 5, pp. 423–430, Oct. 1971.

20. P. A. Cook, "Modified Multivariable Circle Theorems," in *Recent Mathematical Developments in Control*, ed. by D. J. Bell, New York: Academic Press, pp. 367–373, 1973.

21. P. A. Cook, "On the Stability of Interconnected Systems," *Int. J. Control*, vol. 20, no. 3, pp. 407–415, 1974.

22. P. A. Cook, "Circle Criteria for Stability in Hilbert Space," *SIAM J. Control*, vol. 13, no. 3, pp. 593–610, May 1975.

23. C. Corduneanu, *Integral Equations and Stability of Feedback Systems.* New York: Academic Press, 1973.

24. J. B. Cruz and W. R. Perkins, "A New Approach to the Sensitivity Problem in Multivariable Feedback System Design," *IEEE Trans. on Automatic Control,* vol. AC-9, no. 3, pp. 216–223, July 1964.

25. J. B. Cruz (editor), *Feedback Systems.* New York: McGraw-Hill, 1972.

26. J. B. Cruz (editor), *System Sensitivity Analysis.* Stroudsburg, Pa.: Dowden, Hutchinson, and Ross, 1973.

27. C. A. Desoer and M. Vidyasagar, *Feedback Systems: Input-Output Properties.* New York: Academic Press, 1975.

28. P. Dorato and A. H. Levis, "Optimal Linear Regulators: The Discrete Time Case," *IEEE Trans. on Automatic Control,* vol. AC-16, no. 6, pp. 613–620, Dec. 1971.

29. E. J. Davison, "The Robust Control of a Servomechanism Problem for Linear Time-Invariant Multivariable Systems," *IEEE Trans. on Automatic Control,* vol. AC-21, no. 1, pp. 25–34, Feb. 1976.

30. B. Francis, "The Multivariable Servomechanism Problem from the Input-Output Viewpoint," *IEEE Trans. on Automatic Control,* vol. AC-22, no. 3, pp. 322–328, June 1977.

31. R. J. Fitzgerald, "Divergence of the Kalman Filter," *IEEE Trans. on Automatic Control,* vol. AC-16, no. 6, pp. 736–747, Dec. 1971.

32. M. I. Freedman, P. L. Falb, and G. Zames, "A Hilbert Space Stability Theory Over Locally Compact Abelian Groups," *SIAM J. Control,* vol. 7, no. 3, pp. 479–495, Aug. 1969.

33. A. Gelb (editor), *Applied Optimal Estimation.* Cambridge, Mass.: MIT Press, 1974.

34. A. Gelb and W. E. Vander Velde, *Multiple-Input Describing Functions.* New York: McGraw-Hill, 1968.

35. A. S. Gilman and I. B. Rhodes, "Cone-Bounded Nonlinearities and Mean-Square Bounds," *IEEE Trans. on Automatic Control,* vol. AC-18, no. 3, pp. 260–265, June 1973.

36. A. S. Gilman and I. B. Rhodes, "Cone-Bounded Nonlinearities and Mean-Square Bounds—Quadratic Regulation Bounds," *IEEE Trans. on Automatic*

Control, vol. AC-21, no. 4, pp. 472–483, Aug. 1976.

37. G. Guardabassi (editor), *Sensitivity, Adaptivity, and Optimality*. Ischia, Italy: Proc. 3rd IFAC Symposium, June 18–23, 1973.

38. P. P. Gusak and M. M. Simkin, "Nonlinear Filtering Performance Estimation," *Automation and Remote Control*, vol. 36, no. 12, pp. 2008–2014, Dec. 1975.

39. W. Hahn, *Stability of Motion*. New York: Springer-Verlag, 1967.

40. I. N. Herstein, *Topics in Algebra*. Lexington, Mass.: Xerox, 1975.

41. G. Hirzinger and J. Ackerman, "Sampling Frequency and Controllability Region," *Comput. and Elect. Eng.*, vol. 2, pp. 347–351, 1975.

42. J. M. Holtzman, *Nonlinear System Theory, A Functional Analysis Approach*. Englewood Cliffs, N.J.: Prentice-Hall, 1970.

43. I. M. Horowitz, *Synthesis of Feedback Systems*. New York: Academic Press, 1963.

44. I. Horowitz and M. Sidi, "Synthesis of Cascaded Multiple-loop Feedback Systems with Large Plant Parameter Ignorance," *Automatica*, vol. 9, pp. 589–600, Sept. 1973.

45. C. H. Houpis and C. T. Constantinides, "Relationship between Conventional-Control Theory Figures of Merit and Quadratic Performance Index in Optimal Control Theory for a Single-Input/Single-Output System," *Proc. IEE*, vol. 120, no. 1, pp. 138–142, June 1973.

46. A. H. Jazwinski, *Stochastic Processes and Filtering Theory*. New York: Academic Press, 1970.

47. C. D. Johnson, "Optimal Control of the Linear Regulator with Constant Disturbances," *IEEE Trans. on Automatic Control*, vol. AC-13, no. 4, pp. 416–421, Aug. 1968.

48. C. D. Johnson, "Further Study of the Linear Regulator with Disturbances Satisfying a Linear Differential Equation," *IEEE Trans. on Automatic Control*, vol. AC-15, no. 2, pp. 222–228, April 1970.

49. C. D. Johnson, "Accommodation of External Disturbances in Linear Regulator and Servomechanism Problems," *IEEE Trans. on Automatic Control*, vol. AC-16, no. 6, pp. 635–634, Dec. 1971.

50. E. I. Jury, *Theory and Application of the z-Transform Method*. New York: Wiley, 1964.

51. S. J. Kahne, "Low Sensitivity Design of Optimal Linear Control Systems," *Proc. Fourth Annual Allerton Conference on Circuit Theory and System Theory*, Univ. of Illinois, Monticello, Ill., Oct. 5–2, 1966.

52. R. E. Kalman, "When is a Linear Control System Optimal?" *Trans. ASME* ser. D (*J. Basic Eng.*), vol. 86, pp. 51–60, March 1964.

53. E. Kreindler, "On the Definition and Application of the Sensitivity Function," *J. Franklin Inst.*, vol. 285, no. 1, pp. 26–36, Jan. 1968.

54. H. Kwakernaak, "Optimal Low-Sensitivity Linear Feedback Systems," *Automatica*, vol. 5, pp. 279–285, 1969.

55. H. Kwakernaak and R. Sivan, *Linear Optimal Control Systems.* New York: Wiley Interscience, 1972.

56. E. L. Lasley and A. N. Michel, "Input-Output Stability of Interconnected Systems," *IEEE Trans. on Automatic Control*, vol. AC-21, no. 1, pp. 84–89, Feb. 1976.

57. W. H. Lee, "Linear Tracking Systems," B.S. thesis, MIT, Cambridge, Mass., June 1976.

58. W. H. Lee and M. Athans, "The Discrete-Time Compensated Kalman Filter," Rpt. No. ELS-P-748, Electronic Systems Laboratory, MIT, Cambridge, Mass., May 1977.

59. W. S. Levine and M. Athans, "On the Determination of Optimal Constant Output-Feedback Gains for Linear Multivariable Systems," *IEEE Trans. on Automatic Control*, vol. AC-15, no. 1, pp. 44–49, Feb. 1970.

60. W. S. Levine, T. L. Johnson, and M. Athans, "Optimal Limited State-Variable Feedback Controllers for Linear Systems," *IEEE Trans. on Automatic Control*, vol. AC-16, no. 6, pp. 785–793, Dec. 1971.

61. A. H. Levis, R. A. Schlueter, and M. Athans, "On the Behavior of Optimal Linear Sampled-Data Regulators," *Int. J. Control*, vol. 13, no. 2, pp. 343–361, 1971.

62. D. G. Luenberger, "Observers for Multivariable Systems," *IEEE Trans. on Automatic Control*, vol. AC-11, no. 2, pp. 190–197, April 1966.

63. A. G. J. MacFarlane, "Return-Difference and Return-Ratio Matrices and Their Use in the Analysis and Design of Multivariable Feedback Control Systems," *Proc. IEE*, vol. 117, no. 10, pp. 2037–2049, Oct. 1970.

64. A. G. J. MacFarlane, "A Survey of Some Recent Results in Linear Multivariable Feedback Theory," *Automatica*, vol. 8, pp. 455–492, 1972.

65. A. G. J. MacFarlane and J. J. Belletrutti, "The Characteristic Locus Design Method," *Automatica*, vol. 9, pp. 575–588, 1973.

66. P. D. McMorran, "Extension of the Inverse Nyquist Method," *Electronics Letters*, vol. 6, pp. 800–801, 1970.

67. A. I. Mees and P. E. Rapp, "Stability Criteria for Multiple-Loop Nonlinear Feedback Systems," *Proc. IFAC MVTS Symposium*, New Brunswick, Canada, July 1977.

68. L. Meier, R. E. Larson, and A. J. Tether, "Dynamic Programming for Stochastic Control of Discrete Systems," *IEEE Trans. on Automatic Control*, vol. AC-16, no. 6, pp. 767–775, 1971.

69. S. M. Melzer and B. C. Kuo, "Sampling Period Sensitivity of the Optimal Sampled-Data Linear Regulator," *Automatica*, vol. 7, pp. 367–370, 1971.

70. R. W. Miller, "Asymptotic Behavior of the Kalman Filter with Exponential Aging," *AIAA Journal*, vol. 9, no. 3, pp. 537–539, March 1971.

71. B. P. Molinari, "The Stable Regulator Problem and Its Inverse," *IEEE Trans. on Automatic Control*, vol. AC-18, no. 5, pp. 454–459, Oct. 1973.

72. B. C. Moore and G. Klein, "Eigenvector Selection in the Linear Regulator Problem: Combining Modal and Optimal Control," in *Proc. 1976 IEEE Conf. on Decision and Control*, Dec. 1–3, Clearwater Beach, Fla.

73. J. B. Moore and B. D. O. Anderson, "Applications of the Multivariable Popov Condition," *International Journal of Control*, vol. 5, no. 4, pp. 345–353, 1967.

74. P. J. Moylan and B. D. O. Anderson, "Nonlinear Regulator Theory and an Inverse Optimal Control Problem," *IEEE Trans. on Automatic Control*, vol. AC-18, no. 5, pp. 460–465, Oct. 1973.

75. P. J. Moylan, "Implications of Passivity in Nonlinear Systems," *IEEE Trans. on Automatic Control*, vol. AC-19, no. 4, pp. 373–381, Aug. 1974.

76. J. R. Munkres, *Topology, A First Course*. Englewood Cliffs, N.J.: Prentice-Hall, 1975.

77. H. Nyquist, "Regeneration Theory," *Bell Syst. Tech. J.*, Jan. 1932.

78. A. Papoulis, *Probability, Random Variables, and Stochastic Processes*. New

York: McGraw-Hill, 1965.

79. J. Park and K. Y. Lee, "An Inverse Optimal Control Problem and its Application to the Choice of Performance Index for Economic Stabilization Policy," *IEEE Trans. on Systems, Man, and Cybernetics*, vol. SMC-5, no. 1, pp. 64–76, Jan. 1975.

80. R. V. Patel, B. Sridhar, and M. Toda, "Robustness in Linear Quadratic Design with Application to an Aircraft Control Problem," *Proc. Tenth Asilomor Conf. on Circuits, Systems, and Computers*, Nov. 1976.

81. R. V. Patel, M. Toda, and B. Sridhar, "Robustness of Linear Quadratic State Feedback Designs," in *Proc. Joint Automatic Control Conference*, San Francisco, Calif., June, 1977.

82. W. R. Perkins and J. B. Cruz, "The Parameter Variation Problem in State Feedback Control Systems," *Trans. ASME*, ser. D (*J. Basic Eng.*), 87, pp. 120–124, March 1965.

83. W. R. Perkins and J. B. Cruz, "Feedback Properties of Linear Regulators," *IEEE Trans. on Automatic Control*, vol. AC-16, no. 6, pp. 659–664, Dec. 1971.

84. E. Polak and D. Q. Mayne, "An Algorithm for Optimization Problems with Functional Inequality Constraints," vol. AC-21, pp. 134–193, 1976.

85. E. Polak and R. Trahan, "An Algorithm for Computer-Aided-Design Problems," in *Proc. 1976 IEEE Conf. on Decision and Control*, Dec. 1976.

86. D. W. Porter and A. N. Michel, "Input-Output Stability of Time-Varying Nonlinear Multiloop Feedback Systems," *IEEE Trans. on Automatic Control*, vol. AC-19, no. 4, pp. 422–427, Aug. 1974.

87. I. B. Rhodes and A. S. Gilman, "Cone-Bounded Nonlinearities and Mean-Square Bounds—Estimation Lower Bounds," *IEEE Trans. on Automatic Control*, vol. AC-20, no. 5, pp. 632–642, Oct. 1975.

88. H. H. Rosenbrock, "Design of Multivariable Control Systems Using Inverse Nyquist Array," *Proc. IEE*, vol. 116, pp. 1929–1936, 1969.

89. H. H. Rosenbrock, *State-space and Multivariable Theory*. New York: Wiley Interscience, 1970.

90. H. H. Rosenbrock, "Progress in the Design of Multivariable Control Systems," *Trans. Inst. Meas. Control*, vol. 4, pp. 9–11, 1971.

91. H. H. Rosenbrock and Peter D. McMorran, "Good, Bad, or Optimal?" *IEEE Trans. on Automatic Control*, vol. AC-16, no. 6, pp. 552–554, Dec. 1971.

92. H. H. Rosenbrock, "Multivariable Circle Theorems," in *Recent Mathematical Developments in Control*, ed. by D. J. Ball, New York: Academic Press, 1973.

93. H. H. Rosenbrock and P. A. Cook, "Stability and the Eigenvalues of $G(s)$," *Int. J. Control*, vol. 21, no. 1, pp. 99–104, 1975.

94. W. Rudin, *Real and Complex Analysis*. New York: McGraw-Hill, 1974.

95. M. G. Safonov and M. Athans, "Gain and Phase Margin for Multiloop LQG Regulators," Rpt. No. ESL-P-654, Electronics Systems Laboratory, MIT, Cambridge, Mass., March 1976.

96. M. G. Safonov and M. Athans, "Gain and Phase Margin for Multiloop LQG Regulators," in *Proc. 1976 IEEE Conf. on Decision and Control*, Clearwater Beach, Fla., Dec. 1–3.

97. M. G. Safonov and M. Athans, "Gain and Phase Margin for Multiloop LQG Regulators," *IEEE Trans. on Automatic Control*, vol. AC-22, no. 2, April 1977.

98. A. P. Sage, *Optimum Systems Control*. Englewood Cliffs, N.J.: Prentice-Hall, 1968.

99. N. R. Sandell, "Optimal Linear Tracking Systems," Rpt. No. ESL-R-456, Electronics Systems Laboratory, MIT, Cambridge, Mass., Sept. 1971.

100. N. Sandell and M. Athans, "On Type-L Multivariable Linear Systems," *Automatica*, vol. 9, no. 1, pp. 131–136, Jan. 1973.

101. N. R. Sandell and M. Athans, "Solution to Some Nonclassical LQG Stochastic Decision Problems," *IEEE Trans. on Automatic Control*, vol. AC-19, no. 2, pp. 108–116, April 1974.

102. N. R. Sandell and M. Athans, "Design of a Generalized P-I-D Controller by Optimal Linear Control Theory," unpublished.

103. Y. Sawaragi and K. Ogino, "Game-Theoretic Approach to Sensitivity Design of Optimal Systems," *Proc. 3rd IFAC Symposium on Sensitivity, Adaptivity, and Optimality*, Ischia, Italy, June 18–23, 1973.

104. F. C. Schweppe, *Uncertain Dynamic Systems*. Englewood Cliffs, N. J.: Prentice-Hall, 1973.

105. H. W. Sorenson, "On the Development of Practical Nonlinear Filters," *Information Sciences*, vol. 7, no. 3/4, pp. 253–270, Fall, 1974.

106. M. K. Sundareshan and M. Vidyasagar, "L_2-Stability of Large-Scale

Dynamical Systems—Criteria Via Positive Operator Theory," *IEEE Trans. on Automatic Control,* vol. AC-22, no. 3, pp. 396–399, June 1977.

107. T. -J. Tarn and Y. Rasis, "Observers for Nonlinear Stochastic Systems," *IEEE Trans. on Automatic Control,* vol. AC-21, no. 4, pp. 441–448, Aug. 1976.

108. M. Toda, R. Patel, and B. Sridhar, "Closed-Loop Stability of Linear Quadratic Optimal Systems in the Presence of Modeling Errors," 14th Allerton Conference on Circuits and Systems, Sept./Oct. 1976.

109. E. Tse, "Observer-Estimators for Discrete-Time Systems," *IEEE Trans. on Automatic Control,* vol. AC-18, no. 1, pp. 10–16, Feb. 1973.

110. J. C. Willems, *The Analysis of Feedback Systems.* Cambridge, Mass.: MIT Press, 1971.

111. J. C. Willems, "Mechanisms for the Stability and Instability of Feedback Systems," *Proc. IEEE,* vol. 64, no. 1, pp. 24–35, 1976.

112. J. L. Willems, *Stability Theory of Dynamical Systems.* New York: Wiley, 1970.

113. P. K. Wong, *On the Interaction Structure of Linear Multi-Input Feedback Control Systems,* M.S. thesis, MIT, Sept. 1975.

114. P. K. Wong and M. Athans, "Closed-Loop Structural Stability for Linear-Quadratic Optimal Systems," *IEEE Trans. on Automatic Control,* vol. AC-22, no. 1, pp. 94–99, 1977.

115. M. A. Woodhead and B. Porter, "Optimal Modal Control," *Measurement and Control,* vol. 6, pp. 301–303, 1973.

116. R. Yokoyama and E. Kinnen, "The Inverse Problem of an Optimal Regulator," *IEEE Trans. on Automatic Control,* vol. AC-17, no. 4, pp. 497–504, Aug. 1972.

117. P. C. Young and J. C. Willems, "An approach to the Linear Multivariable Servomechanism Problem," *Int. J. Control,* vol. 15, no. 5, pp. 961–979, 1972.

118. G. Zames, "On the Input-Output Stability of Time-Varying Nonlinear Feedback Systems. Part I: Conditions Using Concepts of Loop Gain, Conicity, and Positivity," *IEEE Trans. on Automatic Control,* vol. AC-11, no. 2, pp. 228–238, April 1966.

119. G. Zames, "On the Input-Output Stability of Time-Varying Nonlinear Feedback Systems. Part II: Conditions Involving Circles in the Frequency

Plane and Sector Nonlinearities," *IEEE Trans. on Automatic Control*, vol. AC-11, no. 3, pp. 465–476, July 1966.

120. W. M. Wonham, *Linear Multivariable Control.* New York: Springer-Verlag, 1974.

121. M. Toda and R. V. Patel, "Performance Bounds for Stationary Linear Continuous Filters in the Presence of Modeling Errors," submitted to *IEEE Trans. on Automatic Control*, 1977.

122. R. Patel and M. Toda, "Modeling Error Analysis of Stationary Discrete-Time Filters," Submitted to *IFAC VII Triennial World Congress*, Helsinki, 1978.

123. A. G. J. MacFarlane and I. Postlethwaite, "The Generalized Nyquist Stability Criterion and Multivariable Root Loci," *Int. J. Control*, vol. 25, pp. 81–127, 1977.

124. A. G. J. MacFarlane and B. Kouvaritakis, "A Design Technique for Linear Multivariable Feedback Systems," *Int. J. Control*, vol. 25, pp. 837–874, 1977.

125. L. V. Kantorovich and G. P. Akilov, *Functional Analysis in Normed Spaces.* New York: Pergamon, 1964.

126. C. A. Harvey and G. Stein, "Quadratic Weights for Asymptotic Regulator Properties," *IEEE Trans. on Automatic Control*, vol. AC-23, no. 3, pp. 378–387, 1978.

Index

www.ingramcontent.com/pod-product-compliance
Lightning Source LLC
Chambersburg PA
CBHW051239050326
40689CB00007B/991